LEARNING
AMERICAN
HISTORY

Arthur Link, General Editor for History

LEARNING AMERICAN HISTORY

Critical Skills for the Survey Course

Michael J. Salevouris
Conal Furay

Webster University
St. Louis, Missouri

Harlan Davidson, Inc.
Wheeling, Illinois 60090-6000

Library of Congress Cataloging-in-Publication Data

Salevouris, Michael J.
    Learning American history : critical skills for the survey course
    / Michael J. Salevouris, Conal Furay.
        p.   cm.
    Includes bibliographical references.
    ISBN 0-88295-920-4
    1. United States—History—Examinations, questions, etc.
I. Furay, Conal.   II. Title.
E178.25.S24   1997
973' .072—dc20   96-43462
                                                            CIP

Cover design: DePinto Graphic Design   Cover images: Astronaut James B. Irwin on the moon, August 1, 1971, *courtesy NASA*. A Native American, as depicted in Theodor DeBry's 1590 book of engravings. Women suffragists, *courtesy Library of Congress*.

Manufactured in the United States of America
01 00 99 98 97 1 2 3 4 5 TS

To our wives,
Peggy & Jean

CONTENTS

PREFACE

TO THE STUDENT

As Lord Acton wrote well over a century ago, history should be "not a burden on the memory but an illumination of the soul."[1] Without history our sense of possibilities would be impoverished, and our personal and social identities stunted and incomplete. History is society's collective memory. Without that collective memory our society would be as rootless and adrift as an individual with amnesia. Individually and collectively what we are is the product of what we have been. "A country without a memory" said philosopher George Santayana, "is a country of madmen."

This book is designed to show students that the study of history is much more than memorizing names and dates. The critical skills employed in the serious study of history are essential components of a sound college education and can be valuable assets for you in your career endeavors. The world is changing so rapidly that today's knowledge is soon outdated. The future will belong to those students who continue to learn and adapt to new circumstances after they have earned their degrees. Those who can communicate clearly, solve problems, think critically, and understand the increasingly multicultural and interdependent nature of our world will hold the key to surviving into the twenty-first century.

TO THE INSTRUCTOR

(Students: You should read this too! Forewarned is forearmed!)

This book is designed as a supplementary text for college and university students taking introductory courses in American history. It is not an American history text per se, but a workbook which, after a brief survey of the defining traditions in American historiography (Chapter 1), introduces students to the nature of history and historical thinking (Chapters 2–4), the methods of historical inquiry (Chapters 5–7), and the elements of effective historical writing (Chapters 8–10). Chapter 11 discusses techniques for evaluating history on film and video, and may be assigned at any point in the course in which students are asked to assess critically a historical film or documentary. (There is a film analysis worksheet but no exercises in this chapter.) A series of appendices provide advice on reading history books, writing book reviews and term papers, and doing oral history projects.

The exercise materials follow the chronological sequence of the typical American history survey course, allowing instructors to insert relevant skill-development and skill-assessment exercises at appropriate points in a particular course. The exercise content in each two-chapter sequence relates to a specific chronological segment of American history, although we have made no attempt to shoehorn the exercises into a precise chronological order.

Our aim is not to train potential graduate students, but to help the typical undergraduate student who takes a course in history attain a deeper understanding of how history is made and what it means to think "historically." A theme we develop throughout this book is that the study of history involves much more than the accumulation and mastery of bits of information. It involves a dynamic process of reconstruction and interpretation that requires well-honed critical and communication skills—skills that are, by the way, useful in courses other than history and useful in numerous professional contexts.

The danger of trying to be all things to all people is that, in the end, everyone may be disappointed. Yet the diversity of available survey texts, academic calendars, course patterns, and student competencies has led us to write *Learning American History* in such a way that instructors can easily adapt the book to their individual teaching styles and to differing student needs. Since many students take just one semester of American history, or take chronological units out of sequence, we have designed the book to be used in a single semester. Although chapter narratives tend to use examples drawn from the first half of American history (through the 1860s and 1870s), each chapter has two sets of exercises: the Part I exercises are designed to accompany first-semester American history

---

1 J. E. Dalberg, Lord Acton, *Lectures on Modern History* (London: Macmillan and Co., 1906), quoted in William McNeill, *The Rise of the West* (New York: NAL, 1965), 282.

courses (before 1877), and the Part II exercises to accompany courses in post–Civil-War American history (1865–Present).

Instructors who want to use the book over a two-semester sequence may:

- Assign the Part I exercises in the first semester and the Part II exercises in the second semester. In effect, students would do each type of exercise two times.
- Assign the Part I exercises in the first semester (same as above), and utilize selective advanced-level exercises and materials in the Appendices in the second semester.
- Distribute the chapters/appendices over two semesters, and assign the set of exercises (Part I or Part II) that is most chronologically appropriate at any given point in the class. This tactic will be necessary because spreading the chapters over an academic year will create occasional discrepancies between the material being studied in class and the content of the exercises.

Instructors should also use a good deal of discretion in assigning specific exercises (or even chapters). Depending on your students, some exercises might be too hard, or too easy. In other cases there may be more exercise material than you want to use. Simply omit those you deem inappropriate.

In choosing the content for the exercises we have tried to be cognizant of the dramatic changes that have taken place in historical scholarship in recent decades. As Eric Foner observes in the introduction to an essay series on *The New American History:*

> In the course of the past twenty years, American history has been remade. Inspired initially by the social movements of the 1960s and 1970s . . . and influenced by new methods borrowed from other disciplines, American historians redefined the very nature of historical study. . . . If anything is characteristic of the recent study of American history, it is attention to the experience of previously neglected groups—not simply as an addition to a preexisting body of knowledge but as a fundamental redefinition of history itself.[2]

Consequently, we have tried to include a representative selection of exercise materials that address the historical experiences of women, workers, and traditionally ignored minorities. We have also attempted to choose materials that dramatize the myriad ways our history is interconnected with that of the rest of the globe. The doctrine of American exceptionalism has been an inspiring conceit, but not especially accurate as a thesis defining the American experience then or now.

We must underscore the fact that many of the exercises do not have categorically "right" answers. Unfortunately, experience teaches that however open-ended the question, students will still be able to propose answers that are simply "wrong." However, there is a much wider range of answers which, though not the best, are not entirely wrong either. Ideally students should have the opportunity to discuss their answers in a classroom setting. This is time consuming, but necessary if students are to realize that their defense of an answer is often much more important than the answer itself. In fact, we have often been convinced by the arguments and insights of our own students that our initial judgment on the allowable range of responses to a given question was too narrow.

Finally, a few comments are necessary regarding our way of approaching the task of strengthening student writing. Given the varied demands on survey teachers' time and energy, it is difficult for them to teach writing in all its dimensions. As a practical matter, therefore, we have focused the writing chapters on the paragraph—the common denominator of organizational skill in writing. Of course, a sound paragraph is part of a larger whole called an essay. But doing a paragraph well requires the same sorting out of ideas and subordinating them to a larger theme as is necessary in essay writing. Certainly it is a good place to start. For students and instructors who wish to carry the matter further, we have included appendices on writing book reviews and term papers.

---

2 Eric Foner, ed., *The New American History* (Washington, DC: American Historical Association, 1990), vii–viii.

ACKNOWLEDGMENTS

In writing this book we incurred many debts. To the following we express our thanks: Publisher Andrew Davidson for his encouragement and continued support; former Harlan Davidson Editor-in-Chief Maureen Hewitt, who suggested the project to us; Production Editor Lucy Herz; Harry James Cargas, a colleague who graciously allowed us to use his essay on the writing of term papers; Art Silverblatt, another faculty colleague who made useful suggestions for the chapter on film and television; Ellen Eliceiri, head reference librarian at Eden-Webster Library, for advice and counsel on how best to present a library as a research apparatus; American history survey students who endured trial runs of the entire manuscript and made helpful suggestions; Ruth Nolle, departmental secretary, for her efficiency in all matters relating to the production of the manuscript; Webster University, for its generous policy of supplying computers to all interested faculty; and to Victoria Lopata, former student, who brought one of us (initials CF) out of computer illiteracy.

Michael Salevouris
Conal Furay
Webster University, 1996

CREDITS

Permissions

Excerpts from *A People's History of the United States* by Howard Zinn, copyright © 1980 by Howard Zinn; and excerpt from *The European Witch Craze of the 16th and 17th Centuries* by H. R. Trevor-Roper, copyright © 1967 by H. R. Trevor-Roper. Reprinted by permission of HarperCollins Publishers, Inc.

Excerpt from *The Handmaid's Tale,* by Margaret Atwood, copyright © 1985 by O. W. Toad, Ltd., First American Edition 1986; and excerpt from *The Patton Papers,* volume 1 edited by Martin Blumenson, copyright © 1972 by Martin Blumenson. Reprinted by permission of Houghton Mifflin Co. All rights reserved.

Excerpts from "A Study in Nativism," by Stanley Coben are reprinted with permission from the *Political Science Quarterly,* 79 (1964): 52–75.

Excerpt from *The National Experience: A History of the United States,* Second Edition by John M. Blum and Bruce Catton, copyright © 1968 by Harcourt Brace and Company, reprinted by permission of the publisher.

Excerpts from the following books published by Harlan Davidson, Inc., are reprinted by permission of the publisher:

David E. Kyvig and Myron A. Marty, *Your Family History: A Handbook for Research and Writing,* © 1978; Arthur S. Link, et al., *A Concise History of the American People,* Vol. I., © 1984; C. Joseph Pusateri, *A History of American Business,* 2d ed., © 1988; Arnoldo De León, *Mexican Americans in Texas,* © 1993; Glenda Riley, *Inventing the American Woman,* Vol. I, © 1986; William T. Hagan, "How the West Was Lost," *Indians in American History,* ed. Frederick E. Hoxie, © 1988; Roger L. Nichols, *Black Hawk and the Warrior's Path,* © 1992; Paul K. Conkin, *The New Deal,* 3d ed., © 1992; June Sochen, *Mae West: She Who Laughs, Lasts,* © 1992; Philip Weeks, *Farewell My Nation,* © 1990; R. Kent Newmyer, *The Supreme Court Under Marshall and Taney,* © 1968; Michael Perman, *Emancipation and Reconstruction, 1862–79,* © 1987; William B. Pickett, *Dwight David Eisenhower and American Power,* © 1995; John Hope Franklin, *The Emancipation Proclamation* © 1995; Dewey W. Grantham, *Recent America,* © 1987; Ralph B. Levering, *The Cold War: A Post–Cold War History* © 1994; Allan M. Winkler, *Home Front U.S.A.,* © 1986.

List of Illustrations and Credits

Chapter 1 The meeting of Cortes and Montezuma. *Courtesy Stock Montage, Inc.*

Chapter 2 Sand Creek Massacre *Courtesy Colorado Historical Society*

Chapter 3 Whipping Quakers at the cart's tail, Boston. *Courtesy Stock Montage, Inc.*

Chapter 4 Trial of George Jacobs for witchcraft, 1692. *Courtesy Peabody Essex Museum, Salem, Mass.*

Chapter 5 First battle of Manassas-Bull Run, Civil War. *Courtesy Library of Congress, LCUSZ62-5454*

Chapter 6 Battle of Lexington, Revolutionary War. *Courtesy Library of Congress, LCUSZ62-2727*

Chapter 7 Le Retour de Martin Guerre. Courtesy Museum of Modern Art/Film Stills Archive. Daniel Vigny, 1983

Chapter 8 U.S. troops fire a salute over fifteen officers and men killed at Kaneohe by Japanese, December 7, 1941. *Courtesy National Archives, 80-G-32854*

Chapter 9 JFK watching Caroline and John Kennedy dance in the Oval Office. *Courtesy John F. Kennedy Library*

Chapter 10 Marines in the streets of Hue, Vietnam, 1968. *Courtesy Defense Dept. Official USMC Photo*

Chapter 11 The Birth of a Nation. Courtesy Museum of Modern Art/Film Stills Archive

THE WRITING OF AMERICAN HISTORY   *1*

"The writing of history reflects the interests, predilections, and even prejudices of a given generation."

JOHN HOPE FRANKLIN

"God alone knows the future, but only an historian can alter the past."

AMBROSE BIERCE

Let us begin with a different version of an old folktale.

Once upon a time in a faraway kingdom, a wealthy widower took as his second wife a woman of honor and dignity who was admired by all who knew her. She had two young daughters, neither of them handsome, but much like their mother in character. The man also had a daughter whose beauty stunned all who saw her. In her presence other women were more than a little envious. Of course she was always the center of attention and came to expect that as her due.

When the new family began to live together everything went well at first, just so long as all were on their best behavior. But they did not live happily ever after. The father, knowing that he must win the affection of his new stepdaughters, treated them with utmost kindness and gave them much attention. His beautiful young daughter began to resent all this, and became increasingly jealous of his attention to them.

It is strange, some would say, that a young woman so richly endowed with physical beauty would act this way, but such is the irony of human nature. She began to treat her stepsisters very badly, being mean to them and saying ugly things that were simply not true. To her father she would hint that his new stepdaughters laughed behind his back at his too-solemn efforts to win their friendship. To her stepmother she would complain that the two girls made up

stories about her and told them to her suitors. (Though she cared nothing for these young men, all of them thoroughly intimidated by her beauty.) And when she was with her stepsisters she would make veiled references to their plainness and sometimes openly criticize their dress and appearance. In short, jealousy consumed her and she grew increasingly difficult to live with.

One day the king decreed an annual celebration, with a grand ball to climax the festive event. He invited to his palace all the important families of the kingdom. The ball was to be something special, with the young prince and all of the court to be there. When the father told his family about the invitation, everyone was very excited, but then his daughter began to have misgivings. She had come to hate her stepsisters and did not want to be with them in public, though secretly she yearned to be at the ball because the prince would be there. And with her beauty there was a chance. . . . Finally, though, her jealousy and resentment dominated, and she announced that she would not attend the ball with the family.

There is more to the story, of course, especially how this young beauty contrived to be at the ball, how she captivated the prince, then mysteriously disappeared as midnight approached. Desperately in love now, the prince searched and finally found her after looking throughout the kingdom. Much more could be said about this mean-spirited young woman, of how she refused to invite her family (including her father) to the royal wedding and ignored them ever after, destroyed the young prince by her self-centered ways, and more.

But enough is enough. What you have been reading is the story of Cinderella written from a different, much more cynical point of view, rather than the conventional fairy-tale version. And, just as it is in storytelling, point of view is the essence of history writing. Every historian has a certain point of view, and although the facts don't change, the choice of which facts to select, and how they are presented, is strongly conditioned by point of view.

This chapter is concerned with how, at different times, American history has been differently told, depending on the climate of opinion that prevailed when any given history was written.

In other words, your grandparents did not hear the same story as your parents, and the story you hear is different from the other two. In many cases the facts are the same, but the framework on which the facts are hung—the interpretation—is different. In other cases, one historian may emphasize different subject matter than another. To describe such variations, historians often use the term "historiography," or "the writing of history."

Writings about the American past can be broken into four major categories, each category roughly corresponding to a specific period of American history. *Traditional history*, which is nationalistic and self-congratulatory in tone, was the dominant tradition in the nineteenth century. Around the turn of the century *Progressive history* began to challenge a number of the Traditionalists' most cherished assumptions about the American experience. *Consensus history* was the perspective that grew out of American military and economic successes during and after the Second World War, and various types of *New history* have appeared during the last few decades of professional history writing. We will discuss each of these categories in turn, but it is important to realize that the equation of categories and periods is far from exact. In a given period, for example, one historian might write from a point of view that reflected attitudes from an earlier time period, while during that same period another historian might present a point of view that wouldn't be important until years later. The points of view presented here are the main schools of thought about the American past.[1]

THE TRADITIONALISTS

The American Revolution and the events that followed had a tremendous impact on the early period of American history writing. The magnitude of the Revolution was perhaps best expressed by Oliver Wendell Holmes in his poem "Concord Hymn," which commemorated the Massachusetts site of the first armed skirmish between British troops and colonial militiamen:

> Here once the embattled farmers stood,
> And fired the shot heard round the world.

"The shot heard round the world" involved a number of firsts, at least as the Traditionalist historians perceived the Revolution. It was the first break in European dominance of the Western hemisphere; the first crack in the British colonial system; the first time a subject people acted in unified way to throw off the yoke of im-

perial authority; the first practical manifestation of the doctrine of natural rights being superior to the rights of governmental authority; and, given the success of the Revolution, the first modern nation to exist under a written constitution that severely restricted arbitrary government.

The history writing of the early and mid-nineteenth century reflected the pride people had about these accomplishments. All of the themes mentioned above were developed in the histories written during this time. Some traced the origins of freedom to the Germanic cultures of the early Middle Ages. Others focused on English institutional patterns transplanted to and perfected in America. But all saw the United States as a strongly unified nation with all of its citizens committed to its further perfection. In an age far more sensitive to the role of divine providence in human affairs than is our own, these historians

---

1 The discussion that follows is broadly based on the periodization sketched in Ernst Breisach's *Historiography: Ancient, Medieval, and Modern* (Chicago: The University of Chicago Press, 1983), 224–395. Another useful overview of the evolution of American historiographic traditions is provided by Joyce Appleby, Lynn Hunt, and Margaret Jacob in *Telling the Truth About History* (New York: W. W. Norton, 1994), chs. 3–4. See also Bernard Sternsher, *Consensus, Conflict, and American Historians* (Bloomington: Indiana University Press, 1975); Gene Wise, *American Historical Explanations* (Minneapolis: University of Minnesota Press, 1980).

spoke of Americans as a newly chosen people, a people with a God-given mission to spread their values of democracy and liberty across the globe. All of this added up to histories deeply energized by idealism, nationalism, and patriotism. It was not only the historians who saw America in this glowing light. Novelists, poets, and politicians also perceived Americans as a missionary people whose task it was to redeem the world from tyranny. In a sense America was "God's New Israel."[2]

THE PROGRESSIVE HISTORIANS

By the end of the nineteenth century a different world was forming. As scientific study gained prominence, it had a direct impact on many fields, including history and its related disciplines—economics, political science, and sociology. The Industrial Revolution had transformed the United States from a nation of small farmers to the world's leading economic power. In the wake of this massive change came the distresses of modern capitalism (unemployment, periodic recession, overcrowded cities, and selfish corporate behavior), which spurred a demand for government economic regulation. The social climate of the United States had also changed substantially. Factories attracted a massive influx of people to the cities. Factory workers were exiles from the declining American countryside and new immigrants, especially those from southern and eastern Europe.

All of this had a direct impact on the history profession, especially the movement of academia in the direction of the sciences. Historians of the traditional period, though often without formal training in history, were superb stylists whose vivid prose captivated readers. Now historians began to write in the dry academic style of a scientific treatise. Adoption of the scientific model generated a skepticism that led to rejection of the Traditionalist view of America as a harmonious nation seeking to fulfill its mission.

Progressive historians, named for a political reform movement of the time, believed that "scientific" history could be enlisted in the service of political and social reform. If one could analyze and understand a human situation, they thought, one could ultimately manage and control it. Thus social engineering would, in theory, be as possible as mechanical or chemical engineering, and the social engineers would be the scientifically trained scholars and academics. Historians, from this perspective, could—and should—serve as agents of change, as reformers of an America gone awry. Hence it is not surprising to find the Progressive historians enthusiastically supporting the reformist measures of the Progressives and, later, the New Deal of Franklin Roosevelt.

Progressive historians emphasized economic forces rather than diplomacy, politics, or the military—the themes of their Traditionalist counterparts. Class conflict also played a role in Progressive history writing, but not in the dogmatic Marxian terms that came much later in the century.

Instead of telling a story of an America glorified by its steady progress toward democracy and freedom, the Progressive historians wrote of an America that was in a state of polar conflict between the privileged classes and the common people. This epic drama was played out in the realms of both ideas and institutions. Ideologically there was a clash between the common people, seeking to make good the traditional American beliefs in equality and democracy, and powerful elites determined to protect their political and economic privileges. Also in conflict were the dream of creating "good" institutions and the existing reality of evil institutions that were corrupting American life. The Progressive historians, like their political namesakes, were more embarrassed by America not having fully achieved its ideals than they were appreciative of the advances America had made.

One of the most famous examples of Progressive history was Charles A. and Mary R. Beard's *The Rise of American Civilization*, a two-volume survey of the American past published in the 1920s.[3] In the Beards' view the American Revolution was ultimately the result of the colonists' determination to end the domination of British business interests. At last, in 1783, the job was done, but a very few years later, in 1787, Ameri-

---

2 This theme is developed in a variety of ways in the following works: Edward M. Burns, *The American Idea of Mission* (New Brunswick: Rutgers University Press, 1957); Russel B. Nye, *This Almost Chosen People* (East Lansing: Michigan State University Press, 1966); Conrad Cherry, *God's New Israel* (Englewood Cliffs, NJ: Prentice-Hall, 1971).

3 Charles A. and Mary R. Beard, *The Rise of American Civilization* (New York: The Macmillan Company, 1927).

can business and propertied interests, alert to the dangers of too much democracy, gathered at Philadelphia and wrote a Constitution that successfully reestablished their political and economic control. This the Beards called "the conservative counter-revolution," suggesting that the framers of the Constitution were motivated by economic self-interest.

According to the Beards, the nineteenth century saw more of the same. During the era of Andrew Jackson (1828–36), a farmer-laborer coalition won some victories against the monied interests, but these were minor in comparison with the overwhelming power of business and industrial interests during and after the Civil War (1861–65). The Beards regarded the Civil War as having been economically motivated—a "Second American Revolution," which further concentrated power into the hands of wealthy capitalists to the detriment of "social democracy."[4]

In general, the Beards represented most of the main themes of the Progressive historians. Meticulous in their research, they wrote histories that focused on conflict; they gave expanded coverage to the interests, frustrations, and achievements of the common people.

Other important Progressive-era historians include Frederick Jackson Turner who, while focusing on the impact of the western frontier in the formation of the American character, emphasized geographical differences to the exclusion of nearly every other influence. James H. Robinson is considered the father of social history, especially among the generation of historians who were active in the 1960s and after. Vernon Louis Parrington emphasized recurrent encounters between progress and privilege. Carl Becker tended to see the American past as a form of class conflict. All of these historians had great confidence in America's future, if only "selfish interests" could be throttled and displaced from their seats of power by an electorate politically inspired by the Progressive historians' understanding of American history and the conflict inherent in it.

CONSENSUS HISTORY

The American public mind underwent a change in the 1940s. Having survived the trauma of the Great Depression during the thirties, Americans emerged toughened and confident of the future. American contributions—human and material—had been instrumental in defeating the aggressor states of Germany, Italy, and Japan in World War II, and the United States came out of the war as the unquestioned world leader politically, militarily, and economically. In this climate of wartime and postwar euphoria the Progressive historians were out of step with the public mood. Their story of an America in more or less continual conflict, particularly class conflict, seemed inappropriate to a generation that had stood united in the face of powerful enemies.

Historians of the time reflected the national mood with what may be called Consensus history. This reading of the American past acknowledged conflicts and class competition, but underneath all of this was a fundamental unity of values along with a common commitment to individualism, democracy, and capitalism, even if these were at times messy in their operations. Progressives had focused on the "warts" of the American experience, and in so doing had missed the rich legacy of achievement that characterized American society. Rather than conflict, what was "more distinctive in American political culture . . . were the *limits* of conflict, the wide range of agreement, the moderation that made possible a constitutional consensus."[5] Thus, the Beardian emphasis on economic class conflict was revised in favor of a view that the nation had admirably traveled a hard, tough road toward its ideals, and if these ideals were not yet fulfilled, at least America had gone further toward them than any other modern nation. By contrast with people elsewhere, even the have nots of America had substantial reason for hope.

Richard Hofstadter was a typical Consensus historian who believed that the American historical experience reflected a substantial unity of ideas, values, and practices. These were the

---

4 These opinions irritated many who had grown up with the mix of patriotism and self-congratulation that characterized the earlier histories of the United States. Charles Beard, who taught at Columbia, became the focus of discontent among potential donors, and the president of Columbia, Nicholas Murray Butler, was put in the uncomfortable position of protecting Beard and appeasing university supporters. One day Butler (it is said) was asked by a faculty member, "Have you read Beard's last book?" "I hope so," said Butler, "I hope so." Appleby, et al., *Telling the Truth About History*, 140.
5 Linda K. Kerber, *The Revolutionary Generation: Ideology, Politics, and Culture in the Early Republic* in *The New American History*, ed. by Eric Foner (Washington, DC, AHA, 1990), 3.

foundation stones of the national life—the essential truth of what America is and had been.

In Hofstadter's view, historical conflicts should not be swept under the table, but they should be seen as disturbances within a larger reality. Hofstadter was ambivalent towards social reform. Just like his contemporaries, he believed that because of the complexity of human affairs, many problems resisted legislative solution. The Consensus historians tended to explore the ironies, paradoxes, and uncertainties of life in America. It may be said that they shrugged their shoulders at some of America's problems. However, it is not that they lacked sympathy for the downtrodden; rather, they believed that the human condition is not entirely alterable, even in America.

Other prominent historians of Hofstadter's frame of mind were Perry Miller, Louis Hartz, Daniel Boorstin, Ralph Gabriel, and Clinton Rossiter. Theirs was a more subtle and sophisticated version of the American past than that of the Progressives, reflecting perhaps the insight of philosopher Immanuel Kant: "Out of timber so crooked as that from which man is made nothing entirely straight can be built."

THE NEW HISTORIANS

The 1960s were years of social, political and ideological turmoil, and the history profession was deeply marked by it. Some of the forces bringing change were rooted in the United States, including the long civil rights struggle of African Americans, the rebirth of the feminist movement, and the growing disillusion with America, an attitude fostered by widespread opposition to the Vietnam War. Other currents came from Europe: the spread of trendy philosophies of relativism in academic circles; the increasing popularity of the French *Annales* school of thought that emphasized social structures, attitudes, and customs rather than events as the centerpiece of historical inquiry; and the general admiration among many intellectuals of the statistical methods of the social sciences. With all these forces active it wasn't long before the roof caved in on Consensus history.[6]

This new breed of historians perceived and wrote about the past quite differently from their older colleagues. As products of the vast expan-

sion of educational opportunities that came in the 1950s and 1960s, they were far more diverse in their backgrounds and cultural experiences than previous generations of scholars. Women, African Americans, and the sons and daughters of immigrants were now earning graduate degrees, and their writings reflected a decidedly reformist agenda.[7] They believed that the notion of Americans as one people (whether in values or in basic outlook) was an idealistic conception that had little validity. History, they thought, should reflect the diversity of the American experience, especially the experiences of those who had been powerless and ignored in Traditional accounts. They regarded political history as a story of the elites in American society and thought it should be replaced with social history, which emphasized not only the role of class,

gender, and ethnicity in human affairs, but also the entertainments and attitudes of the common folk—the popular culture. National history was obsolete because cultural differences were more important than what people might have in common.

The New historians' history should ally itself more closely with the social sciences, because psychology, sociology, anthropology, political

---

6 An excellent summary of the emergence of these trends and their impact on the writing of history can be found in Appleby, et al., *Telling the Truth About History*.
7 See especially Appleby, et al., *Telling the Truth About History*, 146–51.

science, and economics shed new light on the lives of average men and women, and the new statistical methods that came out of these disciplines were superior to the more impressionistic methods of Traditional history. As one true believer put it, "social science enabled historians to use numbers to make their assumptions more precise, to define their terms more carefully, [and] to refine research strategies."[8]

The reformist agenda had other implications. Conventional historians' narratives of sequences of events, linked causally into coherent wholes, should (thought the new generation) give way to in-depth descriptions of a narrowly defined phenomenon, place or time, without making cause-effect statements. Finally, to the extent that the first generations of American historians were unabashed patriots, the historians who came of age during the Vietnam experience tended to be quite critical of American foreign policies and military actions, not only in the 1960s, but earlier as well.

The tendencies of the New history are by no means absolutes or agreed upon by all of its practitioners. There are middle-of-the-road historians who find much value in conventional political history, and there are historians whose accounts are based not on quantitative data but on the interpretation of traditional sources like letters and diaries. There are also those, like Marxist historians, who insist that the New history's critique of American and capitalist institutions doesn't go far enough.

Marxist historians' stories of American life are almost entirely shaped by a conviction that all history is based on an economic class struggle. In order to give a feel for how this wing of New historians views the past, it is useful to examine some of their themes. Although we exaggerate for effect, Marxist historians see American history, not as a series of successes and triumphs (as the Traditionalists did), but a series of lost opportunities: the American Revolution, a failure because it did not put power into the hands of the working class; the Civil War, a failure because it did not really emancipate blacks; the late nineteenth century, a misery for everyone except the monied classes; American entry into World War I, an action based strictly on the self-interest of greedy business interests; Franklin Roosevelt's New Deal, a failure because it was insufficiently radical; the Cold War with Russia, a result of American imperialism. In general, the record of America was and is a record of repeated disaster and missed opportunities.

It is not too much to say that the older historians and the New historians coexist uneasily on many campuses. Part of this might be resentment by the older historians over the fact that the new breed has become dominant in American universities.[9] And it doesn't help that the New historians like to say that the older folks must get their collective head out of the sand. The veterans' reaction, predictably, adds fuel to the fire: to the New historians' boast that their social history is "history with the politics left out," the veterans respond that politics is too important to leave out. To the New historians fascination with thick descriptions of individual episodes and phenomena, the veterans claim that such accounts fail to provide the coherence and unity—the "big picture"—that history (in their view) should have. To the New historians' preference for histories of the faceless masses and societal underdogs, the more traditional historians argue that this preoccupation often leads the New historians to make ideological commitments to "oppressed" groups with the result that their finished accounts can be preachy and didactic. Further, to focus the lens on society writ large is to miss the deeds of the great individuals and elites who really did make a difference. Veterans also criticize the New historians' devotion to quantitative methods, which leads them to ignore or bypass materials that yield profit through study by traditional (literary) methods. Finally, while the younger generation argues that their quantitative methods lead to greater precision, the Traditionalists lament the stylistic consequences of that precision. The prose style of the New history, they say, is so laced with the impenetrable jargon of the social sciences that it is wholly lacking in literary grace or elegance.

The conflict, though not so clear cut as the above account implies, is real, current, and con-

8 Alice Kessler-Harris, "Social History," *The New American History*, Eric Foner, ed. (Philadelphia: Temple University Press, 1990), 168.
9 Gertrude Himmelfarb, *The New History and the Old* (Cambridge: Belknap Press of the Harvard University Press, 1987), 4–5. Himmelfarb is a vocal critic of the New history, while the authors of *Telling the Truth About History*, cited above, are practitioners and defenders of the New history, although not uncritically.

tinuing. At the moment the advantage in some ways lies with the New historians—the emphasis on social history in many American textbooks reflects this. But the older historians have not abandoned the field, and it is too soon to count them out.[10]

So ends this brief account of American historical writing. All of this can be extremely confusing when you are just getting started in the study of history. But even if you do not fully understand the nature or implications of some of the points of contention that are still echoing through the halls of universities, keep in mind the central message: history is shaped by the individuals who write it and the currents of the times in which it is written. Point of view and the preoccupations of the times are crucial, whether speaking of history or Cinderella.

EXERCISES

I AGE OF DISCOVERY-EARLY COLONIAL PERIOD, 1492–1650

A *The Varieties of American History*

The following exercise asks you to specify which school of history (Traditionalist, Progressive, Consensus, New) is suggested by each statement. The points of view discussed in the chapter, along with a brief characterization of each, are listed below.

1. *Traditionalist history* Portrays the U. S. as being the first and best among nations; a nation with a *mission* ordained by Providence and destined to lead the world to political perfection. Liberty, democracy, and justice are the defining American values. Heroes: George Washington, John Adams, and Thomas Jefferson as organizers of the American nation; also Andrew Jackson as one who extended democracy.

2. *Progressive history* Emphasizes *conflict* in American life and the suffering of the deprived. Highlights economic motivations, class oppositions, and the common people's ways of life. Reflects an activist mentality dedicated to reform. The study of history is a moral endeavor aimed at improvement of American life; a heavy social science emphasis in writing. Heroes: major reformers such as Woodrow Wilson, F. D. Roosevelt, M. L. King. Villains: big business, the upper classes, conservatives.

3. *Consensus history* Interprets American history as based on a wide range of agreed-upon values (as a nation) instead of class antagonisms. Shared beliefs, principles, and practices are more important than divisions; reform not a central preoccupation because it is limited in what it can accomplish. Reflects awareness of ironies, paradoxes, limitations in the American experience; no earthly Utopias possible. Heroes: Alexander Hamilton, Thomas Jefferson (because he was a man of compromise and believed in fundamental principles), Abraham Lincoln (for the same reason), Dwight Eisenhower, who embodied many mainstream American values. Villains: human nature more than anything else.

4. *New history* Challenges the earlier American historians who are seen as having missed the variety and diversity that characterize the nation—in a sense the "United States" is a misnomer. America's story must be told from the bottom up, with special attention given to groups left out of Traditional histories—women, African Americans, Native Americans, other ethnic minorities—rather than focusing on government and leaders. Many New historians concentrate on social group experiences so singularly that they

---

10 A deeper and more philosophical discussion of the major inroads of many of these trends into the history profession can be found in Peter Novick, *That Noble Dream* (Cambridge: Cambridge University Press, 1988).

often have no heroes, unless they be reformers who have given voice to the aspirations of the oppressed and disenfranchised. As for villains, well, Traditionalist and Consensus historians will do. Also, the "Establishment," responsible as it has been (in their eyes) for the Vietnam War and the oppression and exclusion of many minorities.

Using the numbers given above, characterize as best you can each of the statements below.

CAN HAVE MORE THAN 1 ANSWER

American history that emphasizes:

_____ 1. social history more than political history.

_____ 2. God's special blessings bestowed on America.

_____ 3. conflict overcome by unifying assumptions accepted by the majority.

_____ 4. recurrent conflict between privileged classes and the common people.

_____ 5. blending of races to achieve the perfection of the human race.

_____ 6. idealism unfulfilled throughout American experience.

_____ 7. a story of America as world leader in developing superior political institutions.

_____ 8. varying public tastes as revealed in popular culture.

_____ 9. the hippies of the 1960s reflecting and continuing the essential values of a much earlier Romantic movement in the U.S.

_____ 10. U.S. imperialism as being primarily responsible for the Cold War.

_____ 11. Judeo-Christian values underlying American domestic and foreign policies.

_____ 12. the importance of the social sciences in historical studies.

_____ 13. the experiences of immigrant groups.

_____ 14. American colonists who hated the upper classes yet agreed with them enough to cooperate in a revolution.

_____ 15. population movements, with tables, graphs, and census statistics.

_____ 16. the West as the fundamental unifying experience in all of American history.

_____ 17. the contributions of women and African Americans to the advance of civilization.

_____ 18. recurrent American blunders in foreign policy.

_____ 19. Lincoln's presidency as one dominated by the industrial leadership of the North.

_____ 20. the American experience as a tale of irony.

_____ 21. the importance of popular culture as a reflection of common peoples' ambitions and concerns.

_____ 22. the story of America as a beacon light to the rest of the world.

B *History as Account*

INCLUDE PHRASE THAT MADE YOU PICK IT

A major theme of this chapter has been how much historical accounts vary, depending upon the climate of the times and basic attitudes of individual historians (as well as upon other considerations to be discussed in Chapter 2). However unsettling such variance may

Meeting of Cortes with Montezuma

be to those used to exact and indisputable answers, it is a way of life in history. Thus, when you read history you should try very hard to be sensitive to the manner in which information is presented and to the ultimate meaning the writer wants you to draw from the account.

As an example of how accounts of historical events can differ, we have provided three textbook accounts of the Spanish conquest of Mexico in the early 1500s. As you read the accounts, it is important to realize that if versions of the past differ, you should not come to the conclusion that one is automatically "correct" and the other "false." Truth and falsehood may be at stake, but more frequently differences emerge because authors include and exclude different "facts," and choose to emphasize different aspects of the episode under investigation.

The point of this exercise is to help you perceive similarities and, more important, differences in the accounts you read. First, read all of the questions that follow the third account, then read the accounts themselves and respond to the questions in the spaces provided.

Account 1

The great adventure of mainland conquest began in 1519, when Hernando Cortes and 600 men landed on the site of Vera Cruz, Mexico, which he founded. Cortes then set about a daring conquest of the Aztec Empire. The 200-mile march from Vera Cruz through difficult mountain passes to the Aztec capital of Tenochtitlan (Mexico City), and the subjugation of the Aztecs, was one of the most remarkable and tragic feats in human history.

Cortes had a few assets and made the most of them. An acute judge of character and a gifted diplomat as well as military leader, he landed in a region where the natives were still fighting off the spread of Aztec power and were ready to embrace new allies, especially those who possessed strange animals (horses) and powerful weapons. By a combination of threats and deception, Cortes was able to enter Tenochtitlan peacefully and to make the emperor, Montezuma, his puppet. This state of affairs lasted until the spring of 1520, when the Aztecs rebelled and stoned Montezuma to death. The Spaniards lost about a third of their men as they fought their way out of the city. Their allies remained loyal, however, and Cortes gradually regrouped his forces; in 1521 he took the city again. Thereafter Cortes and his officers simply replaced the former Aztec overlords as rulers over the Indian empire.

George Tindall and David Shi, *America*, brief 2nd ed. (New York: Norton, 1989), 9. Reprinted by permission.

Account 2

What Columbus did to the Arawaks of the Bahamas [killed them], Cortes did to the Aztecs of Mexico, Pizarro to the Incas of Peru, and the English settlers of Virginia and Massachusetts to the Powhatans and Pequots.

The Aztec civilization of Mexico came out of the heritage of Mayan, Zapotec, and Toltec cultures. It built enormous constructions from stone tools and human labor, developed a writing system and a priesthood. It also engaged in (let us not overlook this) the ritual killing of thousands of people as sacrifices to the gods. The cruelty of the Aztecs, however, did not erase a certain innocence, and when a Spanish armada appeared at Vera Cruz, and a bearded white man came ashore, with strange beasts (horses), clad in iron, it was thought that he was the legendary Aztec man-god who had died three hundred years before, with the promise to return—the mysterious Quetzalcoatl. And so they welcomed him, with munificent hospitality.

That was Hernando Cortes, come from Spain with an expedition financed by merchants and landowners and blessed by the deputies of God, with one obsessive goal: to find gold. . . . [Montezuma sent Cortes enormous treasures] but at the same time begg[ed] him to go back. . . .

Cortes then began his march of death from town to town, using deception, turning Aztec against Aztec, killing with the kind of deliberateness that accompanies a strategy—to paralyze the will of the population by a sudden frightful deed. And so, in Cholulu, he invited the headmen of the Cholula nation to the square. And when they came, with thousands of unarmed retainers, Cortes's small army of Spaniards, posted around the square with cannon, armed with crossbows, mounted on horses, massacred them, down to the last man. Then they looted the city and moved on. When their cavalcade of murder was over they were in Mexico City, Montezuma was dead, and the Aztec civilization, shattered, was in the hands of the Spaniards.

Howard Zinn, *A People's History of the United States* (New York: Harper and Row, 1980), 11–12. Reprinted by permission of HarperCollins Publishers, Inc.

Account 3

[After discussing a number of more traditional themes, a recent text adds the following section.]

The Spaniards had the good fortune to land in Central America when the Aztec empire was approaching a decisive moment in its history. By the time Montezuma overcame his initial hesitations and realized that Cortes and his men were not gods, it was too late. However, the Spanish victory was not quickly or easily won. In fact, Cortes might not have succeeded at all if he had not possessed an ally infinitely more powerful than any army and one virtually invulnerable to counterattack. That ally was one which all the European invaders in the Americas possessed. Its name was smallpox. . . .

[N]one of the epidemic diseases which had been perennial killers in other parts of the world had come to the Americas, and the Indians had no immunities to protect them.

The result of the geographical quarantine of the Americas was that at the very outset of the conquest, between one third and one half of the native population died of smallpox, typhus, influenza, or some other epidemic disease unknown in the Americas until the Europeans arrived. . . . In fact, it is virtually certain that Cortes would never have been able to conquer Tenochtitlan if an epidemic had not swept the city before and during the seventy-five days that he held it under siege. . . .

Rather than say that the Spaniards conquered the Aztecs and other Indian civilizations, perhaps it would be more accurate to say that the native Americans were conquered *for* the Spaniards by a plague of sickness of almost incomprehensible proportions.

Arthur S. Link, et al., *A Concise History of the American People*, Vol. I. (Arlington Heights, Ill.: Harlan Davidson, Inc., 1984), 7–8.

Questions

1. Are there common elements on which two or more accounts agree? Specify three of them:

   _____

   _____

   _____

2. This question deals with the ways in which the accounts are different from one another. For each question, write the number of the most appropriate account (#1 Tindall/Shi, #2 Zinn, #3 Link) and the phrase from the passage that justifies your selection.

   Which account:

   a. Gives most emphasis to Cortes' personality?

      _____

   b. Is most specific about the chronology of events?

      _____

   c. Gives some emphasis to the cultural background of the Aztecs?

      _____

   d. Makes reference to the importance of military technology?

      _____

   e. Discusses the political situation existing among the Indian population?

      _____

   f. Pays most attention to economic factors in the situation?

      _____

   g. Gives most attention to the religious aspects of the situation?

      _____

   h. Uses, in your opinion, the most emotion-charged language?

      _____

   i. Plays down the role of Spanish actions and policies in the defeat of the Aztecs?

      _____

3. Write a paragraph in which you indicate which passage you think does the best job of summarizing and explaining the Spanish conquest of Mexico. Give specific reasons for the choice you have made.

Most, though not all, of the words in the puzzle are related to the chapter discussion. You may have to return to the pages of the text for some of the answers.

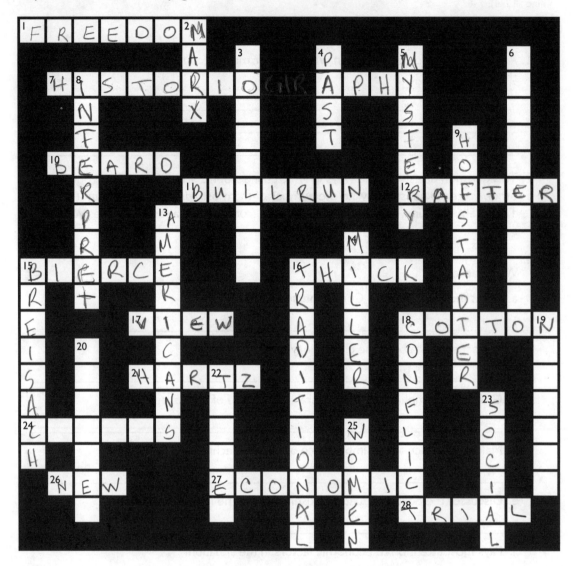

Across Clues

1. Essential ingredient in American life according to Traditionalists.
7. The writing of history; study of historical interpretive traditions.
10. Husband and wife Progressive historians
14. Site of the first skirmish of the American Revolution.
12. One of the support beams of a roof. Rhymes with "after."
15. Author of quotation introducing Chapter 1.
16. Type of detailed description found in the New history
17. All historians write from a distinctive point of _____.
18. Growth of these were a feature of Progressive-era America.
21. Consensus historian mentioned in chapter.
24. Assertions made by historians.
26. Most recent historiographic tradition discussed in chapter.
27. Factor emphasized by Progressive historians.
28. A proceeding in a courtroom.

Down Clues

2. Father of Marxist history.
3. School of history emphasizing unity of American values and traditions.
4. Historians study this.
5. An unsolved puzzle is a _____.   *Quandary?*
6. Reform-minded school of interpretation.
8. What historians do with facts.
9. A typical Consensus historian.
13. Viewed as God's chosen people by Traditionalists.
14. Consensus historian Perry _____.
15. Author whose book influenced the categories used in this chapter. (Hint: check the footnotes.)   *Breisach?*
16. School of interpretation characterized by nationalistic and patriotic sentiments.
18. Class _____ was a major emphasis of the Progressive historians.
19. Another word for researcher and teacher.
20. French school of historical interpretation.
22. Emphasized importance of frontier experience.
23. Type of history with "politics left out."
25. Group given more attention in the New history.

II   RECONSTRUCTION AND INDUSTRIALIZATION, 1865–1898

A   *The Varieties of American History*

See Exercise A in Part I.

B   *History as Account*

A major theme of this chapter has been how much historical accounts vary, depending upon the climate of the times and basic attitudes of individual historians (as well as upon other considerations to be discussed in Chapter 2). However unsettling such variance may be to those used to exact and indisputable answers, it is a way of life in history. Thus, when you read history you should try very hard to be sensitive to the manner in which information is presented and to the ultimate meaning the writer wants you to draw from the account.

As an example of how accounts of historical events can differ, we have provided three textbook passages that deal with the Great Railroad Strike of 1877. As you read the accounts, it is important to realize that if versions of the past differ, you should not come to the conclusion that one is automatically "correct" and the other "false." Truth and falsehood may be at stake, but more frequently differences emerge because authors include and exclude different "facts," and choose to emphasize different aspects of the episode under investigation.

The point of this exercise is to help you perceive similarities and, more important, differences in the accounts you read. First, read all of the questions that follow the third account, then read the accounts themselves and respond to the questions in the spaces provided.

Account 1

That year [1877] there came a series of tumultuous strikes by railroad workers in a dozen cities; they shook the nation as no labor conflict in its history has done.

It began with wage cuts on railroad after railroad, in tense situations of already low wages ($1.75 a day for brakemen working twelve hours), scheming and profiteering by the railroad companies, deaths and injuries among the workers—loss of hands, feet, fingers, the crushing of men between cars.

At the Baltimore & Ohio station in Martinsburg, West Virginia, workers determined to fight the wage cut went on strike, uncoupled the engines, ran them into the roundhouse, and announced no more trains would leave Martinsburg until the 10 percent cut was canceled. A crowd of support gathered, too many for the local police to disperse. B. & O. officials asked the governor for military protection, and he sent in militia. A train tried to get through, protected by the militia, and a striker, trying to derail it, exchanged gunfire with a militiaman attempting to stop him. The striker was shot in his thigh and his arm. His arm was amputated later that day, and nine days later he died.

Howard Zinn, *A People's History of the United States* (New York: Harper and Row, 1980), 240-41. Reprinted by permission of HarperCollins Publishers, Inc.

Account 2

On two occasions attempts were made to bring all railway workers together into a single industrywide union. Each instance resulted in a major work stoppage that culminated in federal intervention. The first occurred in June 1877. . . . The new [Trainmen's Union] mounted a strike against depression-era wage cuts imposed by some of the important roads. The strike began in the East and swept westward to such rail centers as Chicago, Omaha, and St. Louis. . . .

In Pittsburgh, the struggle was especially ugly. A unit of the state militia dispersed one body of strikers, killing twenty-six in the process, only to find itself besieged in a round-house from which it eventually withdrew under fire. It temporarily abandoned the city to a riotous mob, and the ensuing destruction of property totaled in the millions of dollars.

Militia units were soon deployed in other states, and President Rutherford Hayes sent federal troops to Illinois, Indiana, Maryland, Missouri, and West Virginia. They were dispatched in answer to urgent appeals from state governors and calls from federal court judges. It was the first significant occasion in American history in which the army had been ordered out to suppress a strike in time of peace.

C. Joseph Pusateri, *A History of American Business,* Second Edition (Wheeling, IL.: Harlan Davidson, Inc. 1988), 188.

Account 3

Excitement over the Molly Maguires [a militant labor organization] paled beside the near hysteria that gripped the country during the railroad strike of 1877, which began when the Eastern railroads announced a 10 percent wage cut and which soon expanded into something approaching a class war. Strikers disrupted rail service from Baltimore to St. Louis, destroyed equipment, and rioted in the streets of Pittsburgh and other cities. State militias were called out, and in July President Hayes ordered federal troops to suppress the disorders in West Virginia. In Baltimore, eleven demonstrators died and forty were wounded in a conflict between workers and militiamen. In Philadelphia, the state militia killed twenty people when the troops opened fire on thousands of workers and their families who were attempting to block the railroad crossings. In all, over 100 people died before the strike finally collapsed several weeks after it had begun.

The great railroad strike was America's first major, national labor conflict, and it illustrated that disputes between labor and capital could no longer be localized in the increasingly national economy. It illustrated as well the depth of resentment among many American workers and the lengths to which they were prepared to go to express that resentment. And, finally, it indicated the serious problems afflicting the labor movement. The failure of the strike severely weakened the railroad unions and damaged the reputation of labor organizations in other industries as well.

Alan Brinkley, *The Unfinished Nation* (New York: McGraw Hill, 1993), 480. Reprinted by permission of The McGraw-Hill Companies.

Questions

1. There are some common elements on which all the accounts agree. Specify three of them:

   _____

   _____

   _____

2. This question deals with the ways in which the accounts are different from one another. For each question, write the number of the most appropriate account (#1 Zinn, #2 Pusateri, #3 Brinkley) and the phrase from the passage that justifies your selection.

   Which account:

   a. Seems most sympathetic to the railroad workers?

   _____

   b. Is most sympathetic to business and government interests?

   _____

c. Provides most information about the American union movement?

_____

d. Gives the most comprehensive account of the effects of the strike?

_____

e. Minimizes the human suffering caused by the strike?

_____

f. Uses the most emotion-charged language?

_____

3. Write a paragraph in which you indicate which passage you think does the best job of summarizing and explaining the Railroad Strike of 1877. Give specific reasons for the choice you have made.

C *Crossword Puzzle*

See Exercise C in Part I.

THE NATURE
2 OF HISTORY

"[History] is the branch of inquiry that seeks to arrive at an accurate account and valid understanding of the past."

DAVID S. LANDES AND CHARLES TILLY

"As all historians know, the past is a great darkness, and filled with echoes. Voices may reach us from it; but what they say to us is imbued with the obscurity of the matrix out of which they come; and try as we may, we cannot always decipher them precisely in the clearer light of our own day."

MARGARET ATWOOD, *THE HANDMAID'S TALE*

Chapter 1 discussed how the American past has been chronicled in different ways during different eras in American history. As unsettling as that discovery may be, it may be even more unsettling to discover that even within a given period of history there are significant differences between individual historians' versions of the same events. To understand why this is so, we must look more closely at the nature of history itself.

There is no single, unanimously accepted version of American history. There are many versions that often conflict with one another. For instance, Hodding Carter III, Assistant Secretary of State under President Jimmy Carter, was aware at a young age that the American history he was taught in the South differed from what was taught in the North. "It was easy for me as a youngster growing up in Mississippi to know that my eighth-grade state history textbook taught me a lot which didn't jibe with what my cousins in Maine were being taught. We spoke of

the War Between the States. They spoke of the Civil War. . . . But our texts might as well have been written for study on different planets when it came to the status and feelings of the black men and women of the state or nation."[1]

The controversy over a 1991 exhibit at the Smithsonian Institution's Museum of American Art underscores the same point. At issue was the version of the history of the American West that should be presented to the American public. The exhibit, "The West as America: Reinterpreting

Images of the Frontier," challenged many traditional and romanticized American beliefs about the settlement of the West. The move westward, the exhibit suggested, was accompanied by many destructive environmental and social changes that had been overlooked in earlier versions of the frontier experience.

Critics were outraged. Ted Stevens, U.S. Senator from Alaska, fumed, "Why should people come [to the Smithsonian] and see a history that's so perverted?" Daniel Boorstin, an eminent and widely read historian, said the exhibit was "historically inaccurate [and] destructive."[2]

---

1 "Viewpoint," *The Wall Street Journal* (Sept. 23, 1982).
2 "Time to Circle the Wagons," *Newsweek* (May 27, 1991), 70; "Old West, New Twist at the Smithsonian," *The New York Times* (May 26, 1991, Section 2, 1.

This episode was reprised in 1995 when the Smithsonian's National Air and Space Museum planned an exhibit on the dropping of the first atomic bomb in 1945. A firestorm of controversy swirled around the historical narrative that was to accompany the exhibit. Planners and professional historians thought the exhibit should "encourage visitors to undertake a thoughtful and balanced reexamination" of the events in question; veterans' groups and others argued that the commentary was unbalanced and an insult to the soldiers who fought in the war.[3]

Why the controversy? Because people take their history seriously, and they become very uncomfortable if history challenges cherished beliefs and values. The situation can become explosive when historians attempt to record and explain the more unpleasant or even embarrassing episodes in one's own national past. In the early 1980s, for example, the Japanese government ordered a change in their textbooks that played down Japan's record of aggression and war crimes in the 1930s and 1940s, and then backed down in the face of a worldwide protest. The Holocaust is still an extremely sensitive subject in German textbooks. And, in the United States (again, according to Hodding Carter III), "those in charge of such things wanted the textbooks . . . to reflect an American past in which error was almost as foreign to our experience as evil. There was no such thing as racism in those books, or imperialism, or even very much about economic exploitation."[4]

This brings us back to the question: what is history? History—as you encounter it in a classroom or in daily life—is not the past itself, but an account or version of the past. History is the book we read, the lecture we listen to, the television show or film that we watch—or, the museum exhibit we attend. It is also the evening newscast or the daily newspaper. (Philip Graham, the late publisher of the *Washington Post*, said journalism was "the first rough draft of history.")[5]

But history has another meaning besides being an account of the past. There is an ambiguity in the English language that confuses the issue. People sometimes use the word history to mean the past itself—every event that has actually occurred over the centuries. Barbara Tuchman, one of the most accomplished historians of our time, was quite right when she defined history "as the past events of which we have knowledge."[6] However, since we cannot directly study what actually happened, we have to rely on records of those events written by eyewitnesses or participants. These records, called original or primary sources, are the materials that historians use to write their accounts—the books and articles we read. Thus, as James Davidson and Mark Lytle put it, "History is not 'what happened in the past'; rather, it is the act of selecting, analyzing, and writing about the past. It is something that is done, that is constructed, rather than an inert body of data that lies scattered through the archives."[7]

HOW HISTORICAL ACCOUNTS ARE CREATED

History, then, involves an act of creation, but the process is not a simple one. The historian's intellectual task is challenging for two reasons: first, an immense gulf separates the present time from the past historians try to reconstruct and understand; and second, the available evidence is flawed and incomplete.

The key challenge faced by any historian is that the past is lost forever. Unlike scientists who can experiment directly with tangible objects, historians cannot study the past directly, for instance, they can't repeat the Civil War to see if it would come out differently if Robert E. Lee had not made a fatal error at Gettysburg. They will never be able to interview the delegates to the Constitutional Convention, nor visit the Roanoke Island colony founded by Sir Walter Raleigh to find out why the colonists disappeared from the face of the earth. These things did happen, and yet the individuals involved are as inaccessible to the historian as Pharaoh or Julius Caesar. Because of this, the past can only be understood indirectly and imperfectly, and only in terms of the evidence available.

---

3 *The New York Times* (February 5, 1995), E5.

4 *The Wall Street Journal* (Sept. 23, 1982).

5 Quoted in Ken Burns, "The Painful, Essential Images of War," *New York Times* (January 27, 1991).

6 Barbara Tuchman, *Practicing History* (New York: Knopf, 1981), 27.

7 James Davidson and Mark Lytle, *After the Fact: The Art of Historical Detection* (New York: Knopf, 1982), xvii.

Although the past is forever lost, remnants survive as guideposts to those distant events. As Margaret Atwood wrote in her novel *The Handmaid's Tale*, "the past is a great darkness . . . filled with echoes,"[8] and those echoes are all that historians have to work with as they try to reconstruct and explain the human experience. The echoes take many forms: surviving buildings, works of art, weapons, pots, monuments, photographs, recordings, even human remains. But, overwhelmingly, the study of history is based on written records that have survived into our day.

In one sense, too many written records have survived. So many documents are available to

beings who inhabit the earth and you get some idea of the number of events each day that go unrecorded. That is only the beginning of the problem. In the words of historian Louis Gottschalk:

> Only a part of what was observed in the past was remembered by those who observed it; only a part of what was remembered was recorded; only a part of what was recorded has survived; only a part of what has survived has come to the historians' attention; only a part of what has come to their attention is credible; only a part of what is credible has been grasped; and only a part of what has been grasped can be expounded or narrated by the historian. . . . Before the past is set forth by the historian, it is likely to have gone through eight separate steps at each of which some of it has been lost; and

**FROM EVENT TO EVIDENCE:
THE FUNNEL OF DIMINISHING RESOURCES**

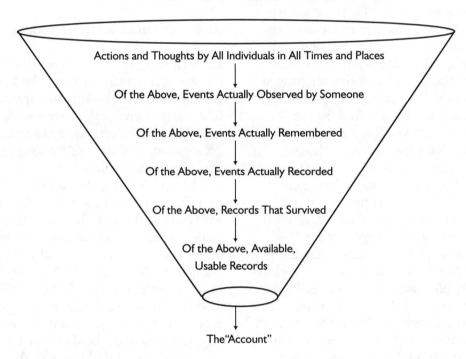

Actions and Thoughts by All Individuals in All Times and Places

Of the Above, Events Actually Observed by Someone

Of the Above, Events Actually Remembered

Of the Above, Events Actually Recorded

Of the Above, Records That Survived

Of the Above, Available, Usable Records

The "Account"

Figure 1

historians that an individual would be hard pressed to read everything relevant to a single topic. But compared to the immensity of the past itself, the surviving records are like a very few drops of water in a very large bucket. For instance, most past events left no records at all! Think of the number of events in your own life for which there is no record but your own memory. Multiply those unrecorded events in your own life by the billions of lives of human

there is no guarantee that what remains is the most important, the largest, the most valuable, the most representative, or the most enduring part. In other words the "object" that the historian studies is not only incomplete; it is markedly variable as records are lost or recovered.[9]

The historian, then, is at the end of a distillation process in which the immensity of the human experience is reduced to a few, sometimes unrepresentative, fragments of the original. (See Figure 1.)

---

8 Margaret Atwood, *The Handmaid's Tale* (New York: Ballantine, 1987), 394.
9 Louis Gottschalk, *Understanding History* (New York: Knopf, 1950), 45–46.

SUBJECTIVITY AND OBJECTIVITY IN THE STUDY OF HISTORY

The immense chasm that separates historians from the past they study and the incomplete and flawed evidence they have to work with leads to the conclusion that all historical accounts are somewhat subjective. Since historians can never get at the full truth about a segment of the past, the best they can do is provide a partial sketch. There is, of course, a relationship between the past-as-it-happened and the historian's account, but the account can never be definitive or complete. "Even the best history," said Civil War historian Bruce Catton, "is not much better than a mist through which we see shapes dimly moving." Or, in the words of W. S. Holt, "History is a damn dim candle over a damn dark abyss."

The historian is also a factor in the equation. Personal biases, political beliefs, economic status, religious persuasion, errors, and idiosyncrasies can subtly and unconsciously influence the way in which sources are interpreted. Conservative Republicans often read and interpret the political history of the United States in a very different way than liberal Democrats. Protestants and Catholics have written distinctive

versions of the religious upheavals known as the Reformation. Northerners and Southerners, as mentioned earlier, continue to have their differences concerning the history of the American Civil War.

Writing history, then, is an act of personal creation, or more accurately, an act of re-creation, in which the mind of the historian is the catalyst; and, whether written or spoken, every piece of history represents the scholarly and creative effort of a single individual. One might even say our history is as much a product of the historians who write it as the people who actually participated in the events it attempts to describe. Small wonder written history is subjective.

At this point you might be asking, "Why study history at all if historical accounts are so far removed from the past they attempt to understand?" What happens to the search for truth if we acknowledge that historical accounts are by nature subjective and incomplete? How can we justify the pursuit of knowledge that appears so shallow and fleeting?

History students should be aware that an element of subjectivity does not invalidate the importance or substance of historical studies. Even though the records of past events are inadequate and difficult to interpret, they do constitute a tangible link between past and present. And, even though historians can never completely eradicate their personal frames of reference, they can still write credible and convincing accounts that are firmly grounded in the existing evidence. As Stephen Jay Gould, the Harvard paleontologist, puts it: "We understand that biases, preferences, social values, and psychological attitudes all play a strong role in the process of discovery. However, we should not be driven to the opposite extreme of complete cynicism—the view that objective evidence plays no role, that perceptions of truth are entirely relative, and that scientific [or historical] conclusions are just another form of aesthetic preference."[10]

This is an important point: history is not fiction. Different historians will interpret the past differently for many different reasons. But in all cases their accounts must be based on all the available relevant evidence. A version of the past that cannot be supported by evidence is worth-

---

10 Stephen Jay Gould, *Wonderful Life: The Burgess Shale and the Nature of History* (New York: W. W. Norton, 1989), 244.

less and will quickly be rejected by other historians. Thus one opinion (no matter how strongly held), is *not* as good as another, and the student of history, whether a beginner or seasoned professional, must learn to discriminate between accounts that are supported by the evidence and those that fail this basic test.

Finally, history is not the only discipline in which conclusions are tentative and constantly open to revision. No field of study is ever static, since all research is, to some degree, conditioned by the climate of the times, the values and attitudes of the researchers themselves, and the discovery of new evidence. Even theories in the so-called hard sciences are influenced by the context of time, place, and circumstance.

CONCLUSION

The realization that history involves the study of individual interpretations or versions of the past can be unsettling. Many of us yearn for the security afforded by unchallenged, definitive answers to a limited and manageable set of questions. To find out that historians are always asking new questions and continually offering new answers to old questions eliminates the possibility of an absolute and singular truth about the human past. At the same time, this is also what makes history so intellectually exciting. History is not the dead study of a dead past; it is not about the memorization of dates, names, and places. History is a living and evolving dialogue about the most important subject of all—the human experience. And all of us are capable in taking part in that dialogue.

The remaining question is, how do you do this? The answer is simple: by learning how historians think and by sharpening the analytical and communication skills that are essential for success in college and professional life. These skills and thought processes are what we call the methods of history.

The methods of history are not especially complicated or confusing. Most of them are common sensical, and can be learned without a great deal of specialized or technical training. Although doing history is not altogether easy, with some time, effort, and enthusiasm even beginning students can become historically literate.

We have seen in this chapter that every piece of history represents an individual account of a segment of the past. A skeptic might ask "Why do historians keep writing new versions of events that have already been examined by dozens or hundreds of previous historians?"

There are a number of reasons for the perpetual rewriting of history: revision is necessary when new information is discovered; the reexamination of old information from a fresh perspective often requires the rewriting of history, since one historian will often interpret the same evidence differently than another; and historians ask new questions of the past that require different sorts of answers. This is often a product of changing times: as our interests change, so do the historical questions that seem most relevant. For instance, since the 1960s more and more American minority groups have demanded equal treatment both before the law and in history books. As a result there has been an explosion in the writing and teaching of women's history, African-American history, Hispanic history, the history of mass culture, and the history of Native Americans, both before and after the coming of the Europeans in 1492.

Two books—Alfred Crosby's *The Columbian Exchange* (1972) and William McNeill's, *Plagues and Peoples* (1976)—provide an example of how new perspectives, new questions and new information can change the way in which we understand our past.[11] A staple of every American history textbook is the story of Hernando Cortes' conquest of the Aztec Empire in Mexico in the early 1500s. Cortes came to Mexico with about 600 men and a few horses and within two or three years he became the master of a huge empire numbering in the millions. Cortes' conquest was traditionally explained as the product of superior technology (guns), Aztec fear of horses (hitherto unknown in the New World), and his ability to find allies among the other Indian peoples of Mexico.

None of these explanations seemed adequate to Crosby or McNeill. "How could such a tiny handful [of Spaniards] prevail?" McNeill asked. Given the relatively few Spaniards who followed Cortes to the New World, how could one explain the ease with which the Spaniards imposed their culture on the defeated Indians? The answer, as the title of McNeill's book hints, is that the Spaniards brought with them a disease—smallpox—that was familiar to Europeans, but not to the Indians. Crosby explains that since the New World had been biologically isolated from the Old World for thousands of years, "the fatal diseases of the Old World killed more effectively in the New, and the comparatively benign diseases of the Old World turned killer in the New." Thus, there came with Cortes "an epidemic whose influence on the history of America is as unquestionable and as spectacular as that of the Black Death on the history of the Old World."[12]

The critical new piece of information came from the field of biology, specifically the study of epidemic disease. Diseases are most destructive when introduced into a community for

---

11 Alfred Crosby, Jr., *The Columbian Exchange: Biological and Cultural Consequences of 1492* (Westport, CT: Greenwood Press, 1972); William McNeill, *Plagues and Peoples* (New York: Anchor, 1976).
12 Crosby, *Columbian Exchange*, 37, 42. See also McNeill, *Plagues and Peoples* , 1–2 and ch. V, passim.

the first time. Tens of thousands of Indians died from smallpox while the Spanish, having survived the disease in childhood, were relatively unaffected.

Another piece of new information—that there were far more Indians in the New World than anyone had previously thought—provided another sobering realization. The number of Indians who died of European diseases during the first century of the age of exploration (roughly the sixteenth century) numbered not in the tens of thousands, but in the tens of millions.[13] Some estimate that, in the century after the landing of Columbus, 90 percent of the native population died of the consequences of epidemic disease! Whole regions were depopulated, leaving vast territories open to the disease-hardened colonists from Europe.

Thus McNeill and Crosby show how new questions (e.g., How has disease influenced the history of the world?), new information (about the behavior of diseases and the size of pre-Columbian populations of the New World), and new societal attitudes (a new environmental and ecological awareness) combined to prompt a radical rethinking of the Age of Discovery and Colonization. These insights are now being incorporated into the textbook accounts you may be reading. (Note especially the third account of Cortes' conquest of Mexico in the Part I exercises of Chapter 1 [p. 10–11].)

---

13 Although the size of the pre–Columbian population of the Americas is still the subject of debate, it seems likely that previous estimates have been unrealistically low. See Leslie Roberts, "Disease and Death in the New World," *Science*, Vol. 246 (December 8, 1989), 1245–47.

EXERCISES

I AGE OF DISCOVERY-EARLY COLONIAL PERIOD, 1492–1650

A *The Nature of History*[14]

Now that you have had the time to think about what "history" actually is, respond to the following statements, indicating whether you agree (A), disagree (D), or are undecided (U). In this exercise, "history" refers to accounts of the past. Be prepared to defend your answer in discussion or in writing.

A___ D___ U___ 1. American history textbooks only provide the basic facts about American history.

A___ D___ U___ 2. Only the discovery of new information makes it necessary to re-write history.

A___ D___ U___ 3. It is possible to come to different conclusions using the same evidence.

A___ D___ U___ 4. Given enough effort it is possible to discover the one true version of an event.

A___ D___ U___ 5. Since it is impossible to know everything about a past event, one opinion about the past is as good as another opinion.

A___ D___ U___ 6. There is no way to determine which historian's interpretation of an event is most accurate.

A___ D___ U___ 7. In history the facts speak for themselves.

A___ D___ U___ 8. Historians interpret the past differently because they have different biases and values.

A___ D___ U___ 9. Historians explain the past differently because they interpret the evidence differently.

A___ D___ U___ 10. Historians should present the facts objectively and not try to interpret them.

A___ D___ U___ 11. Written history records the past as it actually was.

A___ D___ U___ 12. The test of a historian's interpretation is how well the known evidence supports it.

A___ D___ U___ 13. Since history is subjective, it can never teach us anything about the past.

A___ D___ U___ 14. Historians decide which facts are important to include in any account of the past.

A___ D___ U___ 15. It is possible for historians to be perfectly objective if they just write about the known facts.

A___ D___ U___ 16. The use of evidence is influenced by historians' previous experiences and beliefs.

---

14 The concept for this exercise and a number of the questions have been based on Frederick D. Drake, "Using Primary Sources and Historians' Interpretations in the Classroom," *Teaching History*, Vol. 11, No. 2 (Fall 1986), 57–59.

A___ D___ U___ 17. Using historical methods it is possible to understand important episodes in the past.

A___ D___ U___ 18. All historical accounts must recreate the past they are trying to describe.

A___ D___ U___ 19. History can tell us very little about the past because historians disagree with one other.

A___ D___ U___ 20. Historians have an obligation to tell the truth.

B *Fact and Opinion in History*

A major theme of this chapter was the re-creative, often subjective, nature of historical study. The past is real, but accounts of the past reflect historians' differing interests, priorities, values, ideologies, and abilities. A work of history is never *the history* of a subject, but *a history* of the subject—just one of many possible versions. As a student of history you should try to become alert to how the story you read is shaped by the hand of the historian.

Below are a number of statements drawn from a variety of sources. Some of the statements are predominately factual—that is, they purport simply to describe a person or event. Other statements reflect the writer's judgment or interpretation of a person or event—an opinion based on evidence, but an opinion nevertheless. Fitting in the category of opinion are passages which contain factual material but also do one or more of the following: (1) attempt to explain the relationships among the facts presented; (2) characterize individuals or situations; or (3) provide an evaluation of the historical occurrence.

Below label each passage according to whether it is predominantly FACT (F) or predominantly OPINION (O). If a passage contains a relative balance of facts and opinions, write "FO." Underline any segment that you feel is opinion (i.e., explanation, interpretation or judgment). In all cases assume that the opinions are based on solid evidence, and are not arbitrary preferences like the choice of a favorite color or food. The first two statements have been completed as examples.

___F___ 1. Born in 1451, the son of an Italian weaver, Columbus took to the sea at an early age and made up for his lack of formal education by learning geography, navigation, and Latin.

In a sense, no statement is purely factual since the individual writer must choose which pieces of information to include and which words to use. For instance, note how different the tone of the above sentence would be if the writer had said, "Columbus took to the sea totally lacking a formal education." Such a statement would have implicitly portrayed Columbus as a person unprepared for his journey.

However, for the purposes of this exercise, let's ignore this technicality. We labelled this statement "Fact" because it simply provides basic information without any comment on its meaning or significance.

___O___ 2. Columbus' dazzling fame, at least from the American perspective, has blinded us to other achievements of seafaring discovery as great or even greater in that first Age of the Sea.

This sentence clearly provides the author's judgment (opinion) that the achievements of sailors other than Columbus were ultimately more important than those of Columbus himself. Hence we have labelled the statement "Opinion," and underlined the interpretive part of the statement. Note the characterization of Columbus' fame (dazzling), and the reminder that Columbus' achievement was not unique. Note also that there is an element of fact in the statement, namely the reference to the fame that Columbus enjoys in America.

Now do the same thing with the statements below, and be prepared to defend your answers in discussion.

_____   3. The pre–Columbian agriculturalists [native Americans] developed the American food plants from an assemblage of wild plants which was very different from that which the inventors of agriculture in the Old World had.

_____   4. Before they could settle an area of the Americas, therefore, the Europeans had to invade it, conquer its inhabitants, and evict them from their land. Such a struggle for the control of land and resources was, by its very nature, a brutal one that cost many thousands of lives.

_____   5. These independent adventurers [the Spanish Conquistadors] carved out small settlements on Cuba, Hispaniola, Jamaica, and Puerto Rico in the 1490s and early 1500s.

_____   6. The most important Indian leader in Virginia was Powhatan, who dominated virtually all the Indian tribes along the Virginia coast and whose influence extended from Maryland to the Carolinas.

_____   7. Whatever the exact number [of native Americans, or Indians], the crucial fact so often overlooked in studying colonial history is that the Indian population along the west coasts of both continents [North and South America], in Central America, and—to a lesser degree—on the east coast of North America, was considerable—seventy-five people per one hundred square kilometers. Europeans were <u>not</u> entering empty continents, as is so often implied.

_____   8. The oldest of these [myths about the Indians] is the myth of the Noble Red Man or the Child of Nature, who is credited either with a habit of flowery oratory of implacable dullness or else with an imbecilic inability to converse in anything more than grunts and monosyllables. . . . It was in the earliest period of the Noble Red Man concept that the Indians probably exerted their most important influence upon Western Civilization.

_____   9. Human beings had been in the New World for at least 15,000 years. During much of that time, as was the case in the beginning everywhere, they advanced but little from a Paleolithic hunting culture.

_____   10. The Plains Indians did some farming but gradually became more and more nomadic as they followed the buffalo herds. Dogs, their only domesticated animal, pulled the Plains Indians' possessions along on a pair of A-shaped poles, later called a *travois* by the French. These same poles were utilized to form the framework of their teepees.

_____   11. Mexican Americans in Texas descend from people whose ancestry is Spanish and Mexican Indian. After the Spanish conquest of present-day Mexico in the early sixteenth century, Iberian males intermixed with Indian women. Cultures also blended, and those people of a blended heritage and culture moved northward from Mexico and laid the foundation for what would become Mexican-American communities in the United States.

_____   12. These cases of working, professional, and entrepreneurial women are not consistent with the customary image of docile colonial women in their prim white caps and serviceable dresses quietly caring for their homes and families. Yet many colonial writers and speakers exerted a good deal of energy promoting this image of the passive and domestic woman.

Sources

1. George Tindall and David Shi, *America*, brief 2nd ed. (New York: Norton, 1989), 4.
2. Daniel Boorstin, *The Discoverers* (New York: Knopf, 1978), 175.

3. Alfred Crosby, Jr., *The Columbian Exchange* (Westport, CT.: Greenwood Press, 1972), 5.

4, 6. Arthur S. Link, et al., *A Concise History of the American People* (Arlington Heights, IL.: Harlan Davidson, Inc., 1984), 2, 17.

5. Robert A. Divine, et. al., *America Past and Present* (Glenview, IL.: Scott, Foresman, 1984), 15.

7, 10. Jerome R. Reich, *Colonial America*, 2nd ed. (Englewood Cliffs, NJ.: Prentice Hall, 1989), 25, 20.

8, 9. Oliver La Farge, "Myths That Hide the American Indian," in John A Garraty, ed., *Historical Viewpoints*, Vol. I, 2nd ed. (New York: Harper Row, 1975), 3, 4.

11. Arnoldo De León, *Mexican Americans in Texas* (Wheeling, IL.: Harlan Davidson, Inc. 1993), 5.

12. Glenda Riley, *Inventing the American Woman*, Vol. I (Wheeling, IL.: Harlan Davidson, Inc. 1986), 18.

II   RECONSTRUCTION AND INDUSTRIALIZATION, 1865–1898

A   The Nature of History

See Exercise A in Part I.

Alternate Exercise A

Which one statement in Exercise A (Part I) do you agree with most strongly? Write a paragraph explaining your reasons.

B   Fact and Opinion in History

A major theme of this chapter was the re-creative, often subjective, nature of historical study. The past is real, but accounts of the past reflect historians' differing interests, priorities, values, ideologies, and abilities. A work of history is never the history of a subject, but a history of the subject—just one of many possible versions. As a student of history you should try to become alert to how the story you read is shaped by the hand of the historian.

Below are a number of statements drawn from a variety of sources. Some of the statements are predominately factual, that is they purport simply to describe a person or event. Other statements reflect the writer's judgment or interpretation of a person or event—an opinion based on evidence, but an opinion nevertheless. Fitting in the category of opinion are passages which contain factual material but also do one or more of the following: (1) attempt to explain the relationships among the facts presented; (2) characterize individuals or situations; or (3) provide an evaluation of the historical occurrence.

Below label each passage according to whether it is predominantly FACT (F) or predominantly OPINION (O). If a passage contains a relative balance of facts and opinions, write "FO." Underline any segment that you feel is opinion (i.e., explanation, interpretation or judgment). In all cases assume that the opinions are based on solid evidence, and are not arbitrary preferences like the choice of a favorite color or food. The first two statements have been completed as examples.

_____F_____ 1. Harriet Tubman (1823–1913) [was] the runaway slave who before the war led three hundred slaves out of the South by the Underground Railroad.

In a sense, no statement is purely factual since the individual writer must choose which pieces of information to include and which words to use. Note how the above sentence would have been changed by calling Harriet Tubman a "criminal runaway slave" instead of simply a "runaway slave." For the purposes of this exercise, however, try to ignore this technicality. We labelled this statement "Fact" because it provides basic information without any assessment of its meaning or significance.

_____FO_____ 2. In June 1863 she [Harriet Tubman] led a band of black soldiers up the Combahee River in South Carolina, burning plantations and freeing more than eight hundred slaves. <u>Her behavior was bold and courageous, and quite untypical of women's usual wartime role. But then Harriet Tubman, the Moses of her people, had always behaved extraordinarily.</u>

This passage is a mixture of fact and opinion. The first sentence is factual. The rest of the passage (underlined) is the historian's interpretation of Harriet Tubman's actions in 1863 and previously. The interpretation includes both a characterization and an evaluation of Tubman in relation to other women. Also, note that the interpretation (opinion) is strongly supported by the evidence—i.e., the factual statement that precedes it.

Sand Creek Massacre

_____ 3. Under multiple blows, the fabric of Indian political and social life gave way. A half century of American control saw the California Indian population steadily decline until it was less than one-fifth of what it had been in 1848. *Genocide* is a term of awful significance, but one which has application to the story of California's Native Americans.

_____ 4. When [Frances Willard] accepted the presidency of the WCTU [Women's Christian Temperance Union] in 1879, she began her sustained effort to shape a new consciousness in the United States—woman consciousness. She was all the while a profoundly conservative defender of duty, individuality, dignity and self-respect.

_____ 5. In the early 1870s Irish-America began to emerge from the destitution and discrimination which had characterized the preceding quarter-century. . . . By the 1880s literate immigrants and their children supported at least one Irish-American newspaper in nearly every major city in the North and Midwest (New York alone boasted five), and by the early twentieth century a higher proportion of Irish-American youths were attending college than were those of WASP parentage.

_____ 6. There were 5½ million immigrants in the 1880s, 4 million in the 1890s, creating a labor surplus that kept wages down. The immigrants were more controllable, more helpless than native workers; they were culturally displaced, at odds with one another, therefore useful as strikebreakers. Often their children worked, intensifying the problem of an oversized labor force and joblessness. . . . With everyone working long hours, families often became strangers to one another.

_____ 7. The American Century began in the 1890s.

_____ 8. The Utes were Rocky Mountain Indians, and for a generation they had watched the invading white men move into their Colorado country like endless swarms of grasshoppers. . . . [E]ach year these strange men from the East became more numerous, invading the Utes' mountains to dig for yellow and white metal.

_____ 9. The Land Commission first advertised the farms on the Marshall Tract in January and February 1870. Eleven freedmen and their families established conditional ownership of their farms before spring planting that year. They were among a vanguard of some 14,000 Negro families who acquired small farms in South Carolina through the Land Commission program between 1868 and 1879.

_____ 10. Traditional interpretations of industrialization require refinement. Familiar accounts are likely to ignore the dependence of early mills on women for their labor force, yet even Alexander Hamilton recognized that a crucial factor in the development of new factories was that their owners could count on a steady supply of female workers at low rates of pay. Women were among the first self-conscious laborers in America.

Sources

1, 2. June Sochen, *Herstory: A Record of the American Woman's Past,* 2nd ed. (Sherman Oaks, CA: Alfred, 1981), 139.

3. William T. Hagan, "How the West Was Lost," *Indians in American History,* ed. Frederick E. Hoxie (Wheeling, IL.: Harlan Davidson, Inc. 1988), 193.

4. Norman Clark, *Deliver Us from Evil: An Interpretation of American Prohibition* (New York: Norton, 1976), 85.

5. Kerby A. Miller, *Emigrants and Exiles: Ireland and the Irish Exodus to North America* (New York: Oxford University Press, 1985), 495.

6. Howard Zinn, *A People's History of the United States* (New York: Harper, 1980), 261. Reprinted by permission of HarperCollins Publishers, Inc.

7. Walter LaFeber, "The Lion in the Path," *Constitution* (Spring-Summer, 1991), 14.

8. Dee Brown, *Bury My Heart at Wounded Knee* (New York: Bantam, 1970), 349.

9. Elizabeth Rauh Bethel, "Promised Land," *The American Record,* Vol. I, 2nd ed., ed. William Graebner and Leonard Richards (New York: Alfred A. Knopf, 1982), 349.

10. Linda Kerber and Jane De Hart, eds., *Women's America,* 3rd ed. (New York: Oxford University Press, 1991), 99.

HISTORICAL THINKING | 3

"Nothing capable of being memorized is history."

R. G. COLLINGWOOD

"[Evolutionary history is] a staggeringly improbable series of events, sensible enough in retrospect and subject to rigorous explanation, but utterly unpredictable and quite unrepeatable."

STEPHEN JAY GOULD

R. G. Collingwood and Stephen Jay Gould, in the quotations above, summarize nicely the maddening paradox inherent in the study of history. Historians attempt to explain, not memorize, the past, but the events they try to explain are unique and unrepeatable—they happen only once in precisely that way at precisely that time.

Because history is made up of unique and nonrepeatable events, historical explanations differ from those found in the sciences. Science tries to discover explanations that are universally applicable to all similar situations in all times and places—i.e., water freezes at 32 degrees Fahrenheit at standard temperature and pressure. Science also values explanations that allow us to predict the future: tomorrow, or next year, water will still freeze at 32 degrees. Historians can't make such universal generalizations because the events of history are embedded in a web of particular circumstances that will never repeat themselves in precisely the same way.[1]

Although historians cannot predict the future, they *can* explain events after they occur, using methods that allow them to reconstruct the past with some precision. Gould, both scientist and historian, argues that historical explanations are as valid as those based on the experimental scientific method:

> Historical explanations take the form of narrative: E, the phenomenon to be explained, arose because D came before, preceded by C, B, and A. If any of these earlier stages had not occurred, or had transpired in a different way, then E would not exist (or would be present in a substantially altered form, E′ requiring a different explanation). . . . This final result is therefore dependent, or contingent, upon everything that came before—the unerasable and determining signature of history.[2]

Historical explanations, then, must be firmly embedded in the concrete circumstances of time and place. Every human event is a link in a chain that reaches far into the past, and, at any given point in time, there are myriad forces and individuals that determine the final shape of the event in question. Thinking historically, consequently, involves placing events in their appropriate historical context and identifying the multiple forces or causes that produced the final result.

MULTIPLE CAUSATION IN HISTORY

If you study philosophy you will discover that cause is a slippery and confusing term that is difficult to define to everyone's satisfaction. Still, cause is a concept and a word that most of us can't do without. Every day we attempt to explain events that interest us—the slump of the local baseball team, the neighbors' divorce, the defeat of the local bond issue—and it is that commonsense meaning of the term that we will

---

1 For the sake of simplicity, this paragraph overstates the differences between history and the sciences. Sciences such as astronomy and geology, like history, rely heavily on the study of records of past events—the light and radio waves that originated eons in the past and the rock formations that offer mute testimony to geologic upheavals thousands of years ago. Also, scientific theories are less absolute and universal than the lay public often assumes. Like historical interpretations, scientific theories often reflect the culture and intellectual climate of a particular time and place.

2 Gould, *Wonderful Life,* 283. Reprinted by permission.

be using in this book. "Cause," said historian Carl Gustavson, "is a convenient figure of speech for any one of a number of factors which help explain why a historical event happened."[3]

The Spanish conquest of Mexico, discussed earlier, provides a good example of how confusing the issue of causality can become. To the question "Who (or what) destroyed the Aztec empire?" historians have identified a number of possible culprits: superior European technology, Indian disunity, the idea that Cortes was a legendary Aztec god, infectious disease, the inadequacies of Montezuma as a leader, etc. As we nod our heads in agreement we realize that we have only begun to scratch the surface, for we can also look a bit further back and ask, "What

factors brought Cortes to the New World in the first place?" What economic, technological, military, diplomatic, and ideological impulses set Europeans to exploring the globe? Why did Spanish soldiers, and not English, French, or Italian soldiers, step ashore at Veracruz in 1519? And, why did Cortes land at that spot and not some other? Was it intentional? Did winds drive him off course? Was it an arbitrary decision or an accident?

This brief example dramatizes the point that no single cause ever provides an adequate explanation of a historical event. Not only do historians have to look beyond the immediate cause— i.e., further back into the past—they also have to consider a broad range of possible causal factors.

ASKING QUESTIONS

How is this done? Most simply by asking a series of questions, like a detective, and seeing which answers fit best. As James Thurber said,

"It is better to know some of the questions than all of the answers."

The following questions should almost always be asked about any given episode in history.[4] Some of these may prove to be irrelevant when applied to a given event, but if you ask (and answer) all of them you will be on your way to becoming historically literate. After determining the immediate trigger of an event, you should ask:

1. *What individuals had an important impact on the outcome?*

This is not the place to debate whether the individual makes the times (the so-called "Great Man Theory" of history) or the times make the individual. Whichever the case, individual human actions, personalities, characters, and motives do influence the course of history. While it would be a mistake to simply patch together accounts of the deeds of historical heroes or villains, it would be equally a mistake to assume that individuals are merely victims of forces they cannot control. On a more practical level, one of the best ways to begin studying a historical event is to read about the most prominent individuals (e.g., Cortes, Montezuma) who seemed to make a difference.

Single individuals certainly have influenced the course of history. But individuals in groups or as a collective whole have a much enhanced power to divert the course of history into new channels.

2. *Were there any powerful ideas or belief-systems (ideologies) that were influential?*

The adage that people "do not possess ideas, rather they are possessed by them" has much truth, especially if ideas are taken to include not only the influential theories of philosophers and scientists, but the popular ideals, beliefs, attitudes, and values shared by a society or large portions of it. Frequently people are not even conscious of the ideas and values that influence their decisions, and it is often ideas that are not explicitly recognized that exert the most powerful influence on human behavior. The alert historian will always be reading between the lines to try to ferret out elements of the dominant world view at a particular time in history.

---

3 Carl G. Gustavson, *A Preface to History* (New York: McGraw-Hill, 1955) 55.
4 The list is based on, but not identical to, the questions suggested by Carl Gustavson. See *Preface to History*, 62.

One of the most passionate modern debates about the American Revolution concerns the origin and nature of the ideas that became the basis of English and American political culture in the eighteenth century. One set of ideas, usually associated with the English philosopher John Locke and the English Common Law emphasized individualism, competition, the protection of property, and self-interest. The other set of ideas (called "republicanism"), whose origins can be traced ultimately to ancient Rome and Renaissance Italy, emphasized "self-sacrifice and self-control in the interest of the common good."[5]

Historians may disagree whether eighteenth-century American revolutionary ideals owe more to one or the other of these intellectual and cultural traditions, but they are unanimous that ideas played a vital role in the politics of the eighteenth century.

Individual books can often have a dramatic impact. In the nineteenth century Harriet Beecher Stowe's *Uncle Tom's Cabin* changed northern perceptions of slavery before the Civil War, and Alfred Thayer Mahan's famous work, *The Influence of Sea Power upon History* (1890) prompted the U.S. government, and others around the world, to invest staggering sums of money in battleship construction. Upton Sinclair's, *The Jungle* (1906) is often credited (too simplistically) with prompting President Theodore Roosevelt and Congress to draft and pass the Meat Inspection Act of 1906.

When historians try to get a feel for the climate of the times or the explicit ideas that take a society by storm, they should look for both emergent ideas of compelling power and traditional ideas that maintain an enduring hold on people's loyalties.

3. *Were there economic forces or interests that influenced the course of events?*

We all know that individuals often make decisions based on economic interests. "What's in it for me?" they ask. But when historians talk about economic factors in history, they have something more in mind. Economics refers to the processes by which a society and its members make a living and major changes in the way goods and wealth are produced or distributed. Both of these factors can radically affect the course of history. Thus economic factors are those that involve large numbers of people, and often polarize groups (farmers and cattle ranchers), classes (peasants and landowners), and nations. Historians must ask what economic forces and what group economic interests caused people to behave as they did.

So important are economic factors in influencing human affairs that some writers have suggested that changes in the economic basis of society and in economic relationships are the key to history. Karl Marx and Friedrich Engels argued this viewpoint over a century ago when they wrote the famous sentence: "The history of all hitherto existing society is the history of class struggles."[6] This is too simple (remember, no single cause is an adequate historical explanation), but Marx and Engels were correct in making their generation and ours appreciate how important economic factors are as causal factors in history.

4. *Were technological developments or constraints important?*

Related to economic factors are technological developments that influence a society's production processes and its lifestyle. Such developments can bring sharp changes in a society's direction, as happened in America in 1793. Before that date slavery was commonly regarded in the South as a crumbling system. Southerners lacked a profitable cash crop to support the expenses of the institution. Then, while visiting at a South Carolina plantation, young Eli Whitney put together a simple but ingenious device called a cotton gin. It made what was then called green-seed cotton a viable crop—at exactly the time when English mills were voraciously consuming every fiber of cotton that could be produced. Thus, cotton became "map-maker, trouble-maker, history-maker,"[7] and insured the survival of the South's "peculiar institution."

5. *Was there a religious dimension to the situation?*

Religion has played such a major role in American history, not to mention the history of

5 See Linda K. Kerber, *Revolutionary Generation*, 4–7. The book that did most to prompt a reappraisal of the role of Lockean individualism in American history was J. G. A. Pocock, *The Machiavellian Moment: Florentine Republican Thought and the Atlantic Republican Tradition* (Princeton, NJ: Princeton University Press, 1975).

6 *The Communist Manifesto* (New York: Penguin, 1986), 79.

7 Anne O'Hare McCormick, *New York Times Magazine*, June 1, 1930, 1.

much of the world, that it deserves a category to itself. The truth of this will be dramatized by the briefest reflection on the pieces of American history you have studied thus far. The Conquistadors' motives, for example, have often been characterized as "greed, glory, and the gospel"—the quest for wealth, glory, and converts to Christianity. A century later the English Puritans immersed themselves in the stories of the Old Testament, thought of themselves as the new Hebrews or chosen people, and came to America to found a New Jerusalem. Still later, the eighteenth-century religious revival know as the Great Awakening, had, according to one American history text, "a far greater impact on the lives of the common people than did the Enlightenment."[8] In fact, almost nothing in the Colonial Period can be studied without reference to religion.

6. *What role did organized groups play?*

David Potter is correct in saying that the historian deals with human beings less as individuals than as groups—religious groups, cultural groups, ideological groups, interest groups, occupational groups, or social groups.[9] And, there are few historical situations that can be understood without careful consideration of the role that group interests have played in shaping the course of events. Human affairs might be viewed as a battleground in which opposing groups with differing interests strive to achieve their goals.

7. *Was there an institutional factor that must be taken into account?*

The word institution can mean several things: (1) an established custom or practice (i.e., the "institution" of marriage), (2) an organization that plays a public or political role (the Catholic Church, the Department of Defense, the Supreme Court), or (3) a building (prisoners are "institutionalized" in a penitentiary). We restrict our comments to the sort of institutions encompassed by the second definition: powerful, established, often public service organizations. Institutional factors, consequently, reflect the influence of those organizations in society.

Groups (see question 6 above) create institutions in order to pursue their collective interests.

While the membership of groups is fluid and ever-changing, an institution often achieves a kind of permanence and, in time, "it also tends to develop its own policies and spirit . . . which transcend the period in office of any individual. . . . The institution molds the psychology and conduct of its officials."[10] In other words, institutions often develop an identity and personality of their own, and established institutional routines, rules, behaviors, and interests can have a profound influence on events.

As an example, large entrenched bureaucracies can often frustrate the best attempts of individuals and groups to initiate change. The Bolsheviks, who won the Russian Revolution, tried

to refashion their society in the 1920s. Many of their efforts, however, were resisted by entrenched and traditionalistic bureaucrats. Lenin, the first leader of the newly named Soviet Union, complained that though he had in place a "vast army of governmental employees," he lacked any real control over them, and that "down below . . . the bureaucrats function in such a way as to counteract our measures."[11]

---

8 Robert A. Divine, et al., *America Past and Present* (Glenview, IL: Scott, Foresman, 1984), 98.
9 David M. Potter, "The Historian's Use of Nationalism and Vice Versa," *American Historical Review*, Vol. 67 (July, 1962), 924.
10 Carl G. Gustavson, *Preface to History*, 81–82.

8. *Was the physical environment a factor in the situation?*

Obviously, all human actions take place on a particular stage, and the stage set is going to influence the action. American regional differences, for instance, are as much a product of differences of climate and terrain as they are a product of the different cultures and peoples that settled the land.

9. *What contingent factors were involved?*

You should always consider the extent to which coincidence, unforeseen circumstance, accidents, and specific decisions that might have been made another way influenced the events of the time. History is full of occasions where we can say, "if only such-and-such particular occurrence hadn't happened, or happened that way, things would have turned out differently." One must be wary of "what if?" history, but occasionally asking a "what if" question highlights the importance of contingency in history. For example, how might things have happened differently during the American Revolution had the Americans lost the battle of Saratoga and France had consequently decided not to intervene on the colonists' side? Would the United States have ratified the Treaty of Versailles in 1920 had Woodrow Wilson pursued a policy of political conciliation? These are things we will never know, but considering alternative outcomes helps illustrate that nothing in history is inevitable.

CHANGE AND CONTINUITY IN HISTORY

Most of the preceding questions emphasize the concept of change. What new ideas, trends, actions, inventions, etc. created the dramatic changes that we study in history—the Pilgrim exodus, the Salem witch trials, the Great Awakening, the American Revolution? The study of history is the study of how and why things change. Yet a moment's reflection about your own day-to-day life should convince you that all changes occur in a context in which countless things stay the same. Change, therefore, has no meaning when considered in isolation; change and continuity are simply opposite sides of the same historical coin.

Because the word change implies passing from one stage or condition to another, a historian should investigate what was there before the change took place. Specifically, the historian must be aware of the established ways of the society in question: common beliefs and attitudes, fixed elements of the social structure, long-existing economic arrangements, relatively permanent governmental patterns, and the like. Without knowledge of such basic continuities, any concept of change is meaningless.

EXERCISES

I THE COLONIAL ERA, 1650–1776

A *Asking Questions*

To discover the multiple causes involved in any historical episode you should ask questions that force you to consider the role of (1) individuals, (2) ideas, (3) economic forces or motivations, (4) technological developments, (5) religion, (6) organized groups, (7) institutions, (8) the physical environment, and (9) contingencies. However, the categories them-

---

11 Merle Fainsod, "The Pervasiveness of Soviet Controls," in Michael Dalby and Michael Werthman, *Bureaucracy in Historical Perspective* (Glenview, IL: Scott Foresman, 1971), 121. Years later Nikita Khrushchev, leader of the USSR from 1958 to 1964, lamented the obstructionism inherent in large institutional bureaucracies: "It is very difficult indeed to carry through specialization and cooperation in production where there are so many ministries and departments, because the departmental interests of the numerous ministries and central boards raise obstacles in the way." E. Strauss, "Varieties of Bureaucratic Control," in Fainsod, *Bureaucracy*, 86.

selves are somewhat artificial and they clearly overlap. For instance, when you ask a question about the impact of Puritan beliefs you are asking a question about the impact of ideas (#2), religion (#5), and an organized group (#6).

Below are a number of questions you might ask in order to understand a historical event or circumstance, and each question touches more than one of the general categories noted above. In the space provided list what you consider to be the main category and at least one, two (better), or three (best) additional relevant categories. The first one is completed for you as an example.

1. What economic theories influenced the policies being investigated?

   economic forces, ideas
   _____

2. What important traditional beliefs continued to hold the loyalty of influential individuals and groups?

   _____

3. What motivated such-and-such individual to act in a given way?

   _____

4. Did intellectuals (i.e., teachers, writers, thinkers) or a specific intellectual influence the outcome in any way?

   _____

5. Did labor and management strife play a role?

   _____

6. Was any key figure motivated by greed?

   _____

7. How did the change in climate influence the poorest farmers of the region?

   _____

8. Were any religious groups advancing ideas intended to sway the opinion of a court or legislature?

   _____

9. Did new manufacturing techniques upset existing trade patterns, or create significant population movements?

   _____

10. Which interest-group leaders were most effective in advancing the interests of their groups?

    _____

B   *Multiple Causality in History*

Using your American history textbook, identify as many different causal factors for the following episodes as you can. Specify at least three causal factors, more if possible, using only the textbook account. Indicate (in parentheses) which of the general categories listed under Exercise A (individuals, ideas, economic forces, etc.) is represented by each of the factors you identify.

Note to instructors: The specific topics below can be replaced with others as long as students have enough material to consider multiple causes.

Whipping of Quaker at the cart's tail.

1. The Great Awakening (1730s–1740s)

   _____

   _____

   _____

   _____

2. The French and Indian War (1754–63)

   _____

   _____

   _____

   _____

3. The Salem witch trials (1692)

   _____

   _____

   _____

   _____

C *Constructing a Historical Explanation*

One of the defining events in the history of the United States was the American Revolution. Historians have argued for generations about the precise mix of causes which led to the increasing alienation between England and its American colonies, and the ultimate break in 1775–76. In this exercise, we want you to use your American History textbook to help you identify as many causes as you can of the split between England and America.

1. First, list the most significant causes (individuals, ideas, situations, etc.) under the appropriate headings below. Attempt to list at least one cause—preferably more—under as many categories as possible. Be prepared to defend your selections in class.

   a. Individuals

   _____

   b. Ideas (formal ideas and popular beliefs)

   _____

   c. Economic forces or motivations

   _____

   d. Technological developments/factors

   _____

   e. Religious factors

   _____

   f. Group interests

   _____

   g. Institutional interests

   _____

   h. Environmental factors

   _____

   i. Contingent factors

   _____

   _____

2. Of the various factors you have identified, which ones would you consider to be immediate or short-term causes? That is, which events, forces, individuals, and groups were important in triggering the actual parting of the ways that took place in 1775–76? Which factors would you label as long-term, or situational causes—i.e., those circumstances, attitudes, institutions, etc. that for many years had been driving Britain and its American colonies apart?

   Short-term causes:

   _____

   _____

   _____

   _____

   Long-term causes:

   _____

   _____

   _____

   _____

3. Generally historians deny that complex events can be explained by singular or simple causes, and most would reaffirm the principle of multicausality in history. However, historians passionately disagree when they attempt to determine which of the many causes or factors they have discovered are the most important. Such arguments about the priority of importance of various causal factors is at the center of the enterprise of history.

Even though your knowledge of American history during the colonial period is incomplete, we would like you to try your hand at determining which causal factors are most and least important. Your task is to decide which of the factors you noted above are most important, and which are least important. Using the spaces provided list the factors which you consider "important" or "most important," and those which you consider "unimportant" or "least significant." Be prepared to defend your selections.

Note to instructors: You might consider allowing small groups to work on this question and then have them defend their conclusions in a classroom discussion with other groups.

Most important causal factors:

_____

_____

_____

_____

Least important causal factors:

_____

_____

_____

_____

D *Optional Writing Exercise*

On a separate sheet of paper, write a paragraph-length essay defending your selection of one of the causes you listed as "most important."

II EMPIRE AND WORLD WAR, 1890–1920

A *Asking Questions*

See Exercise A in Part I.

B *Multiple Causality in History*

Using your American history textbook, identify as many different causal factors for the following episodes as you can. Specify at least three causal factors, more if possible, using only the textbook account. Indicate (in parentheses) which of the general categories listed under Exercise A, Part I (individuals, ideas, economic forces, etc.) is represented by each of the factors you identify.

Note to instructors: The specific topics below can be replaced with others as long as students have enough material to consider multiple causes.

1. Spanish-American War

_____

_____

_____

_____

2. The Progressive Movement

_____

_____

_____

_____

3. American entry into World War I

_____

_____

_____

_____

C   *Constructing a Historical Explanation*

On August 26, 1920, the 19th Amendment was ratified, thereby granting the vote to women for the first time in American history. In this exercise, we want you to use your American history textbook to help you identify as many causes as you can for the passage of women's suffrage. To do justice to this topic you will have to consider the evolving role of women in American society during the nineteenth and early twentieth centuries and changing attitudes on gender issues during the same period.

1. First, list the most significant causes (individuals, ideas, etc.) under the appropriate headings below. Attempt to list at least one cause—preferably more than one—under as many categories as possible. Be prepared to defend your selections in class.

   a. Individuals

   _____

   b. Ideas (formal ideas and popular beliefs)

   _____

   c. Economic forces or motivations

   _____

   d. Technological developments/factors

   _____

   e. Religious factors

   _____

   f. Group interests

   _____

g. Institutional interests

_____

h. Environmental factors

_____

i. Contingent factors

_____

2. Of the various factors you have identified, which ones would you consider to be immediate or short-term causes? That is, which events, forces, individuals and groups most immediately influenced the outcome of the ratification process in 1920? Which factors would you label as long-term or situational causes—i.e., those circumstances, attitudes, institutions, etc. that, in effect, set the stage for the ultimate success of the women's suffrage movement?

Short-term causes:

_____

_____

_____

_____

Long-term causes:

_____

_____

_____

_____

3. Generally historians deny that complex events can be explained by singular or simple causes, and most would reaffirm the principle of multicausality in history. However, historians passionately disagree when they attempt to determine which of the many causes or factors they have discovered are the most important. Such arguments about the priority of importance of various causal factors is at the center of the enterprise of history.

Even though your knowledge of this period of American history is incomplete, in this exercise we would like you to try your hand at determining which causal factors are most and least important. Your task is to decide which of the factors you noted above are most important, and which are least important. Using the spaces provided list the factors which you consider "important" or "most important," and those which you consider "unimportant" or "least significant". Be prepared to defend your selections.

Note to instructors: You might consider allowing small groups to work on this question and then have them defend their conclusions in a classroom discussion with other groups.

Most important causal factors:

_____

_____

_____

_____

Least important causal factors:

_____

_____

_____

_____

D *Writing Option*

On a separate sheet of paper, write a paragraph-length essay in which you explain why the long campaign for women's suffrage succeeded in 1920.

"Men resemble their times more than they do their fathers."

ARAB PROVERB

"History with its flickering lamp stumbles along the trail of the past, trying to reconstruct its scenes, to revive its echoes, and kindle with pale gleams the passion of former days."

WINSTON CHURCHILL
HOUSE OF COMMONS, NOVEMBER 12, 1940

One thing astute international travelers learn quickly is how much trouble can result when they don't know enough about the culture they are visiting. In Bulgaria Americans may be confused until they discover that the conventional head motions for "yes" and "no" are exactly the opposite in that country. Visitors to the Middle East or parts of Asia may unintentionally insult local residents by crossing their legs and pointing the sole of their shoe at someone. In certain cultures it is impolite to point with your index finger (China, Malasia, India), to show up late to dinner (Denmark), to pat a child on the head (Thailand, Singapore), to ask personal questions about an individual's family or health (France), or to address someone by his or her first name (China, Scandinavia, Eastern Europe).[1]

Occasionally such cultural ignorance can have far more serious consequences than personal embarrassment. In 1969, the Japanese Prime Minister, Eisaku Sato, visited Washington to respond to growing American concern over Japanese trade policy. When President Richard Nixon asked Mr. Sato to help limit Japanese exports to the United States, Mr. Sato said "Zensho shimasu," which literally meant, "I will do my best." Unfortunately, President Nixon and other American officials did not realize that, to the Japanese, that phrase really meant "No way." When the Japanese failed to respond to American pressure, the President reportedly called the Japanese Prime Minister a liar.[2] Since 1969 there have been a number of other official misunderstandings between the United States and Japan based on mutually incomprehensible linguistic and cultural styles.

These relatively commonplace incidents dramatize the importance of understanding the broader context (i.e., the overall situation), when we visit another country or converse with someone from another culture. Misunderstandings are inevitable if we interact with people from foreign cultures without making some attempt to understand the bewildering array of customs, practices, laws, and values that seem strange and even illogical to an outsider.

If contextual knowledge is essential in order to understand different cultures, it is even more necessary in order to understand the past. To historians the past is much like a foreign country where things are often done differently.[3] Historians must become fully acquainted with the institutions, cultural habits, and beliefs of both the society and the period they are studying. A distinguishing mark of good historians (and students of history), is their ability to put themselves in the shoes of those who lived long ago and to see past societies as those societies saw themselves. In the words of Robert Darnton, "other people are other. They do not think the way we do. And if we want to understand their way of thinking, we should set out with the idea of capturing otherness."[4]

1 Alice Garrard, "Foreign Faux Pas," *Travel and Leisure* (October, 1985), 164–66.
2 Clyde Haberman, "Japanese Have a Way (Out) with Words," *New York Times*.
3 See for instance, David Lowenthal, *The Past is a Foreign Country* (Cambridge: Cambridge University Press, 1985).
4 Robert Darnton, *The Great Cat Massacre and Other Episodes in French Cultural History* (New York: Basic Books, 1984), 4.

Thinking historically requires that you constantly remind yourself that the past is different from the present; that historical events should never be judged in isolation from the environment or situation in which they took place. Without a leap of sympathetic imagination we risk oversimplifying events or, worse, misunderstanding them completely. A popular story about the Battle of Bunker Hill helps make the point concrete. As the battle began (June 17, 1775), the commander of the American troops allegedly shouted something like: "Don't fire until you see the whites of their eyes!" Whether this piece of popular patriotism is true or false, it illustrates the dangers of taking things out of their proper context. On the surface the order seems to suggest an idealized and heroic vision of the colonial rebels—determined, stalwart, and brave in the face of an attack by disciplined British troops. However, a more intimate knowledge of the conventions and technology of eighteenth-century warfare reveals a more mundane explanation for the famous order. The muskets of the time were so inaccurate that a soldier had no hope of hitting an enemy infantryman unless he could see the "whites of his eyes." Military necessity, not superior military valor, best explains the famous and stirring order. The British commander probably said something similar to his men.

Another incident from the colonial period illustrates the importance of context in the study of history: the Salem witchcraft trials of 1692. Many moderns find it perplexing that people—even in the seventeenth century—could believe their lives were threatened by witches and black magic. The particular outbreak of hysteria in Salem, Massachusetts, seems even more perplexing given the fact that the "bewitched" victims were all seemingly healthy and well-adjusted girls or young women, and the accused were respected members of the community. At first glance the witch hysteria seems impossible to explain rationally. Yet, when one begins to examine the broader context of the time and place, the reasons become clear. (See IA under Exercises.)

The investigator's knowledge, claim Jacques Barzun and Henry Graff, "must include an understanding of how [people] in other eras lived and behaved, what they believed, and how they managed their institutions."[5] History students should not only attempt to see the world through the eyes of those they are trying to study, but should also be able to distance themselves from their own values and assumptions about the world. Such "sympathetic imagination" is a prerequisite for sound historical thinking.

All of this is easier said than done. The historian knows how things came out, but the participants did not. Historians narrate and interpret the past with the advantage of hindsight, and it is much easier to be an armchair quarterback than to play the game itself. The clarity of hindsight makes it very tempting for the historian to make grand generalizations about the incompetence, naiveté, and shortsightedness of those in the past whose vision was not so clear. Allan

Nevins, in *The Gateway to History*, points out the fallacy involved with this sort of analysis. Historical hindsight, Nevins warns, makes past problems seem much more simple (and more easily solvable), than they actually were, and "the leaders that dealt with them . . . smaller men."[6] Hindsight, in short, makes it very difficult for even the best-intentioned investigators to approach the trials and triumphs of past ages with true imaginative sympathy.

It becomes even more difficult to be fair-minded in judging the past when you study an

---

5 Jacques Barzun and Henry Graff, *The Modern Researcher*, rev. ed. (New York: Harcourt, Brace and World, 1970), 116.
6 Allan Nevins, *The Gateway to History* (Chicago: Quadrangle Books, 1963), 257.

individual you personally dislike or an event that you find evil or repugnant from the standpoint of your own value system. David Harris Willson had this problem when he was working on his biography of James I, the English king who ruled 1603–25, chartered the Virginia Company, and created religious policies that drove the Pilgrims first to Holland and then to the New World. This biography, still one of the best treatments of this rather obnoxious king, is a model of impartiality. Willson succeeded in writing a fair and sympathetic treatment of James,[7] in spite of the fact that he never really liked the British king, no matter how hard he tried.

CONTEXT AND MORAL JUDGMENTS IN HISTORY

Many practices that today we consider morally reprehensible have, in different times and places, been commonplace and morally tolerated. Today, for example, the institution of slavery is universally condemned. Yet historically slavery and serfdom were considered to be part of the natural order of things. Slavery was a prominent feature of ancient Greek and Roman societies; in the European Middle Ages (and much later in Russia and Eastern Europe), serfs lived lives not far removed from formal slavery; and, as we all know, slavery was an integral part of the culture of the American South for over two hundred years. In cases such as this, what position should historians take? Should they condemn these societies as "immoral"? Should they accept as valid the societal values and institutions that were operative during the period being studied? Or, should they avoid making moral judgments altogether?

Herbert Butterfield, a British historian, believed that moral judgments were irrelevant to historical understanding. If readers did not recognize the immorality or morality of past deeds, Butterfield argued, the historian's moralistic pronouncements would certainly not change readers' minds. Further, moral judgments would do nothing to help researcher or reader understand the past in any meaningful way. Says Butterfield: "Moral judgments on human beings are by their nature irrelevant to the enquiry and alien to the intellectual realm of scientific history. . . . These moral judgments must be recognised to

be an actual hindrance to enquiry and reconstruction. . . ."[8]

Butterfield and those like him are sometimes called "amoralists," that is, they believe that moral judgments do not serve any useful purpose in a historical narrative. Ranked opposite are those who believe historians have a right and duty to inject moral commentary into their history. They believe that certain moral and ethical norms are universal and transcend time and space. It is appropriate, therefore, to point the finger at evil and condemn it. As Goldwin Smith wrote, "A sound historical morality will sanction strong measures in evil times; selfish ambition, treachery, murder, perjury, it will never sanction

in the worst of times, for these are the things that make times evil—Justice has been justice, mercy has been mercy, honour has been honour, good faith has been good faith, truthfulness has been truthfulness from the beginning."[9] We sacrifice too much, in other words, if we place "understanding" above defending a sound morality.

There are others who occupy a middle ground. They believe it is legitimate and important for historians to provide moral critiques of the past, but they also believe (along with Butterfield) that

---

7 D. H. Willson, *King James VI & I* (New York: Oxford University Press, 1967).
8 Quoted in Hans Meyerhoff, ed., *The Philosophy of History in Our Time* (New York: Doubleday, 1959), 230.
9 Meyerhoff, *Philosophy of History in Our Time*, 225.

the historian should not play the role of the judge. This position is held by American historian John Higham who believes that what he calls moral history can be an important spur to historical understanding. Moral history can help us appreciate the nature and importance of moral imperatives in different times and places. It can show how certain values—honor, courage, concepts of character—changed over time. It can also help us understand the moral alternatives available to leaders at key moments in history. In Higham's words, "The historian is not called to establish a hierarchy of values, but rather to explore a spectrum of human potentialities and achievements."[10] Higham's position, then, is somewhat "relativistic." The historian can and should venture into the realm of moral judgments, but those judgments must take into account the broad context of the time and place being studied.

And the debate goes on. Wherever your sympathies lie on this issue, it is necessary to keep in mind that there is no easy answer. It is the historian's job to understand and interpret the past, and this is most difficult if basic moral values are in conflict. Perhaps the best advice is this: be aware of the dilemma.

In summary, difficult though it may be, you should always try to avoid making judgments out of context. Just as you would never pass judgment on the questionable actions of your friends until you had heard their side of the story (that is, the context that influenced their decisions and actions), you should not come to conclusions in history without paying due attention to the context in which events took place.

---

10 John Higham, *Writing American History* (Bloomington, IN: Indiana University Press, 1970), 150–56.

The question of context is not only important in the university classroom, but in professional life as well. Journalism is the "first rough draft of history," and journalists who ignore the lessons of context do so at their own risk. It is difficult to report and assess the significance of world events if those events are studied independent of cultural and historical context. Likewise government officials would be well-advised to consider the big picture whenever considering specific policies and proposals. And doctors must know as much as possible about a person's life—the context—in order to prescribe the best treatment.

Failure to appreciate the importance of context can cost money, as numerous corporations have discovered. Many businesses have made embarrassing and costly marketing errors simply because they were unaware of critical cultural differences in foreign markets. To cite some examples:

- Very few people in Southeast Asia responded to Pepsodent's promise to make their teeth whiter. Why? Well, in that area of the world, where many people chew betel nuts, discolored teeth are a status symbol.

- General Foods had trouble marketing Jell-O in England. It turns out that British shoppers buy gelatin in cakes, not in powdered form.

- One firm tried advertising refrigerators in the Moslem Middle East by using pictures of the refrigerator full of appetizing food, including a very prominent ham. Of course, Moslems do not eat pork.

- Advertising disasters have also resulted from ignorance of the significance of certain colors in various countries. In Japan, for instance, white is the color of death. In Africa green is the color of disease.

(The examples of business marketing errors were drawn from: "Business Blunders: Some Funny but All Costly," *St. Louis Post-Dispatch*, November 13, 1980.)

1 THE COLONIAL ERA, 1650–1776

A Context in the Study of History

In a sense, the search for the relevant context is a refinement of the search for multiple causes discussed in the preceding chapter. Just as different causal factors help us explain events in history, the context, or overall situation in which events occur, also helps us explain what we are studying. When we talk about context, we are referring to the ideas, values, assumptions, situations and objects that every age takes for granted and consequently are easily overlooked by latter-day historians. The context is like background noise: often ignored but always present.

This exercise is intended to help you appreciate the importance of trying to understand past events within the proper historical context. The event in this case is the witchcraft hysteria that shook Salem, Massachusetts in 1692.

The Salem Witch Trials: Introduction

In the 1600s, belief in witchcraft was widespread in Europe and in the European colonies of North America. In fact, the age of European exploration and colonization (the sixteenth and seventeenth centuries), marked the period of the most violent "witch" persecutions in western history. This is ironic because the 1500s and 1600s were also the centuries that gave birth to the modern scientific outlook.

Witchcraft is difficult to define. But generally a witch was a person who had the power to do good or evil (primarily evil) by manipulating supernatural forces. In late medieval Europe (the 1400s and 1500s), churchmen added the conception that a witch was a person who had formed a pact with the devil in order to harm people and undermine the true Christian faith.

On Trial for Witchcraft

In many parts of Europe witches were hunted with evangelistic fervor. Neighbors denounced neighbors, authorities tortured suspected witches to wring confessions of evildoing, and witch trials and executions were commonplace. Literally thousands of men and women, mostly women, were consumed in bonfires lit by antiwitch zealots. The most grisly witch persecutions took place on the European continent. England and the American colonies escaped the worst excesses of the antiwitch hysteria, but not entirely. In England, accusations and criminal persecutions of witches were quite common, and English witch beliefs accompanied the immigrants who were coming to the New World in increasing numbers. The Salem trials of 1692 are the most famous American example of the witch delusions of the time.

Today the witch mania seems incomprehensible. How could the contemporaries of Copernicus, Galileo, Locke, and Newton fall for such a base superstition? How could they believe in black magic, pacts with the devil, witches riding brooms to secret rendezvous? How could they torture and execute thousands of innocent people on the pretext that they were witches? How could the villagers of Salem, Massachusetts try and execute members of their own community with precious little evidence that the accused had done anything wrong?

We want you to begin to try to answer these questions by reading the passages below. Of course, you can't even approach a complete answer given the brevity of the sample passages, but you can begin to appreciate the importance of understanding the total environment in which the witch trials took place.

1. Read the passages below (marked "Supplementary Information") and try to identify the background ideas, attitudes, situations, and social and political relationships that one needs to be aware of in order to explain the Salem trials of 1692. Note: to explain is not the same as to justify. Whether a person approves or disapproves of what the citizens of Salem, Massachusetts did, it is an obligation of the historian to understand and explain the event.

   In the spaces provided record the important contextual insights of each passage. As you do so, be sure to indicate clearly how the material in each passage adds to our understanding of the witchcraft hysteria of the time.

Supplementary Information

A. We should remember also that the seventeenth century firmly believed in a dualistic universe: in a material or visible world, and a spiritual or invisible world as well. Heaven was still a concrete reality, as were the Angels who inhabited it; so was Hell and its Devils. . . . Like other learned men of his time, [English philosopher John] Locke not only believed in a world of spirits, but that spirits can appear in this material world: "that Spirits can assume to themselves bodies of different bulk, figure, and conformation of parts." To be sure, Locke warned that "universal certainty" concerning the world of spirits was beyond us; we could know it, he thought, only as it impinges on our senses. But that, of course, is precisely what was thought to happen in witchcraft.

   Contextual Insights:

   _____

   _____

B. In a society technologically more backward than ours the immediate attraction of the belief in witchcraft is not difficult to understand. It served as a means of accounting for the otherwise inexplicable misfortunes of daily life. Unexpected disasters—the sudden death of a child, the loss of a cow, the failure of some routine household task—all could, in default of any more obvious explanation, be attributed to the influence of some malevolent neighbour. There was virtually no type of private misfortune which could not thus be ascribed to witchcraft, and sometimes the list of injuries might be extremely miscellaneous. . . . But a supernatural explanation was particularly seductive in the field of medicine, where human impotence in the face of a variety of hazards was only too obvious.

Contextual Insights:

_____

_____

C. When we read the confessions of sixteenth- and seventeenth-century witches, we are often revolted by the cruelty and stupidity which have elicited them and sometimes, undoubtedly supplied their form. But equally we are obliged to admit their fundamental "subjective reality." For every victim whose story is evidently created or improved by torture, there are two or three who genuinely believe in its truth. . . .

That external suggestion alone does not account for witches' confessions is clear when we descend to detail. Again and again, when we read the case histories, we find witches freely confessing to esoteric details without any evidence of torture, and it was this spontaneity, rather than the confessions themselves, which convinced rational men that the details were true.

Contextual Insights:

_____

_____

D. Recent studies of witchcraft have concentrated on how witchcraft accusations are related to the whole social structure rather than individual tensions. Instead of seeing witchcraft as the result of the conflict between the individual and society, the phenomenon is analysed in terms of the relationship between various groups in society.

[I]t is not surprising to discover a high correlation between Salem Village factionalism and the way the Village divided in 1692 over the witchcraft outbreak. . . . Almost every indicator by which the two Village factions may be distinguished, in fact, also neatly separates the supporters and opponents of the witchcraft trials.

Contextual Insights:

_____

_____

E. To appreciate the light in which the witch appeared to her neighbors it is necessary to recall the importance which the inhabitants of sixteenth- and seventeenth-century England attached to social harmony, and the variety of means they employed to check all signs of dispute or nonconformity. . . . Indeed if the records of Tudor and Stuart village life leave any single impression, it is that of the tyranny of local opinion and the lack of tolerance displayed towards nonconformity or social deviation. Rural society lacked much of the modern concept of privacy and private life. . . . [The witch] was the extreme example of the malignant or nonconforming person against whom the local community had always taken punitive action in the interests of social harmony.

Contextual Insights:

_____

_____

F. [Women accused of Witchcraft in New England were] women [who] stood to inherit, did inherit, or were denied their apparent right to inherit substantially larger portions of their fathers' or husbands' accumulated estates than women in families with male heirs. Whatever actually happened to the property in question . . . these women were aberrations in a society with an inheritance system designed to keep property in the hands of men.

Finally, inheriting or potentially inheriting women were vulnerable to witchcraft accusations not only during the Salem outbreak, but from the time of the first formal accusations in New England at least until the end of the century. . . . The Salem outbreak created only a slight wrinkle in this established fabric of suspicion.

Contextual Insights:

_____

_____

Sources

A. Chadwick Hansen, *Witchcraft at Salem* (New York: Mentor, 1969), 28–29. Reprinted by permission of George Brazilier, Inc.

B. Keith Thomas, *Religion and the Decline of Magic* (New York: Scribner's, 1971), 535–36. Reprinted by permission of Prentice Hall.

C. H. R. Trevor-Roper, *The European Witch-Craze of the Sixteenth and Seventeenth Centuries and Other Essays* (New York: Harper and Row, 1969), 123–24. Reprinted by permission of HarperCollins Publishers, Inc.

D. A. D. J. Macfarlane, *Witchcraft in Tudor and Stuart England* (New York: Harper and Row, 1970), 246; and Paul Boyer and Stephen Nissenbaum, *Salem Possessed* (Cambridge, MA: Harvard Univ. Press, 1974), 185.

E. Thomas, *Religion and Decline of Magic*, 526–30. Reprinted by permission of Prentice Hall.

F. Carol F. Karlsen, *The Devil in the Shape of a Woman: Witchcraft in Colonial New England* (New York: Vintage, 1987), 101, 115–16; also excerpted in Linda K. Kerber and Jane S. DeHart, eds., *Women's America*, 3rd ed. (New York: Oxford University Press, 1991), 65–66, 70. Reprinted by permission of W. W. Norton & Co., Inc.

2. Some of the passages above help put the Salem trials into context by providing information about some of the popular ideas (beliefs, world view) of the time; others talk about the social relationships within the seventeenth-century village; others tell us something about the particular circumstances in Salem itself. Indicate which passages (A-F) belong primarily in each of the categories below. If you think a given passage belongs in more than one category, list it more than once. If you think a passage does not fit in the first three categories (a, b, c), list it under "Other" (d), and be prepared to explain your decision.

   Passages (A–F) that *primarily* provide more information about seventeenth-century:

   Ideas/Beliefs:_____

   Village Society:_____

   Salem:_____

   Other:_____

3. Discussion: Which contextual factor, of those represented in the passages excerpted above, contributes most to helping you understand the witch persecutions of that time? Why is that factor, in your judgment, more important than other possible choices?

   Essay Option: Write a brief paragraph summarizing the specific contextual insights that were most useful in helping you understand the Salem witchcraft trials of 1692.

Moral Judgments in History (Optional):

1. In Chapter I review the three brief passages that recount Hernando Cortes' conquest of Mexico (IB under "Exercises," p. 9). Do any of those accounts contain implicit moral or ethical judgments about the events in question (i.e., judgments as to whether actions were "right" or "wrong")? Do the authors seem to be passing judgment morally and ethically on the actions of the Aztecs or Spaniards? Record your conclusions in the spaces below. If you conclude that an author does make moral or ethical judgments, indicate which passage(s) prompted you to come to that conclusion.

Account 1 ("The great adventure. . ."):

_____

_____

_____

Account 2 ("What Columbus did to the Arawaks . . ."):

_____

_____

_____

Account 3 ("The Spaniards had the good fortune . . ."):

_____

_____

_____

2. Essay or Discussion Option: What moral stance does your textbook take when discussing interactions between the European colonists and the indigenous Native Americans (Indians) in the seventeenth and eighteenth century? Is the behavior of the colonists portrayed in a positive or negative way? Indian behavior? Is your text morally neutral or does it make any explicit or implicit moral judgments?

II   EMPIRE AND WORLD WAR, 1890–1920

A   *Context in the Study of History*

In a sense, the search for the relevant context is a refinement of the search for multiple causes discussed in the preceding chapter. Just as different causal factors help us explain events in history, the context, or overall situation in which events occur, also helps us explain what we are studying. When we talk about context, we are referring to the ideas, values, assumptions, situations and objects that every age takes for granted and consequently are easily overlooked by latter-day historians. The context is like background noise: often ignored but always present.

This exercise is intended to help you appreciate the importance of trying to understand past events within the proper historical context. The "event" is the famous "Red Scare" of 1919–1920.

The Palmer Raids and the "Red Scare" of 1919–20: Introduction

The "Red Scare" was a short-lived outburst of antiforeign and antiradical sentiment triggered by a series of highly publicized bombings and bomb attempts in 1919. Among the targets was the home of the U.S. Attorney General, A. Mitchell Palmer, whose home was bombed on June 2. Palmer retaliated with a series of raids designed to round up and deport foreign radicals who were perceived to be Communists or "reds." Thousands of recent immigrants were caught in the net of the Palmer Raids. Federal officials searched homes and offices, often without warrants, detained people in jails or detention centers without benefit of bond or counsel, and ultimately deported hundreds of innocent people. How can this intemperate outburst, in the shadow of the war fought (in Woodrow Wilson's words) "for democracy, . . . [and] for the rights and liberties of small nations," be explained?

1. Read the passages below (marked "Supplementary Information") and try to identify the background ideas, attitudes, situations, and social and political relationships that one needs to be aware of in order to explain the "Red Scare." Note: To explain is not the same as to justify. Whether a person approves or disapproves of Palmer and his raids, it is an obligation of the historian to understand and explain the event.

In the spaces provided record the important contextual insights of each passage. As you do so, be sure to indicate clearly how the material in each passage adds to our understanding of the events of 1919–20.

Supplementary Information

A. [T]he nation suffered a sharp economic depression in late 1918 and early 1919, caused largely by sudden cancellations of war orders. Returning servicemen found it difficult to obtain jobs during this period, which coincided with the beginning of the Red Scare. The former soldiers had been uprooted from their homes and told that they were engaged in a patriotic crusade. Now they came back to find "reds" criticizing their country and threatening the government with violence.

Contextual Insights:

_____

_____

B. [T]he Seattle general strike [of 1919] took place in the midst of a wave of postwar rebellions all over the world. A writer in *The Nation* commented that year:

The most extraordinary phenomenon of the present time . . . is the unprecedented revolt of the rank and file. In Russia it has dethroned the Czar. . . . In Korea and India and Egypt and Ireland it keeps up an unyielding resistance to political tyranny. In England it brought about the railway strike, against the judgment of the men's own executives. In Seattle and San Francisco it has resulted in the stevedores' recent refusal to handle arms or supplies destined for the overthrow of the Soviet Government. In one district of Illinois it manifested itself in a resolution of striking miners, unanimously requesting their state executive "to go to Hell."

Contextual Insights:

_____

_____

C. [T]he traditional Protestant code of morality was almost universal in a nation that still derived overwhelmingly from British and West European ancestry.

After 1890 this changed with incredible speed. The breath-taking growth of industry resulted in a vast expansion of cities, and the industrial cities overflowed with immigrant laborers from Eastern and Southern Europe. Most of the new arrivals were Catholics and peasants with a moral code that, if neither less strict nor more humane, was yet noticeably different. Overcrowding and poverty meant slums; slums meant political bosses and organized crime. The new immigrant groups came to be voting blocs of more significance than were native-born Americans in one city after another, and acquired influence even in Washington. . . . The farm boy came to the city, and he was often revolted and outraged by what he saw there.

Contextual Insights:

_____

_____

D. Hatred of the enemy is a thing striven for in wartime. It is also often accompanied by a hatred of all foreign people, of all who are alien in any way. . . . Theodore Roosevelt spoke for nationalists everywhere when he dealt with this issue on a number of occasions in 1917: "The Hun [German] within our gates masquerades in many disguises; he is our dangerous enemy; and he should be hunted down without mercy." "Every man," he wrote in 1918, "ought to love his country. . . . [But] he is only entitled to one country. If he claims loyalty to two countries, he is necessarily a traitor to at least one country."

Contextual Insights:

_____

_____

E. *Saturday Evening Post,* February 7, 1920:

We must rid ourselves of the notion that America is some kind of a world institution for the care of nuts; . . . that her citizenship is open to anyone to accept or reject as his own whims and interests dictate; . . . that we can make a few passes over anyone regardless of race and presto! an American. . . .

[People] do not understand that many of these alien peoples are temperamentally and racially unfitted for easy assimilation; that they are living in an age two or three centuries behind ours. . . . This matter of Americanization is only partly a question of education. Many second-generation Americans from Central and Eastern Europe, men with college degrees, are quite unassimilated to American ideals. Temperamentally and racially they are still Russian or Balkan or German. So further immigration must not only be rigidly limited in volume but we must analyze the possibilities and desirability of different races in a way that we have never done before.

Contextual Insights:

_____

_____

F. Psychological experiments indicate that a great many Americans—at least several million—are always ready to participate in a "red scare." These people permanently hold attitudes which characterized the nativists of 1919–20: hostility toward certain minority groups, especially radicals and recent immigrants, fanatical patriotism, and a belief that internal enemies seriously threaten national security. . . . [M]illions of Americans are both extraordinarily fearful of social change and prejudiced against those minority groups which they perceive as "threatening intruders." A number of anthropologists have come to conclusions about the roots of nativism which complement these psychological studies. Since the late nineteenth century, anthropologists have been studying the religious and nativistic cults of American Indian tribes and of Melanesian and Papuan groups in the South Pacific. Recently, several anthropologists have attempted to synthesize their findings and have shown striking parallels in the cultural conditions out of which these movements arose.

Contextual Insights:

_____

_____

Sources

A. Stanley Coben, "A Study in Nativism: The American Red Scare of 1919–20," *Political Science Quarterly*, LXXIX (March 1964), 67.

B. Howard Zinn, *A People's History of the United States* (New York: Harper and Row, 1980), 371. Reprinted by permission of HarperCollins Publishers, Inc.

C. Ray Ginger, *Six Days or Forever?* (London: Oxford University Press, 1958), 8–9.

D. H. C. Peterson and Gilbert Fite, *Opponents of War, 1917–1918* (Seattle: University of Washington Press, 1957), 81. Reprinted by permission of the University of Washington Press.

E. David A. Shannon, ed., *Progressivism and Postwar Disillusionment: 1898–1928*, Vol. 6 of *A Documentary History of American Life*, ed. by David Donald (New York: Johns Hopkins University Press, 1966), 277.

F. Coben, "Nativism," in *Political Science Quarterly*, 53–54.

2. Some of the passages above help put the Red Scare into context by providing information about popular ideas (beliefs, attitudes, world view) of the time; others focus on social and economic forces that changed American society after the Civil War; still others tell us about the particular circumstances of the time that made the Red Scare possible. Indicate which passages (A–F) belong primarily in each of the categories below. If you think a given passage belongs in more than one category, list it more than once. If you think a passage does not fit in the first three categories (a, b, c), list it under "Other" (d), and be prepared to explain your decision.

   Passages (A–F) that *primarily* provide more information about:

   Ideas/Beliefs:_____

   Social and Economic Changes:_____

   The Period of the Scare (1918–20):_____

   Other:_____

3. Discussion: Which contextual factor, of those represented in the excerpted passages, is most helpful in helping you understand the Red Scare? Why is that factor, in your judgment, more important than other possible choices?

   Essay Option: Write a brief paragraph summarizing the specific contextual insights that were most useful in helping you understand the Red Scare of 1919–20.

B *Moral Judgments in History (Optional):*

1. In Chapter 1 review the three brief passages that recount the Great Railroad Strike of 1877 (IIB under "Exercises," p. 13). Do any of those accounts contain implicit moral or ethical judgments about the events in question (i.e., judgments as to whether actions were "right" or "wrong")? Do the authors seem to be passing judgment morally and ethically on the actions of the strikers? The authorities? The owners? Record your conclusions in the spaces below. If you conclude that an author does make moral or ethical judgments, indicate which passage(s) prompted you to come to that conclusion.

Account 1 ("That year [1877] there came. . ."):

_____

_____

_____

Account 2 ("On two occasions . . ."):

_____

_____

_____

Account 3 ("In order to cope . . ."):

_____

_____

_____

2. Essay or Discussion Option: What moral stance does your textbook take when discussing interactions between the American government and the indigenous Native Americans (Indians) in the late-nineteenth century? Is the behavior of the government portrayed in a positive or negative way? Indian behavior? Is your text morally neutral or does it make any explicit or implicit moral judgments?

GATHERING INFORMATION 5

"Knowledge is of two kinds. We know a subject ourselves, or we know where we can find information upon it."

DR. SAMUEL JOHNSON (1709–84)

"My library was dukedom large enough."

PROSPERO, *THE TEMPEST*
WILLIAM SHAKESPEARE

In those times and places when the art of writing was unknown, people had to rely on their memories to store important information, and the ability to memorize large amounts of information was a highly prized skill. In many oral cultures (e.g., the early Greeks, the Irish Celts, early Native Americans, and the first African Americans), stories, myths, family genealogies, and historical experiences were committed to memory and passed orally from generation to generation.

Today, though memorization has become a lost art, our need to store and retrieve information has never been greater. Our very survival depends on our ability to sort through the avalanche of information that inundates us daily from books, newspapers, television, and the Internet. Indeed, the mark of today's educated individual is less the ability to memorize than the ability to find and use relevant information as needed. You've probably already discovered this; on your own campus you need information and lots of it.

The library is the most important educational resource on the campus, and you should know it well. Not only does the library house the books, journals, documents, films, videos, and audiocassettes that serve as the lifeblood of learning, it can also serve as your entry ramp into cyberspace—the so-called "electronic information superhighway." Finally, don't overlook the library as a pleasant (and increasingly colorful) place to browse, study, think, and even socialize.

The only way to learn how to use a library properly is to use one. This is true even for seasoned scholars who may be quite ignorant of sections of libraries (or library services), they rarely use. Jaroslav Pelikan, an eminent historian of Christian doctrine, once dumbfounded a Yale University library employee by asking where the periodicals room was. Pelikan explained that he knew, "where the incunabula" [rare books] were, but since he never used recent magazines in his research, he had no idea where to find the periodicals room. Like Pelikan, you will learn how to locate library resources and use library services as the need arises. Be assured that mastering the skills of accessing library resources will be well worth it in the long run. The faster you are able to collect your sources, the less time any research project will take.

There are four basic things you must know to begin: (1) the layout of your library, (2) how books are classified, (3) how to initiate a search for the information you need, and (4) whom to ask for help if you reach a dead end.

LAYOUT OF THE LIBRARY

First, play the role of a tourist in your own library. Ask for any available informational guides or pamphlets; then wander around and note the location of the following:

1. The main desk and reference desk
2. The catalog (electronic or card)
3. Computer terminals providing access to electronic indexes and services
4. The reference area (printed encyclopedias, indexes, dictionaries, map atlases, etc.)
5. The periodicals room or area.
6. The book stacks—especially those relevant to your immediate needs
7. The reserve room or reserve shelves
8. The audiovisual (A–V) area

THE CLASSIFICATION SYSTEM

As overwhelming as a library may seem at first glance, the thing to remember is that there is a place for everything, and those who understand the organizational scheme will be able to make the library work for them.

The Library of Congress system is by far the most common system of classification in college and university libraries. Introduced around the turn of the twentieth century in Washington, D.C., this system uses 21 letters of the alphabet to designate the following general categories:

A. General works
B. Philosophy/Religion
C. Auxiliary Sciences of History

D. UNIVERSAL HISTORY
E–F. AMERICAN HISTORY

G. Geography/Anthropology
H. Social Sciences
J. Political Science
K. Law
L. Education
M. Music
N. Fine Arts
P. Language and Literature
Q. Science
R. Medicine
S. Agriculture
T. Technology
U. Military Science
V. Naval Science
Z. Bibliography/Library Science

Subcategories can be created by adding a second letter to the general designation. For instance:

D	History (general)
DA	Great Britain
DB	Austria, Liechtenstein, Hungary, Czechoslovakia
DC	France
	Etc.

You don't have to memorize the entire system, but it is a good idea to know the designation(s) for your own field of study. Also don't ignore the benefits and pleasures of simply browsing through the stacks. Browsing makes the system more comprehensible, and, for those who enjoy the atmosphere of a good bookstore, it can be a satisfying and intellectually rewarding experience.

INITIATING THE SEARCH

Understanding your library's classification system will help you locate the relevant book collections, but to find specific works on specific topics you will have to turn to the catalog—the most important research tool in the library. For generations libraries used card catalogs, but in recent years electronic catalogs have made the traditional card catalog increasingly obsolete. It is no longer the card drawer, but the computer terminal, that will be your first stop when attacking a classroom assignment or research project.

The catalog gives you access to listings of all the materials held by your library. With a computerized catalog you simply type an author's name, a title, a subject, or a key word, and the computer will show what is in the collection. When you see a promising title, a simple command will display an array of information on that source: among other things, the classification number, whether it is in the reference or general collection, the number of pages, whether the book is illustrated, the date of publication, and, related subject areas. You might also be able to find out if it is already checked out or on order.

Looking up a specific title or the works of a given author is relatively easy, but finding all the relevant books on a given subject or topic is not always so simple. The electronic catalogs allow you to enter key words based on your subject, and you can combine key words in order to narrow the limits of your search. For instance, in our library, when we typed in the word "War" we got over 700 "hits" or matches; when we typed in "Civil War" there were 111 "hits"; and when "United States Civil War" was the entry, our list had been narrowed to 63.

If you have struck gold with a well-chosen subject or keyword entry, don't assume your search is complete. Try to think of additional subject headings that might yield results. To continue with our example of the U.S. Civil War, when we typed in the name of "Abraham Lincoln," dozens more entries appeared, many of which were not included in the Civil War lists mentioned above. Often the catalog itself will tell you to "see also" this or that subject. The information display on a specific book will also include alternate subject headings that you might want to try. Browsing through relevant sections of the book stacks can also help you turn up sources you didn't discover during the catalog search.

THE REFERENCE SECTION

The catalog is only the first step in your search for information. Next you should try to find journal and periodical articles on your subject, and perhaps relevant books that are not currently in your library's collection. To do this you have to consult various indexes and bibliographies (i.e., lists of books and articles) found in your library's reference section.

As Montaigne noted, without much exaggeration, "There are more books upon books than upon all other subjects." Unfortunately, books that list other books are not especially exciting reading. They are, however, quite necessary if you are going to do a thorough job of research. Keep in mind, though, that these indexes, bibliographies, and abstracts do not contain the actual historical information you are seeking; they are intended to help you find the books and articles that do contain that information.

Many of the most useful indexes are now available either online (i.e., via direct electronic link to a centralized data base) or on CD-ROM (**C**ompact **D**isk with **R**ead **O**nly **M**emory). These are CDs, just like those you buy at the local mu-sic store, which contain massive amounts of information that can be read by computers. Most libraries provide computer terminals that will allow you to tap a number of these major indexes (see the list of resources on pages 61–63), allowing you to do the subject and keyword searches discussed earlier. You will be able to find not only new materials in your own library, but important books and articles that your library might not have. The latter you may wish to order through interlibrary loan or see in another library.

At the end of this chapter there is a short list of indexes, bibliographies, and abstracts useful to

the history student. Some titles that merit special mention are the periodical indexes which do for journal and magazine articles what the catalog does for books. The most important are the *Readers' Guide to Periodical Literature* and the publication known variously as the *International Index* (to 1965), the *Social Sciences and Humanities Index* (to 1974), and now, separately, the *Social Sciences Index* and the *Humanities Index*. Although recent parts of these indexes (the late 1990s) are available electronically, the printed volumes of these publications will still be of use to history students who often need reference materials from the more distant past.

The *Readers' Guide, Social Sciences Index,* and *Humanities Index* list articles alphabetically by author and under one or more subject headings. The *Readers' Guide* will help you find articles published in the more popular magazines (e.g., *Time, Newsweek,* etc.), and the *Social Sciences Index* and *Humanities Index* will list articles that appear in the more scholarly journals. A key is provided in the front of these volumes to help you understand the sometimes-confusing abbreviations they use to save space.

In addition to these guides to books and articles, the reference section also has countless volumes that contain a wealth of actual historical information. Included in this group are dictionaries, encyclopedias, biographical dictionaries, map atlases, and statistical compilations. Somewhere in your reference collection there is a book that contains the answer to just about any informational question you might have. In the category of dictionaries, for instance, there are historical dictionaries, pronunciation dictionaries, slang dictionaries, and rhyming dictionaries. There are dictionaries of forgotten words, new words, common words, foreign words, technical words, crossword-puzzle words, uncouth words, and even words used by criminals.

SURFING IN CYBERSPACE: THE INTERNET

Computer literacy is now an essential survival skill in our increasingly technological society. Since computer networks now give researchers access to more information than people can ever use, never again will you be able to say, "I couldn't find any information on that subject."

As one newspaper columnist wrote recently, "What I found confirmed my worst fears; there is more information out there than I could possibly process."[1]

Computer networks can make your life as a student much easier. You will be able to access your library's catalog using the computer in your room, and begin to assemble a preliminary bibliography without ever physically entering the library. But this only scratches the surface of possibilities. There are now literally thousands of computer networks around the world that you can access using the Internet.

The Internet presents history students with a world of research opportunities never before available. It can help you search the catalogs of libraries all over the world, plug into historical bulletin boards and discussion groups, read journal articles and newsletters, examine an array of original documents and photographs, and survey the full text of court cases or the stories appearing in contemporary newspapers and magazines. You will still have to use traditional books and periodicals in your research, but the Internet will allow you to tap resources that previous generations of students could only have dreamt about.

---

1 Christine Bertelson, "On-Line Journey Leaves Traveler Seeking Real Talk," *St. Louis Post-Dispatch,* October 18, 1994: B1.

The Internet presents to history students a world of research opportunities never before available—and pitfalls to match. On the plus side, the information to which you have access is no longer limited by physical location. You can live in the deserts of Utah or the wilds of the Northwest Territory and access information in libraries, universities and museums around the world. On the other hand, just about anyone with a computer can publish on the Internet so that the quality of much of the information out there is suspect. Still the Internet is here to stay, and students will have to know how to use it.

It is not our intention to write an in-depth primer on Internet use. There are plenty of them out there, and they often run to hundreds of pages. Also, the world of cyberspace is changing so rapidly, anything written today will be outdated tomorrow. However, there are a few introductory points that might be helpful.

For our purposes it is sufficient to note that your passport to the information contained in the worldwide network of computer connections is called the World Wide Web (WWW), which allows computer users to browse through the almost infinite variety of information available on the Internet. The WWW provides easy access to information. To cruise the Web you also need a software program that allows your computer to read the information you discover. There are two ways to use the system once you are hooked into the Web.

1. You can do keyword searches that will result in a number of "hits" (i.e., a list of addresses with some mention of your subject). When you click your mouse on one of those selections you will be linked to a "home page" (the entry door) of someone who has put information—or links to other information—on the Web. Any word or phrase highlighted in a different color (usually blue or red) represents an avenue to further information on that subject. A click of the mouse will get you in.

2. If you know the actual address of the link you want to access, you can click the "Open" icon in the menu bar at the top of the page, and type the address into the box that is provided. Click "Open" or press "Return" to complete the process.

Much of the information in this section is based on "Historians and the Web: A Guide," by Andrew McMichael, Michael O'Malley, and Roy Rosenzweig, published in *Perspectives*, the American Historical Association's newsletter. The following list of history-related web sites is printed here with the permission of the authors.[2]

World Wide Web Sites for Historians

54 Years Ago Archives:
http://www.webcom.com/~jbd/ww2.html

About the World Wide Web:
http://www.afcom.com

American Freedom Coalition:
http://www.afcom.com

American Historical Association:
http://web.gmu.edu/chnm/aha

American Historical Review:
http://www.indiana.edu/~amhrev/

American Memory:
http://lcweb2.loc.gov/amhome.html

Anti-imperialism in the United States:
http://web.syr.edu:80/~fjzwick/ail98-35.html

---

2 Andrew McMichael, Michael O'Malley, and Roy Rosenzweig, "Historians and the Web: A Guide," *Perspectives* (January, 1996), 16.

Bacon's Rebellion:
http://grid.let.rug.nl/~welling/usa/documents/bacon.html

Carnegie Mellon University:
http://english-server.hss.cmu.edu/History.html

Center for History and New Media:
http://web.gmu.edu/chnm

Central Connecticut:
http://neal.ctstateu.edu/history/world_history/world_history.html

Civil War:
http://www.access.digex.net/~bdboyle/cw.html

Congressional Record:
http://thomas.loc.gov/

Crossroads:
http://www.georgetown.edu/crossroads/crossii.html

Cybrary of the Holocaust:
http://www.best.com/~mddunn/cybrary/

Declaration of Independence:
gopher://wiretap.spies.com:70/00/Gov/US-History/decind.txt

Eighteenth Century Studies:
http://www.english.upenn.edu/~jlynch/18th.html

Electronic Text Center:
http://www.lib.virginia.edu/etext/ETC.html

Essays in History:
http://www.lib.virginia.edu/journals/EH/EH.html

French and Indian War:
http://web.syr.edu/~laroux/

History Departments:
http://web.gmu.edu/departments/history/research/depts.html

Hong Kong:
http://www.arts.cuhk.hk/His.html

Instructional Development Office:
http://ww2.ido.gmu.edu/IDO/search.html

Interlinks:
http://www.nova.edu/Inter-Links

Internet:
http://home.mcom.com/assist/about_the_internet.html

Korean War:
http://www.onramp.net/~hbarker/

The Labyrinth:
http://www.georgetown.edu/labyrinth

Letters from an Iowa Soldier in the Civil War:
http://www.ucsc.edu/civil-war-letters/home.html

Louisiana State University:
http://www.cwc.lsu.edu/

Lycos:
http://www.lycos.com

Mirsky's Worst of the Web:
http://mirsky.turnpike.net/wow/Worst.html

Mississippi State University:
http://www.msstate.edu:80/Archives/History/USA/usa.html

Naval Ocean Systems Center:
http://white.nosc.mil/museum.html

On-line Museums:
http://www.comlab.ox.ac.uk/archive/other/museums.html

Project Muse:
http://muse.jhu.edu

Ragged Dick:
gopher://wiretap.spies.com/oo/library/classic/ragged.txt

Second Treatise on Government:
http://www.jim.com/jamesd/2ndtreat.html

Social Sciences Data Collection:
http://ssdc.ucsd.edu/

University of Geneva:
http://cuiwww.uniqe.ch/meta-index.html

University of Kansas:
http://history.cc.ukans.edu/history/WWW_history_main.html

University of Rochester:
http://www.history.rochester.edu

University of Tennessee:
http://cobweb.utcc.utk.edu/~hoemann/warweb.html

Valley of the Shadow:
http://jefferson.village.virginia.edu/vshadow/vshadow.html

Vietnam War:
http://www.ionet.net/~uheller/vnbktoc.shtml

Voice of the Shuttle:
http://humanitas.ucsb.edu/

Web Crawler:
http://webcrawler.com/

World Wide Web:
http://www.w3.org

Yahoo:
http://www.yahoo.com

CHOOSING THE BEST SOURCES

Once you have found relevant information on your subject, you might ask yourself, "How do I select a usable and representative sample of sources from the vast mountain of information available?" Remember, if you have been conscientious in your search, you will have more information than you need and it will be necessary to choose the most appropriate materials. There are no hard and fast rules, but the following tips might prove helpful.

1. Don't let the perfect be the enemy of the good. It is better to have enough sources and get your assignment in on time than to try to read all the sources and never begin writing.

also helpful to check book reviews to identify the most respected works in the field.

4. You will probably discover some scholarly controversies involving your topic; try to do justice to the differing interpretations.

SOME PLACES TO BEGIN

The following section contains a sample list of reference books and will best serve you when you actually begin a research project. Sources available online or on CD-ROM are indicated in brackets. Many more resources will be available in electronic versions in the near future.

Indexes and Bibliographies: Finding Your Source Materials
This is a selective list of some of the best places to begin your search for the sources you will use

Battle of Bull Run/Manassas

2. Making the proper selection usually requires preliminary research and reading. You have to get to know a topic before you can discern the books and articles historians judge to be the most important on your subject.

3. In selecting books and articles (remembering there are exceptions to all that follows): choose the most up-to-date research over outdated works and works with substantive source references and bibliographies. It is

on your research project.

America: History and Life [CD-ROM]. Citations and abstracts of periodical articles on the U.S. and Canada from prehistoric times to the present.

The American Historical Association's Guide to Historical Literature, 3rd ed. An excellent place to begin a bibliographical search. The 3rd edition was published in 1995.

Book Review Digest. Contains brief book review excerpts and can help you decide which books are the best on your subject. It is also indispensable in helping you decide which complete book reviews to read.

Harvard Guide to American History, Volumes 1 & 2. A bibliographical guide to the literature on American history. The opening chapter provides an excellent introduction to research methods and materials.

Historical Abstracts [Online]. Provides brief summaries of scholarly articles that have appeared in periodical literature from around the world. The history of the United States is covered in the section "American: History and Life." Good for finding articles relevant to your research and getting a preview of the content.

New York Times Index. [Online; CD-ROM] Excellent source for the beginner. This is a thorough index of the articles that have appeared in the *New York Times* since 1851. It is important to follow the directions under each subject heading in order to find the full citation.

A Reader's Guide to Contemporary History (Bernard Krikler and Walter Laqueur, eds.).

Reader's Guide to Periodical Literature. [Online; CD-ROM] An excellent source; discussed on page 57. Note, however, that this index covers popular, nontechnical magazines (e.g., *Time*, *Newsweek*, etc.) representing many important fields of study.

Social Sciences Index [Online; CD-ROM] and the *Humanities Index* [Online; CD-ROM] (originally the *International Index* and, then, the *Social Sciences and Humanities Index*). Discussed on page 57. Excellent guides for the student of history and politics since these indexes concentrate on more scholarly, specialized periodicals.

The Social Sciences: A Cross-Disciplinary Guide to Selected Sources (Nancy L. Herron, ed.). Discusses reference materials for history as well as political science, law, and other social sciences.

Dictionaries and Encyclopedias: Finding General Information

The few titles listed below will help you get an initial overview of any topic you are researching. These sources are useful for getting started and for filling in the odd fact here and there, they are much too general, however, to serve as the core sources for your research. For those with personal computers, there are CD-ROM versions of certain dictionaries and encyclopedias.

In addition to the standard encyclopedias—*Britannica* [CD-ROM], *Americana* [CD-ROM], *Colliers*—the following reference works are excellent resources for the student of history.

Dictionary of American Biography. A multivolume collection of scholarly articles on prominent Americans who died before 1945. The articles have bibliographies that can serve as a guide to further research.

Dictionary of American History. An eight-volume work with brief, signed, articles on aspects of American history. Each entry contains a brief bibliography.

Dictionary of National Biography. This is the British equivalent of the *Dictionary of American Biography*. It is especially useful if you are studying the long colonial period of American history. The lack of any national designation in the title often confuses American students. The DNB (as it is known) was the first such biographical dictionary and everyone knew which nation was referred to in the title. British postage stamps, likewise the first in the field, also do not carry the name of the country of origin. Check it out some time.

Encyclopedia of American History (Richard B. Morris, ed.). A condensed overview of the major events in American history. A good way to get a brief account of the events and chronology from colonial times to the present.

An Encyclopedia of World History (William Langer, ed.). Does the same thing for world history that Morris does for American history.

Harper Encyclopedia of U.S. History. An excellent source of articles on many aspects of U.S. history.

International Encyclopedia of the Social Sciences. Articles in the realm of political science, economics, anthropology, law, sociology, and psychology. Much historical research touches on these related disciplines, and, since history is the mother of the social sciences, it is quite appropriate to dip into such materials.

Oxford English Dictionary. [CD-ROM] A comprehensive multivolume English-language dictionary that traces the historical evolution of the meanings of words. When reading and interpreting documents from previous centuries it is important to know how that age understood certain words, rather than how we understand them. Look up the word "enthusiasm" in the *OED* and see what we mean.

The Reader's Companion to American History. (Eric Foner and John A. Garraty, eds.) Like many other standard one-volume reference works, but with a larger dose of articles on social history—e.g., the history of the family, minorities and women.

Guidebooks to Other Useful References
For more definitive listings and descriptions of other bibliographies, indexes, and informational references, consult the following:

Benjamin, Jules R. *A Student's Guide to History*, 5th ed. New York: St. Martin's Press, 1991. See especially "Appendix A: Basic Reference Sources for History Study and Research."

Fritze, Ronald H., Brian E. Coutts, and Louis A. Vyhnanek. *Reference Sources in History: An Introductory Guide*. Santa Barbara, CA: ABC-Clio, 1990. Designed to replace *The Historian's Handbook* (see below).

Li, Tze-Chung. *Social Science Reference Sources*, 2nd ed. Westport, CT: Greenwood, 1990. A guide on how to find reference works and how to use them.

Navigating the Internet
Braun, Eric. *The Internet Directory*. New York: Fawcett Columbine, 1994.

Kehoe, Brendan P. *Zen and the Art of the Internet: A Beginner's Guide*, 2nd ed. Englewood Cliffs, NJ: Prentice Hall, 1993.

Krol, Ed. *The Whole Internet: User's Guide & Catalog*. Sebastopol, CA: O'Reilly and Associates, 1992.

LaQuey, Tracy and Jeanne C. Ryer. *The Internet Companion: A Beginner's Guide to Global Networking*. Reading, MA: Addison-Wesley, 1994.

Levine, John. *Internet for Dummies Quick Reference*. Peterborough, NH: IDG Books, 1994.

This section has been compiled with the generous assistance of Ellen Eliceiri, Head of Reference and Public Services, Webster University.

EXERCISES

I CREATION OF A NATION, 1776–1820

A The Search for Sources[3]

The catalog is the logical place to begin a search for research materials. But, to get the full benefit of a catalog search, you should check a variety of possible subject headings. For instance, a person researching the topic of the Salem witchcraft trials should not only look for books under the heading "Salem", but under subject headings such as "witchcraft," "U.S.—History—Colonial Period," "magic," "sorcery," and "occult sciences," as well.

For each of the topics below, list four or more catalog subject headings in which relevant materials are listed. Don't guess! Go to the catalog and check out the categories yourself.

Example:

Research Topic: *The Spanish Conquest of Mexico (1500s)*

Possible Catalog Subject Headings (Examples):

Spain—History	Indians of Central America
U. S.—History	Indians of Mexico
America—Discovery and Exploration	Aztecs
Latin America—History	Hernando Cortes
Indians—Transpacific Influences	

---

3 For the concept of exercise B the authors are indebted to William Coyle, *Research Papers*, 2nd ed. (Indianapolis, IN: Odyssey Press, 1965), 103–106.

♡ *Reader's Guide to Periodicals*

1. Topic: ~~The Military History of the American Revolution~~

    Possible Catalog Subject Headings:

    women

    consumers

    history

    trade

    economics, women

2. Topic: ~~The Campaign for a Bill of Rights~~   *The Seneca Falls Bill of Rights*

    Possible Catalog Subject Headings:

    Bill of Rights

    rights

    Seneca Indians

    government.

    _____

3. Topic: Women in Eighteenth-Century America

    Possible Catalog Subject Headings:

    American women

    women history

    Indian women

    18th century

    _____

4. Topic: The Slave Trade, 1787–1820

    Possible Catalog Subject Headings:

    Slave trade

    west Africa

    Anti-slavery movements

    slavery

    _____

B   *Using the Reference Collection*

Using the reference collection, answer the following questions and list the source you used for each answer. Do not use general encyclopedias (e.g., *Britannica*) or any single source for more than one answer. You may use specialized encyclopedias (e.g., *Encyclopedia of American History*). The object of this exercise is to acquaint you with as wide a variety of reference works as possible. For each answer, indicate whether you found it in a printed volume or an electronic data base.

You might want to review the list of possible references on pp. 61–63. In addition to the specific sources listed on those pages, the following categories of reference works might be helpful:

Atlases (maps plus much more useful geographic and demographic information)

Dictionaries of Famous Quotations

Almanacs and Yearbooks (information on the year just past plus many statistics)

Dictionaries of Dates

Readers Guide to Periodicals

1. Locate a magazine or journal article written after 1990 (list author, title, date, name of periodical) about the Constitutional Convention. Locate another article on the same topic written before 1980.

"Time for a people's convention", G. Vidal, The Nation 254:73+; Jan. 27, 1992 / "Thomas Jefferson, won't you please come home?" L.N. Cutler, Annals of the American Academy of Political and Social Science, 396: 25-39, July 1971

Source(s) Readers' Guide to Periodical Literature, 1992 / March 1971-Feb. 1972

PE 1625 Oxford Eng. dictionary

2. What did the word "enthusiasm" mean in the 18th century?

Rapturous intensity of feeling in favour of a person, principle, cause, etc.

Source p.296, The Oxford English Dictionary, Volume V

3. List three reference works (not including general encyclopedias) in which you can find a biographical sketch of Tecumseh, the Shawnee leader who tried to create an Indian confederacy in the early 1800s. Include the volume numbers (where relevant) and page numbers of the essays. Pocahontas or Sacagawea

Source

Source

Source

Readers Guide

4. Locate an article on slavery in the American South written after 1980 and appearing in a historical journal. Cite the title of the article, the author, the journal, and the date.

Source "The Response of the Slaves." G.J. Heuman. History Today. 34: 31-5 April 1984

p. 1645, Readers' Guide to Periodical Literature, March 1984 - Feb. 1985

Book Review Index/Digest

5. Locate a book review of J. G. A. Pocock, *The Machiavellian Moment: Florentine Republican Thought and the Atlantic Republican Tradition, 1975*. Simply provide the citation for the magazine or journal in which the review appeared, including the author of the review and the date.

Virginia Quarterly Review, Autumn 1975 vol 51 p.628

Source Book Review Digest

6. Who wrote: "I have sworn upon the altar of God, eternal hostility against every form of tyranny over the mind of man."

Jefferson, letter to Dr. Benjamin Rush (Sept. 23, 1800)

Source

P. 388.15, Bartlett's Familiar Quotations

7. When (date and year) and where was James Oglethorpe, the founder of Georgia, born?

_____

Source

_____

C *Notetaking*

Gathering information in a usable form requires well-developed notetaking skills, and, effective notetaking skills are also extremely useful in the classroom and on the job. But notetaking skills aren't inborn; like everything else, they must be learned.

Notetaking is not the same thing as copying; it requires active intellectual effort. A good note is not a literal transcript of a text or lecture, but a summary, written in your own words, which reflects your understanding of what you have read or heard. Doing it this way requires thought and effort on your part, but the rewards are worth it. "What you have accomplished is threefold: you have made an effort at thought, which has imprinted the information on your mind; you have practiced the art of writing by making a para-phrase; and you have at the same time, [if you are writing a paper], taken a step toward your first draft, for here and now these are your words, not a piece of plagiarism thinly veiled by a page reference."[4]

This exercise is designed to give you some experience in taking good notes. As you do the following segments, keep in mind that a good note summarizes the important points and it should be written in your own words. You should not try to copy the original text or lecture verbatim. Before beginning examine the following example of the right way and the wrong way to take notes.

Original Passage

For most Americans . . . this was the deeply felt meaning of the Revolution: they had cre-ated a new world, a republican world. No one doubted that the new polities would be republics, and as Thomas Paine pointed out, "What is called a *republic,* is not any *particular form* of government." Republicanism meant more for Americans than simply the elimina-tion of a king and the institution of an elective system. It added a moral dimension, a uto-pian depth, to the political separation from England—a depth that involved the very char-acter of their society. "We are now really another people," exclaimed Paine in 1782. (Gor-don S. Wood, *The Creation of the American Republic, 1776–1787* [New York: W. W. Norton, 1969], 47–48.) Reprinted by permission of W. W. Norton & Co., Inc.

---

4 Barzun and Graff, *Modern Researcher,* 30.

> G. Wood, <u>Creation</u>
>
> Meaning of Revolution
>
> Most Americans felt Revolution had created a new, republican, world. They wanted to create republics, but as Thomas Paine said, a republic "is not any particular form of government." Republicanism meant to Americans more than elimination of king and institution of an elective system; it had moral dimension and implied change in "the very character of their society."
>
> pp. 47-48

This note is OK as far as it goes. It records all the essentials, but it is more a literal transcription than a summary. Such a note requires very little work on the part of the researcher. Remember, a good note should be a summary written in your own words. Now take a look at another note based on the same passage.

Sample Note # 2

> Wood, <u>Creation</u>
>
> Meaning of the Revol.
>
> To Americans Revol. meant creation of a new world. A republic meant elimination of king and use of elections, but Wood argues it also meant a moral transformation of soc. itself. Quotes Paine: "We are now really another people."
>
> pp. 47-48

This note is much better. It is shorter (by more than a third) and it translates the key ideas into the words of the researcher. In this sort of note some true intellectual work has been done, in that the passage had to be fully understood in order to be effectively summarized in different language. When it comes time to write a paper there will be no temptation to use the author's words (other than the quoted extract from Tom Paine) since the note already reflects the style and words of the student.

Notice the use of abbreviations, a legitimate and time-saving practice. Also, the source and page number have been recorded along with a one-line heading that indicates the general topic of the note.

For each of the passages below write a research note that summarizes the key ideas in your own words.

1. "Undoubtedly this narration of Black Hawk's early life omits much that would help [us] understand his later attitudes and actions, but several clear indications of his personality and world view do emerge. He thought of himself as a traditional Sauk. He personified tribal rivalries throughout much of his life. Thus, because the Osages had been long-time enemies of the tribe they became his enemies. He practiced the ceremonies, dances, and mourning customs with determination, often going far beyond minimal expectations, as in mourning his father for five years instead of the usual six months. He grew to manhood during an era when the Sauks and their tribal neighbors still enjoyed a good degree of isolation and freedom from the demands of the European powers then trying to divide the continent among themselves.

Roger L. Nichols, *Black Hawk and the Warrior's Path*, Harlan Davidson, Inc., 1992, 18–19.

_____

_____

_____

_____

2. Study of the pamphlets confirmed my rather old-fashioned view that the American Revolution was above all else an ideological, constitutional, political struggle and not primarily a controversy between social groups undertaken to force changes in the organization of the society or the economy. It confirmed too my belief that intellectual developments in the decade before Independence led to a radical idealization and conceptualization of the previous century and a half of American experience, and that it was this intimate relationship between Revolutionary thought and the circumstances of life in eighteenth-century America than endowed the Revolution with its peculiar force and made it so profoundly a transforming event.

Bernard Bailyn, *The Ideological Origins of the American Revolution*. Copyright © 1967 by the President and Fellows of Harvard College. Reprinted by permission of Harvard University Press.

_____

_____

_____

_____

3. In 1782, weakened and humiliated by the loss of the American colonies, Britain had agreed to a new deal for Ireland.

Britain had no choice. A self-styled Irish Volunteer army had been formed by the Irish ruling class to protect the country against the French. Then, encouraged by the success of the Americans, they demanded some form of self-government or threatened an Irish War of Independence.

Ireland, like America in the previous decade, posed the delicate problem of reconciling the national aspirations of a colony with the strategic needs of the mother country. Yet Ireland, half-independent as she had become, was geographically part of the British Isles. It was to this unique geographical predicament—too far from Britain to be assimilated, too near to be allowed to be separate—that so many of Ireland's anomalies and miseries could be traced.

Thomas Pakenham, *The Year of Liberty: The Story of the Great Irish Rebellion of 1798*, Prentice Hall, 1969, 24–25. Reproduced by permission of Curtis Brown, Ltd., London, on behalf of Thomas Pakenham. Copyright © Thomas Pakenham, 1969.

_____

_____

_____

_____

4. [In saluting an American vessel in 1776] the small voice of [the Dutch island of] St. Eustatius [in the Caribbean] was the first officially to greet the largest event of the century—the entry into the society of nations of a new Atlantic state destined to change the direction of history.

The effect of the American Revolution on the nature of government in the society of Europe was felt and recognized from the moment it became a fact. After the American rebellion began, "an extraordinary alteration took place in the minds of a great part of the people of Holland," homeland of St. Eustatius, recalled Sir James Harris, Earl of Malmesbury, who was British Ambassador at The Hague in the years immediately following the triumph of the American Revolution. "Doubts arose," he wrote in his memoirs, "about the authority of the Stadtholder" (Sovereign of the Netherlands and Prince of Orange) . . . "indeed all authority came under attack when the English colonists in America succeeded in their rebellion."

Barbara Tuchman, _The First Salute_, Alfred A. Knopf / Random House, 1988, 5–6.

_____

_____

_____

_____

II AMERICA BETWEEN TWO WARS, 1918–1941

A _The Search for Sources_

The catalog is the logical place to begin a search for research materials. To get the full benefit of a catalog search, you should check a variety of possible subject headings. For instance, a person researching the topic of the Salem witchcraft trials should not only look for books under the heading "Salem", but under subject headings such as "witchcraft," "U.S.—History—Colonial Period," "magic," "sorcery," and "occult sciences," as well.

For each of the topics below, list four or more catalog subject headings in which relevant materials are listed. Don't guess! Go to the catalog and check out the categories yourself.

Example:

> Research Topic: Japanese Attack on Pearl Harbor
>
> Possible Catalog Subject Headings (Examples):
>
> | | |
> |---|---|
> | Midway—Battle of | Military History—Modern |
> | Naval History | Battles |
> | World War, 1939–1945 | Japan—History |

1. Topic: Labor Unrest in the 1920s

   Possible Catalog Subject Headings:

   _____

   _____

   _____

   _____

   _____

2. Topic: The Scopes Trial

   Possible Catalog Subject Headings:

   _____

   _____

   _____

   _____

   _____

3. Topic: Franklin Roosevelt's Attempt to Pack the Supreme Court in 1937

   Possible Catalog Subject Headings:

   _____

   _____

   _____

   _____

   _____

4. Topic: African Americans during the Great Depression

   Possible Catalog Subject Headings:

   _____

   _____

   _____

   _____

   _____

B *Using the Reference Collection*

Using the reference collection, answer the following questions and list the source (including volume and page number) used for each answer. Do not use general encyclopedias (e.g., *Britannica*) or any single source for more than one answer. You may use specialized encyclopedias (e.g., *Encyclopedia of American History*). The object of this exercise is to acquaint you with as wide a variety of reference works as possible. For each answer, indicate whether you found it in a printed volume or an electronic data base.

You might want to review the list of possible references on pp. 61–63. In addition to the specific sources listed on those pages, the following categories of reference works might be helpful:

Atlases (maps plus much more useful geographic and demographic information.

Dictionaries of Famous Quotations

Almanacs and Yearbooks (information on the year just past plus many statistics)

Dictionaries of Dates

Remember: Include source title, volume number (if relevant) and page citation.

1. Locate a magazine or journal article written in or after 1991 (list author, title, date, name of periodical) about the Japanese attack on Pearl Harbor or about the 50th anniversary of that event. Locate an article on the Pearl Harbor attack written before 1970.

_____

_____

Source(s)

_____

2. List three reference works (not including general encyclopedias) in which you can find a biographical sketch of W. E. B. Du Bois, the turn-of-the-century African-American leader. Include the volume numbers (where relevant) and page numbers of the essays.

Source

_____

Source

_____

Source

_____

3. List three reference works, at least two different from those above (not including general encyclopedias), in which you can find a biographical sketch of Eleanor Roosevelt. Include the volume numbers (where relevant) and page numbers of the essays.

Source

_____

Source

_____

Source

_____

4. Locate an article on Louisiana governor Huey P. Long, written after 1980 and appearing in a magazine or journal. Cite the title of the article, the author, the journal, and the date.

_____

Source

_____

5. Locate a book review of George Marsden's _Fundamentalism and American Culture: The Shaping of Twentieth-Century Evangelicalism, 1870–1925_ (1980). Simply provide the citation for the magazine or journal in which the review appeared, including the author of the review and the date.

_____

Source

_____

6. Who wrote: "No one can make you feel inferior without your consent."

_____

Source

_____

7. When (month, day, year) was F. Scott Fitzgerald born?

_____

Source

_____

C Notetaking

Gathering information in a usable form requires well-developed notetaking skills, and effective notetaking skills are also extremely useful in the classroom and on the job. But notetaking skills aren't inborn; like everything else, they must be learned.

Notetaking is not the same thing as copying; it requires active intellectual effort. A good note is not a literal transcript of a text or lecture, but a summary, written in your own words, that reflects your understanding of what you have read or heard. Doing it this way requires thought and effort on your part, but the rewards are worth it. "What you have accomplished is threefold: you have made an effort at thought, which has imprinted the information on your mind; you have practiced the art of writing by making a paraphrase; and you have at the same time, [if you are writing a paper], taken a step toward your first draft, for here and now these are your words, not a piece of plagiarism thinly veiled by a page reference."[5]

This exercise is designed to give you some experience in taking good notes. As you do the following segments, keep in mind that a good note summarizes the important points and it should be written in your own words. You should not try to copy the original text or lecture verbatim.

For each of the passages below write a research note which summarizes the key ideas in your own words. Before beginning examine the example of note-taking on page 66–67 above.

1. In 1936 [Franklin] Roosevelt clearly had the support of a large majority of the people. When they voted for him, they presumably also voted for the New Deal and its con-

---

5 Barzun and Graff, _Modern Researcher_, 30.

tinuation. Sixty percent approved, whatever their degree of understanding. They confirmed Roosevelt's own sense of righteousness and confirmed his distaste for his more vocal critics. Yet already the courts had nullified or crippled much New Deal legislation. Even by 1935 Congress was becoming restless and increasingly concerned about the power it had surrendered in a time of crisis. . . . Roosevelt detested such flagrant defiance of the majority's will and of his own will. As a person who usually had his way, and now seemed worthy of it by democratic choice and moral right, Roosevelt fought back. As a democrat, he refused to accept the institutional barriers that often nullified the will of the majority or even to fight back by means legitimized by these same institutions.

Paul K. Conkin, *The New Deal,* 3d ed., Harlan Davidson, Inc., 1992, 91.

_____

_____

_____

2. Women of color coped [with the Depression] by using a strategy of downward mobility—that is, they took whatever jobs they could get. Rural black women often left their homes, migrating in larger numbers than black men to urban areas in search of employment. Urban black women also became small-scale entrepreneurs, peddling such goods as home-baked bread or home-raised vegetables on the streets or door to door. Urban black women also responded to economic hard times by gathering into so-called slave markets on street corners each morning, where they offered their labor to the highest bidder on an hourly basis, often for as little as ten cents an hour. In New York City, an observer noted that hundreds of "forlorn and half-starved" girls were lucky to find a few hours' work one or two days each week.

Glenda Riley, *Inventing the American Woman: An Inclusive History,* 2d ed., Vol. 2, Harlan Davidson, Inc., 1995, 255.

_____

_____

_____

3. By 1931, Mae West had polished her public image to perfection. She was a force, a personality who took charge of any and all situations, an initiator who shaped her own destiny. Her every action enforced this view. The name Mae West evoked a clear picture: a funny, seductive woman who loved to talk about sex and to practice it as often as possible. No one was lukewarm toward her; you either liked her or you did not. Few other public personalities at that time commanded a similar name recognition. She benefited from the negative publicity accompanying her allegedly scandalous plays and confirmed most of America's opinion that New York City was the center of sin and corruption. To her credit, she converted this seemingly negative view to a positive one, ensuring her even greater visibility in the unlikely venue of the movies.

June Sochen, *Mae West: She Who Laughs, Lasts,* Harlan Davidson, Inc., 1992, 55.

_____

_____

_____

4. Those who contributed to the literature of the Harlem Renaissance [after World War I] were deeply aware of their belonging to a group that not only was a minority but also was set apart in numerous ways, many of which were degrading. If black writers accepted this separateness, it was not so much because they wanted to be what others wanted them to be; that is, a distinct and even exotic group in the eyes of the

more patronizing whites. Rather, it was because their experiences had given them some appreciation of their own distinct and unique cultural heritage and traditions. The plantation, the slave quarters, the proscriptions even in freedom, the lynchings and the riots, the segregation and discrimination had created a body of common experiences that, in turn, helped to promote the idea of a distinct and authentic cultural community.

John Hope Franklin, *From Slavery to Freedom,* 4th ed., Alfred A. Knopf / Random House, 1974, 374.

_____

_____

_____

_____

_____

_____

EVALUATING EVIDENCE

"The documents are liars."

T. E. LAWRENCE

"The central methodological problem for the historian . . . is to know how to interrogate witnesses, how to test evidence, how to assess the reliability and the relevance of testimony."

ROBIN WINKS

The famous soldier-scholar, T. E. Lawrence (Lawrence of Arabia), once wrote a friend: "The documents are liars. No man ever yet tried to write down the entire truth of any action in which he has been engaged."[1] Lawrence exaggerated, but he certainly had a point. Not all documents lie, but they don't always tell the unalloyed truth either. There exists, says historian Simon Schama, a "teasing gap separating a lived event and its subsequent narration,"[2] and it is that gap that can create a treacherous problem for those who try to wring the truth out of the records of the past.

Whatever their imperfections, documents, and other surviving artifacts, are the basic raw materials of history. In this chapter we will consider the types of sources historians use to learn about the past and to write history. We will also examine some techniques used by the historian to evaluate and interpret the raw data of the past.

THE SOURCES: PRIMARY AND SECONDARY

The problem of weighing evidence is never an easy one, but the difficulty can be eased by an appreciation of the various types of sources historians rely upon in their work. There are two basic categories of sources used by students of history, whether beginners or seasoned professionals.

Primary sources (also called original sources) are those materials that were written or created during the period under investigation. They are the records of contemporaries who participated in, witnessed, or commented on the events you are studying. They are the documents and artifacts—letters, reports, diaries, government records, parish registers, newspapers, business ledgers, works of art, buildings, and a host of others—that make the writing and study of history possible. In sum, primary sources are to the historian what a mountain is to the geologist: the surviving record of events that took place long ago.

Secondary sources are accounts of the past written by historians who use the primary sources as evidence. Secondary sources are the books, articles, essays, and lectures through which we learn most of the history we know. If primary sources are produced by those who lived during the period under investigation, secondary sources are produced by the historians who are doing the investigating. Historians take the raw data found in primary sources and transform it into the written histories that attempt to explain how and why things happened as they did.[3]

The distinction between primary and secondary sources is not always as clear as the above definition implies. For instance, a newspaper is definitely a primary source for the period in

---

1 Barzun and Graff, *Modern Researcher*, 50.
2 Quoted in James Atlas, "Stranger Than Fiction," *The New York Times Magazine*, June 23, 1991, 22.
3 Textbooks and similar works represent a special category of tertiary source. Most general survey texts are not based on research into primary sources so much as they reflect the findings of a wide variety of secondary sources—that is, other history books. An author who attempts to cover American history from pre–Columbian times to the present could not in a lifetime read all the necessary primary sources. Such an author would have to rely on books and articles written by other scholars (i.e., on secondary sources) in order to complete the project. Thus textbooks are a step or two further removed from the original sources than are most secondary works.

which it was published. But a newspaper also has many of the characteristics of a secondary source. Very often journalists are not eyewitnesses to the events they write about. Like historians, journalists must interrogate witnesses—in this case directly—and read pertinent documents in order to construct the story, the history, that appears in the paper.

Another problematic source is the personal memoir or autobiography written by a politician, military officer or movie star. Such memoirs often straddle the line that separates primary and secondary sources. While memoirs and autobiographies are first-person accounts of events, their authors rarely rely totally on their memories, as the name memoir implies. Authors often "recollect" the events of their public life with the help of a variety of documents or with previously published accounts of friends and colleagues. When this happens the memoir writer is functioning like any other historian, and the memoir itself must be considered, at least in part, a secondary source.

Also confusing is the fact that many sources can be categorized either as primary or secondary *depending on the subject being studied*. An example is Charles Beard's famous book, *An Economic Interpretation of the Constitution*, published in 1913. Beard's controversial thesis was that the delegates to the Constitutional Convention in Philadelphia designed the Constitution to protect their own personal economic interests. For scholars studying the origins of the Constitution, Beard's book is a secondary source, and its central thesis has been long debated. However, the book would be a primary source for anyone studying the ideas of Charles Beard himself. That is, if Charles Beard and his ideas were the subject of the study, *An Economic Interpretation of the Constitution* would be a primary source; if the origins of the Constitution were the subject, Beard's book would be a secondary source.

Finally, history students should be aware that many primary sources have been published in book form. In spite of their resemblance in form to secondary sources, these materials remain primary. Remember, the basic question to ask is when did the materials originate?, not when were they published or reprinted? The Declaration of Independence printed in the back of a textbook is still a primary source for the revolutionary period of American history, even though the textbook itself is a secondary source.

USING PRIMARY SOURCES[4]

However inadequate the surviving store of records related to a specific historical episode, so many documents and artifacts have survived (especially from the modern centuries of which American history is a part), that the task of historians is truly daunting. Before historians can use any body of evidence they must thoroughly sort and sift it. Evidence is found in mixed-up bundles, with relevant and irrelevant information thrown together like kernels of grain and their husks. Only a small part of the existing evidence will be relevant to a particular investigation, and the historian must separate the wheat from the chaff.

Equally daunting is the task of coaxing the truth from the sources. Sources can be seductive or coldly aloof. They can mislead, lie, or lure you into a false sense of security. They can be written in the obscure languages or the incomprehensible jargon of the modern bureaucrat, or they can lead the researcher into blind alleys, false turns and dead ends. For all the frustrations, however, unlocking the secrets of these records can be a fascinating task. The historian becomes a detective who seeks out clues found in the primary sources.

Since most primary sources are in written form, historians typically limit themselves to the study of that segment of the past for which we have written records. (The study of preliterate, or prehistoric cultures and societies is the domain of cultural anthropologists and archeologists.) Not all primary sources, however, are documents. Remember our definition: A primary source is something that came into existence during the period that the historian is studying. From this perspective, just about anything that has survived (including your Aunt Edna) is a potential primary source—buildings, tools, works of art, weapons, coins, and, more recently, photographs, films, and recordings. The list below should give you a rough idea of the variety of primary sources historians use.

A quick review of the above list will reveal that not all types of written primary evidence are

---

4 Techniques for reading and analyzing secondary sources are discussed in Appendix A.

inscriptions	works of art
buildings	baptismal and burial records
coins	newspapers
royal charters	magazines
tapes of tv shows	mystery novels
laws	autobiographies/memoirs
government publications	legislative debates
diplomatic dispatches	maps
court records	poetry
police reports	films
advertisements	parents
minutes of organizations	photographs
private letters	folk songs
diaries	language
business records	furniture
railroad schedules	telephone books

equally "primary." That is, some primary sources are inherently less useful and less trustworthy than others. Admittedly newspapers are indispensable primary sources, but we have seen that press accounts are frequently written by journalists who are not themselves eyewitnesses to the stories they write. Journalists, like historians, have to piece together stories from many sources, and such stories are often somewhat distanced from the events they describe. Also problematical are the memoirs and autobiographies we discussed above. They are often written years after the events they describe; and vanity, personal bias, or failing memory can influence the tale an author has to tell. Even individuals who are determined to provide a balanced and accurate account rarely remember the same event in precisely the same way.

In contrast to newspapers and memoirs are those sources which were never intended to be made public. Such information is often the most revealing and valuable to the historian. "The most primary source of all is unpublished material: private letters and diaries or the reports, orders and messages in government archives."[5] Even here the situation is ambiguous, however, because public figures are now conscious that history will judge them, and even their private correspondence may be written to influence the historians who will one day make those judgments. We will discuss this subject in more depth in the next chapter.

PRIMARY SOURCES AND CRITICAL METHOD

The most challenging task of the historian-detective is to draw testimony from the records of the past. Here the historian has two aims, neither of them simple: (1) to determine if a source is *authentic* and, (2) to establish the *meaning and believability* of the contents. The first is accomplished through external criticism; the second through internal criticism.

External criticism, in the words of one historian, "authenticates evidence and establishes texts in the most accurate possible form."[6] Many historical records lack precise dates or correct attribution. Many texts, for various reasons, are inaccurate, and forgeries are not uncommon. Highly specialized techniques are required to authenticate documents and artifacts: carbon dating, linguistic analysis, chemical analysis, and the like. Extensive knowledge of the period in question is also a prerequisite. Beginners rarely have either the background knowledge or the specialized skills for such criticism so that we need not dwell on this aspect of critical method. However, students may safely assume that the documents in the exercises and the sources they might be using in a class are authentic.

Once the authenticity of a document has been established, the historian faces the far more important challenge of reading and interpreting the contents. This is called internal criticism, and the techniques involved are much less mysteri-

---

5 Tuchman, *Practicing History*, 19.
6 R. J. Shafer, ed., *A Guide to Historical Method* (Homewood, IL.: Dorsey Press, 1969), 100.

ous. More than anything else, the process requires a healthy skepticism to weed out inaccuracies, mistakes, and even lies. We have a tendency to believe anything if it is written down, and, the older the document or more ornate the script, the more we tend to believe it. Therefore, it is important to remind ourselves that our venerable ancestors could lie, shade the truth, or make a mistake the same as we.

Documents do not reveal their secrets easily. You must learn to question the evidence like an attorney in a courtroom—from different angles, from different perspectives, relentlessly, suspiciously. What sort of questions should you ask of the evidence? Below is a partial list of some of the most important.[7]

1. *What exactly does the document mean?*

Often the literal meaning differs from the real meaning. Diplomatic communications, for example, are notorious for veiling harsh international disagreements in extremely polite language. Diplomats are trained to phrase messages in such a restrained fashion that even an impending war can be made to sound no more threatening than a neighborly disagreement over the backyard fence. Because of this, the historian must become familiar with the conventions of diplomatic correspondence in order to understand the real meaning of the dispatches.

Another problem facing the historian is that words change meaning from one age to the next. For instance, in *Inventing America; Jefferson's Declaration of Independence*, Garry Wills argues

that Jefferson's famous line about the unalienable right to "the pursuit of happiness" meant something quite different in the eighteenth century than it does today.[8] To discover these sorts of differences you have to know as much as possible about the cultural and political context of the period you are studying.

2. *How well situated was the author to observe or record the events in question?*

This question brings up a number of additional questions. What was the author's physical location? Was he or she a direct eyewitness or did the information come from someone else? What was the author's *social ability* to observe? That is, might the person's social or economic position in the society have influenced how the event was seen? An angry farmer sympathetic to Daniel Shays would view Shays's Rebellion (1787) much differently than a well-to-do Boston merchant or banker. Finally, did the witness have *specialized knowledge* that might enhance the credibility of the testimony? A lawyer's report of a murder trial might be far more insightful than that of a casual observer in the audience. On the other hand, the casual observer might be able to report on things the lawyer missed.

3. *When, how, and to whom was the report made?*

Obviously, the longer the time between the event and the report, the greater the chance a witness's memory will play tricks. In addition, you should ask what the intended purpose of the report was. An army officer reporting to a superior may tell what the commander wants to hear rather than a more disappointing truth. The number of casualties inflicted by American soldiers on the enemy during the Vietnam War (1961–1975) was constantly exaggerated as field commanders turned in unrealistically high body counts to please their superiors at headquarters.

4. *Is there bias, either in the report, or in yourself, that must be accounted for?*

Personal bias can be the enemy of truth on two levels. It is, of course, common for a piece of testimony to be colored by an author's personal beliefs and convictions. In the same way, your own biases can often blind you to much that the

---

7 These questions are based on those printed in Shafer, *Guide to Historical Method*, 137–38.
8 Garry Wills, *Inventing America: Jefferson's Declaration of Independence* (New York: Doubleday, 1978); see also, Davidson and Lytle, *After the Fact*, 74–78.

sources reveal. Knowing about the person who left the account will help you recognize and compensate for the first sort of bias. Knowing yourself is the only way to ensure that your own prejudices don't get in the way of understanding.

5. *What specialized information is needed to interpret the source?*

Many times you will have to look up names, places, dates, and technical terms to get the full meaning of a statement.

6. *Do the reported actions seem probable according to the dictates of informed common sense?*

Here the significant words are "probable" and "informed common sense." We can never get absolutely conclusive answers for many questions in history. The test of the believability of a piece of testimony is the inherent probability of its being true. The issue is not whether a version of events is possible, but whether, given all the evidence, it is probable.

In this process the historian's most important tool is simple common sense seasoned with appropriate relevant information. In the end, the credibility of testimony must be judged in the light of our understanding of how people behave. But there are pitfalls. Our common sense may deceive us unless we also have all the special knowledge necessary to make it work. Reports of eighteenth-century armies marching great distances in short periods of time violate our common-sense notion of what infantrymen can accomplish. Yet such reports are too numerous

to have been fabricated. Clearly, we must supplement our native cleverness with solid information.

7. *Is there corroborating testimony?*

No document can stand alone. Even asking all of the right questions can't ensure that you won't be fooled. You must seek other witnesses

—what lawyers call corroborating testimony—to reinforce and substantiate the first account. Just as corroboration is necessary in the courtroom, it is essential to good history.

The preceding list of questions can be used as a rudimentary guide to help you think critically. But the list is not exhaustive. The more you know about the period in question, human behavior, and the workings of the natural world, the better off you will be.

CRITICAL THINKING: ITS MEANING AND IMPORTANCE

The term "critical thinking" has become something of a buzzword in American educational circles. Course descriptions pledge its achievement as a primary goal; professional literature abounds with references to it as the most significant aim of all education; and, not long ago, the president of Yale University resigned his post to become chief executive of an organization planning to build two hundred private schools devoted to its development. Yet despite all the homage given to the importance of critical thinking, there is no widely accepted definition of what it is.

It is clear that there are certain things that critical thinking is not. It is not the same as creative thinking, which is characterized by finding fresh angles of vision, new combinations of familiar things, the path untrodden. It is not gender based—there is no evidence whatsoever that males are better at it than females, or vice versa. It is not necessarily something one learns in school.

Critical thinking is a process by which we measure things. That might mean deciding whether a given statement is true or false, or determining the appropriateness of a given course of action in response to a problem. It might take the form of evaluating candidates for an elective office. On an exam, a student who evaluates Franklin Roosevelt's Depression-born New Deal has engaged in critical thinking, just as has the trained historian who writes a book on the same subject.

There are certain specific mental activities that can be identified as central elements of critical thinking. Among the most frequently mentioned are:

1. Identification of assumptions that underlie a statement or argument.
2. Drawing of a warranted conclusion from an accepted premise—also known as inference. (See Chapter 7.)
3. Assessment of the quality of available evidence one might use to investigate a specific situation or problem.
4. Determination of whether the known evidence supports a given generalization or interpretation.
5. Selection of criteria by which to evaluate a statement or proposal.

In the long run, practice in evaluating and reasoning will advance your ability to measure the truth or falsity of the propositions you confront daily. This is the enduring product of education. Whatever the future may hold for each of us, the capability of thinking effectively will remain essential. This axiom was neatly summed up by Bernard M. Baruch, American businessman and statesman, who, near the end of a long life, said: "During my eighty-seven years I have witnessed a whole succession of technological revolutions. But none of them has done away with the need for character in the individual or the ability to think."

I CREATION OF A NATION, 1776–1820

A Primary Sources

As noted on pages 75–76, historians make a distinction between primary and secondary sources. Below are sources you might consult if you were preparing a paper on the Constitutional Convention that met in Philadelphia in 1787, and the subsequent ratification of the Constitution. In the spaces provided indicate whether the sources should be classified "primary" (P) or "secondary" (S), for a paper written on this specific topic. If you think a source shares both primary and secondary characteristics, write "PS." The dates in parentheses indicate the year(s) of publication.

_____ 1. Clinton Rossiter, *The Grand Convention* (1966).

_____ 2. C. Ford, ed., *Journals of the Continental Congress: 1774–1789* (1904–1937).

_____ 3. Jonathan Elliot, *The Debates in the Several State Conventions, on the Adoption of the Federal Constitution,* 5 vols. (1876).

_____ 4. Cecelia Kenyon, "Men of Little Faith: The Anti-Federalists on the Nature of Representative Government," *William and Mary Quarterly,* 3rd. Ser., 12 (1955), 3–43.

_____ 5. *The Constitution of the United States of America* in Oscar Handlin, *America: A History* (1968), Appendix, pp. A x – A xxviii.

_____ 6. *The Federalist Papers: Alexander Hamilton, James Madison, John Jay,* Introduction by Clinton Rossiter (1961).

_____ 7. Gary Wills, *Explaining America: The Federalist* (1981).

_____ 8. Forest McDonald, *Alexander Hamilton: A Biography* (1979).

_____ 9. James Madison, *Notes of Debates in the Federal Convention of 1787,* Introduction by Adrienne Koch (1966).

_____ 10. Max Farrand, ed., *Records of the Federal Convention of 1787,* 4 vols. (1911–1937).

If you wrote "PS" by any of the items, briefly give your reason for each such classification.

_____

_____

_____

B Types of Primary Sources

There are many types of primary sources, and each type has its characteristic strengths and weaknesses. This exercise requires that you use your critical intelligence since we have not discussed the potential values and hazards inherent in each type of primary source. For each type of source listed below, indicate one or two reasons why such a source would be of value, and indicate one or two reasons why the researcher should be wary of using the source uncritically (i.e., without the support of corroborating evidence). Put another way, in what ways might each of the following sources aid the researcher and in what ways might each of them mislead the researcher? We have answered the first item to give you a start.

1. Newspaper Stories

   Possible Contributions:

   a. Excellent source for day-to-day events.

   b. Provide a sense of what the public is interested in at the time.

   c. A number of articles can give a sense of underlying values and world view of the paper, and elements of society it addresses.

   d. In many cases reporters are eyewitnesses to events of great importance.

   Possible Weaknesses:

   a. Often articles are not accurate due to deadline pressures and rapidly changing situations. You should follow a story for a few days in order to pick up later corrections.

   b. Editorial or reportorial bias can influence the content or tone of a story. You should try to find out the ideological and political "stance" of a given paper. Also, it's important to ask, What has been left out of the story or the newspaper? Note, this is the flip side of the strength noted in "c" above.

   c. Often articles will tell you what different individuals say about an issue, but make no attempt to help you decide who might be wrong or right if there is a disagreement on a substantive issue.

   d. Often the reporters are not eyewitnesses to the events they report. Their accounts are based on interviews and reading relevant documents. See "d" above.

2. Memoirs/Autobiographies You might want to review page 76 above.

   Possible Contributions:

   _____

   _____

   _____

   Possible Weaknesses:

   _____

   _____

   _____

3. Private Letters

   Possible Contributions:

   _____

   _____

   _____

   Possible Weaknesses:

   _____

   _____

   _____

4. Records of a Government Agency

    Possible Contributions:

    _____

    _____

    _____

    Possible Weaknesses:

    _____

    _____

    _____

5. Political Speeches

    Possible Contributions:

    _____

    _____

    _____

    Possible Weaknesses:

    _____

    _____

    _____

6. Diplomatic Communications (from one government to another)

    Possible Contributions:

    _____

    _____

    _____

    Possible Weaknesses:

    _____

    _____

    _____

7. Church or Government Registry of Births and Deaths

    Possible Contributions:

    _____

    _____

    _____

    Possible Weaknesses:

    _____

    _____

    _____

8. Public Opinion Polls

Possible Contributions:

_____

_____

_____

Possible Weaknesses:

_____

_____

_____

Battle of Lexington

C *Analysis of Evidence*

Lexington Green, April 19, 1775

The first shots of the American Revolution were fired at Lexington, Massachusetts, on April 19, 1775. British troops on their way to destroy colonial military stores in nearby Concord were confronted by colonial militiamen at Lexington Green. Shots rang out and military hostilities began.

Since neither the British nor the American colonists wished to appear the aggressor, both sides denied firing the first shot. Below are four brief accounts of the event. Your task is not to determine who fired the first shot, but to examine the reports with the critical eye of the historian. Again, what points about each account should be noted by the historian wishing to weigh the probable validity of each? Make pertinent observations concerning the authorship, circumstances of composition, content, and potential believability of each piece of evidence. Use the seven questions on pages 78–79 as a basis for your analysis.

1. Robert Douglass, who had been at Lexington, swore to the following deposition on May 3, 1827:

In about fifteen minutes after we entered the tavern, a person came to the door and said the British were within half a mile. I then heard an officer (who I afterwards learned was Captain Parker) call his drummer and order him to beat to arms. I paraded with the Lexington company between the meeting-house and the tavern, and then marched to the common near the road that leads to Bedford; there we were ordered to load our guns. Some of the company observed, "There are so few of us, it would be folly to stand here." Captain Parker replied, "The first man who offers to run shall be shot down." The Lexington company began to break off on the left wing, and soon all dispersed. I think no American was killed or wounded by the first fire of the British, unless Captain Parker might have been. No one of Captain Parker's company fired on the British, to my knowledge, that morning, and I think I should have known it, had they fired. I knew but two men of the Lexington company, and I never heard any person say that the Americans fired on the British that morning at Lexington.

After the British marched toward Concord, I saw eight men who had been killed, among whom were Captain Parker and a Mr. Porter of Woburn.

ANALYSIS:

_____

_____

_____

_____

_____

2. The official deposition of the commander of the colonial militia, John Parker:

Lexington, April 25, 1775

I, John Parker, of lawful age, and commander of the Militia in Lexington, do testify and declare, that on the nineteenth instant, in the morning, about one of the clock, being informed that there were a number of Regular Officers riding up and down the road, stopping and insulting people as they passed the road, and also was informed that a number of Regular Troops were on their march from Boston, in order to take the Province Stores at Concord, ordered our Militia to meet on the common in said Lexington, to consult what to do, and concluded not to be discovered, nor meddle or make with said Regular Troops (if they should approach) unless they should insult us; and upon their sudden approach, I immediately ordered our Militia to disperse and not to fire. Immediately said Troops made their appearance, and rushed furiously, fired upon and killed eight of our party, without receiving any provocation therefor from us.

John Parker

ANALYSIS:

_____

_____

_____

_____

_____

3. British commander Major John Pitcairn's official report to General Gage:

I gave directions to the Troops to move forward, but on no account to Fire, or even attempt it without orders; when I arrived at the end of the Village, I observed drawn up upon a Green near 200 of the Rebels; when I came within about One Hundred Yards of them, they began to File off towards some stone Walls on our Right Flank—The Light Infantry observing this, ran after them—I instantly called to the Soldiers not to fire, but to surround and disarm them, and after several repetitions of those positive Orders to the men, not to Fire &c—some of the Rebels who had jumped over the Wall, Fired Four or Five Shott at the Soldiers, which wounded a man of the Tenth, and my Horse was Wounded in two places, from some quarter or other, and at the same time several Shott were fired from a Meeting House on our Left—upon this, without any order or Regularity, the Light Infantry began a scattered Fire, and continued in that situation for some little time, contrary to the repeated orders both of me and the officers that were present—It will be needless to mention what happened after, as I suppose Col. Smith hath given a particular account of it. I am sir

Boston Camp Your most humble Servant,

26th April, 1775 John Pitcairn

ANALYSIS:

_____

_____

_____

_____

_____

4. Personal account of British ensign Jeremy Lister written in 1832:

However to the best of my recollection about 4 oClock in the Morning being the 19th of April the 5 front [companies] was ordered to Load which we did, about half an hour after we found that precaution had been necessary, for we had then to [fire] . . . and then was the first Blood drawn in this American Rebellion. It was at Lexington when we saw one of their [Companies] drawn up in regular order Major Pitcairn of the Marines second in Command call'd to them to disperce, but their not seeming willing he desired us to mind our space which we did when they gave us a fire they run of[f] to get behind a wall. [W]e had one man wounded of our [Company] in the Leg his Name was Johnson also Major Pitcairns Horse was shot in the Flank we return'd their Salute, and before we proceeded on our March from Lexington I believe we Kill'd and Wounded either 7 or 8 men.

ANALYSIS:

_____

_____

_____

_____

_____

For Discussion:

1. Which pieces of evidence do you find most convincing? Which do you find least convincing? Why?

2. On which "facts" does there seem to be general agreement?

3. What are the central points of disagreement?

Essay:

Based on the evidence above, write a paragraph-length account of the confrontation on Lexington Green. Use as a first sentence: "Historians have long disputed whether the colonial militia or the British regulars fired the first shot of the American Revolution." In your paragraph try to state clearly what can be established beyond doubt (assume the excerpts above are all the sources you have available to you), what is probable given the above evidence, and what cannot be established with certainty.

Sources:

Excerpts 1 and 2 taken from Peter S. Bennett, ed., *What Happened on Lexington Green* (Reading, MA: Addison-Wesley, 1970), 13–14. Excerpts 3 and 4 are from Allen French, *General Gage's Informers* (Ann Arbor: Univ. of Michigan Press, 1932), 53–54; 55.

II **AMERICA BETWEEN TWO WARS, 1918–1941**

A *Primary Sources*

As noted on pages 75–76, historians make a distinction between primary and secondary sources. Below are sources you might consult if you were preparing a paper on President Woodrow Wilson's diplomatic efforts at the Paris peace conference, which met between January and May, 1919. The architects of the Versailles (i.e., Paris) Treaty, along with Wilson, were David Lloyd George of Britain, and Georges Clemenceau of France, and their respective support staffs. In the spaces provided indicate whether the sources should be classified "primary" (P) or "secondary" (S), for a paper written on this specific topic. If you think a source shares both primary and secondary characteristics, write "PS." The dates in parentheses indicate the year(s) of publication.

_____ 1. Arno J. Mayer, *Politics and Diplomacy of Peacemaking: Containment and Counterrevolution at Versailles 1918–1919* (1967).

_____ 2. Arthur S. Link, *Woodrow Wilson: Revolution, War, and Peace* (1979).

_____ 3. Lord Riddell, *Intimate Diary of the Peace Conference and After, 1918–1923 (1933)*.

_____ 4. Charles Seymour, ed. *The Intimate Papers of Colonel House,* 4 vols. (1926–28). *[Edward M. "Colonel" House was President Wilson's closest advisor, and attended the Paris Conference with the president.]*

5. Harold W. Temperley, *A History of the Peace Conference of Paris,* 6 vols. (1920–24).

6. David Lloyd George, *Memoirs of the Peace Conference,* 2 vols. (1939)

7. *The Papers of Woodrow Wilson:* Vols. LIV–LV, Jan. 11–March 16, 1919.

8. *The New York Times,* 1919.

9. David Stevenson, "The Treaty of Versailles," *History Today* (October, 1986), 50–53.

10. Harold G. Nicolson, *Peacemaking 1919* (1934). [*Nicolson attended the conference as part of the British delegation.*]

11. *British and Foreign State Papers,* Vol. 112 (1919).

12. Lloyd E. Ambrosius, *Woodrow Wilson and the American Diplomatic Tradition: The Treaty Fight in Perspective* (1987).

B *Types of Primary Sources*

See Exercise B in Part I.

C *Analysis of Evidence*

The Dispersion of the "Bonus Army": July 28, 1932

One of the most dramatic political events during the Great Depression was the march of the "Bonus Expeditionary Force" (B. E. F.) on Washington, D. C., in 1932. The B. E. F. was composed of thousands of unemployed World War I veterans who came to Washington to demand immediate payment of the cash bonus voted by Congress in 1924, but scheduled for disbursement only in 1945. The Bonus March was one of the first examples of the mass protest marches that have become a familiar feature of the American political scene since the 1960s.

The House of Representatives approved immediate payment, but the Senate voted it down. Thousands of disappointed veterans then left Washington, but thousands more stayed on in vacant government buildings and a squatters camp near the Capitol. The impoverished Bonus Marchers made the administration nervous, and in July it ordered the marchers evicted and the camp razed. During the eviction proceedings a policeman panicked and killed one veteran. On July 28 Secretary of War, Patrick J. Hurley, sent the army, commanded by General Douglas MacArthur, to clear the affected area "without delay." What followed was the expulsion of the Bonus Marchers from Washington, D. C., and a series of controversies that have continued to reverberate through the years. Among the questions that historians have debated are: What was President Herbert Hoover's exact role in the events of July 28? Was excessive force used against the B. E. F.? Were the Bonus Marchers nonviolent ex-veterans or criminals and Communist agitators?

Below are brief accounts of the eviction proceedings against the Bonus Marchers who occupied vacant public buildings. These accounts also include remarks about the people who made up the B. E. F. Your task is not to settle the various controversies noted above, but to examine the evidence with the critical eye of the historian. What points about each account should be noted by the historian wishing to weigh the probable validity of each? Make pertinent observations concerning the authorship, circumstances of composition, content, and potential believability of each piece of evidence. Use the seven questions on pages 78–79 as a basis for your analysis.

1. *The New York Times* interview with General Douglas MacArthur, published July 29, 1932.

General MacArthur's estimate of the situation and his review of the events of this afternoon and evening [July 28] were set forth orally by him substantially as follows:

• • •

At the first point of attack, on Pennsylvania Avenue, not far from the foot of the Capitol, the mob was a bad-looking one. It was one marked by signs of revolution. The gentleness and consideration, with which they had been treated they had mistaken for weakness. They had come to the conclusion that they were to take over the government in some arbitrary way or control it by some indirect method.

If President Hoover had not acted when he did he would have been faced with a serious situation. Another week might have meant that the government was in peril.... Had the President not acted when he did, in General MacArthur's opinion, he would have been derelict in his duty. . . .

In General MacArthur's opinion there was not one "real" veteran soldier out of ten in those cleared from government property today. He regarded the bulk of them as insurrectionists.

ANALYSIS:

_____

_____

_____

_____

_____

2. Major George S. Patton, a junior officer serving in the 3rd Cavalry, records his observations. (No precise date is recorded by Martin Blumenson, editor of *The Patton Papers*.)

After a halt of half an hour at 3rd Street the infantry put on their gas masks and, advancing in assault formation in two waves, using gas grenades, began clearing the buildings. . . . Major Surles then moved his cavalry to push them on. We were doing very well when the infantry halted to reform, and the mob, angry by now . . . were very nasty and brandished clubs, iron bars and bricks, and cursed us in a most whole-hearted manner. The soldiers were magnificent. They set grimly on their horses and made no reply except to poke an occasional Marcher who tried to grab a horse by the head. Things kept looking worse as the infantry was still not up and our flank was turned. Suddenly, without a word of command, the whole line surged forward. Bricks flew, sabers rose and fell with a comforting smack, and the mob ran. We moved on after them, occasionally meeting serious resistance. Once six men in a truck threw a regular barrage of bricks, and several men and horses were hit. Two of us charged at a gallop, and had some nice work at close range with the occupants of the truck, most of whom could not sit down for some days [afterwards].

ANALYSIS:

_____

_____

_____

_____

_____

3. An unnamed "newspaper man in Washington, who found himself in the rear of the B. E. F. during the recent battle," published in *The New Republic,* August 10, 1932.

A block away on Pennsylvania Avenue, the federals, cavalry, tanks and infantry, were marching and counter-marching. They spent perhaps thirty minutes taking up positions. The offensive began with a tear-gas bomb attack on a half-demolished brick garage, which was cleaned out in about ten minutes. Then, to my astonishment and acute rage, a little chap in uniform wearing a gas mask and followed by perhaps three squads of infantry, similarly masked, came crouching and dodging over towards where I was standing and tossed a tear gas bomb at me. It made me mad as hell for about a minute. . . .

I retreated towards 3½ Street with what dignity I could (very little, of course). At 3½ Street, to my confusion, a couple of other fellows and I got charged by a troop of cavalry with drawn sabres. That is something to write home about. A lot of lousy soldiers just makes you mad, but I'm scared to death of horses.

It was perfectly obvious that the bonus army members were going to put up no sort of a show whatever. . . . Personally I'm convinced that the whole temper of the bonus army is that of a Baptist camp meeting. [They believe] Mr. Hoover is an evil man who is disobeying the commands of God in not giving them a bonus. . . . Now you can't make a revolution out of that.

ANALYSIS:

_____

_____

_____

_____

_____

4. Observations by Walter W. Waters, commander of the Bonus Army. *The New York Times,* July 29, 1932.

Just before arrival of the troops, he went to a small restaurant on Pennsylvania Avenue for a cup of coffee.

Asked about the day's happenings he replied: "The men got completely out of control. There was nothing and is nothing I can do to control them."

In his statement later he said: "Every drop of blood shed today or that may be shed in days to come as the result of today's events can be laid directly on the threshold of the White House."

"The B. E. F. had been organized on strictly American lines of respect for law and order and is pledged to uphold American institutions. They were under strictest orders to conduct themselves in orderly manner in the event of attempted forcible evacuation and to offer nothing but a passive resistance, but the administration saw fit to issue orders for forcible evacuation of the Pennsylvania Avenue billet, making no provision for other billets nor allowing us time to make such provision. . . ."

ANALYSIS:

_____

_____

_____

_____

_____

5. President Herbert Hoover, reflecting on the events of 1932 in his *Memoirs*, published in 1952.

That the Bonus March was largely organized and managed by Communists became clear with the passage of time, through disclosures by Congressional committees and repentant Communist leaders who participated in it. Benjamin Gitlow, who was a leader in the Communist party, later published a full account of the movement in which he described the organization of the march and its direction in Washington by a Russian Communist agent from a safe hotel room, and the anger of the director when the attempt failed after the troops took charge without hurting a single veteran.

ANALYSIS:

_____

_____

_____

_____

_____

For Discussion:

1. Which pieces of evidence do you find most convincing? Which do you find least convincing? Why?

2. On which "facts" does there seem to be general agreement?

3. What are the points of disagreement?

Essay:

Based on the evidence above, write a paragraph-length account of the expulsion of the Bonus Army in July, 1932. In your paragraph try to state clearly what can be established beyond doubt (assume the excerpts above are all the sources you have available to you), what is probable given the above evidence, and what cannot be established with certainty.

Sources

Excerpt #1 is taken from *The New York Times*, July 29, 1932, 3. Copyright © 1932 by The New York Times Company. Reprinted by permission; #2 from Martin Blumenson, *The Patton Papers, 1885–1940*, Vol. I (Boston: Houghton Mifflin, 1972), 896; #3 from *The New Republic*, August 10, 1932, 326; #4 from *The New York Times*, July 29, 1932, 1, 3. Copyright © 1932 by The New York Times Company. Reprinted by permission; #5 from Herbert Hoover, *The Memoirs of Herbert Hoover*, Vol. III, *The Great Depression, 1929–1941* (New York: Macmillan and Co., 1952), 230.

INTERPRETING
7 EVIDENCE

"Who does not know that the first law of historical writing is the truth."

CICERO

"History is not a science; it is a method."

CHARLES SEIGNOBOS

A freshman seminar class at our university recently read *The Return of Martin Guerre* by Natalie Zemon Davis, an implausible but true story about sixteenth-century French peasants.[1] The students, nurtured on the notion that history is nothing more than a collection of facts to be memorized, were troubled and even angry when the author speculated about what might have happened. They were uncomfortable when Davis admitted that there were things about her topic we could never know for sure. How could it be history, the students asked, if the historian was forced to admit there were things we could never know for sure?

We have seen that there are always gaps in the historical record, and historical documents cannot speak for themselves. Even when a lot of evidence is available on a specific topic or time period, we cannot always provide definitive answers to many historical questions. When, for example, did President Franklin Roosevelt decide that the United States should enter World War II? Did President Harry Truman, Roosevelt's successor, really have to drop the atomic bomb on Japan in order to bring World War II to a speedy end? These are questions historians still debate, in spite of mountains of surviving records from the World War II period.

INFERENCE AND HISTORICAL METHOD

Doubt and debate are inevitable in history because historians cannot just lift the answers off the pages of the documents they read. They must make inferences or conclusions based on evidence. Even though inferences can be "notoriously unreliable,"[2] the making of legitimate inferences is central to all historical reasoning.

Inference-making skills are especially valuable when you attempt to learn things by reading between the lines, that is, when you try to find out things the records weren't intended to reveal. As Arthur Marwick argues, "a primary source is most valuable when the purpose for which it was compiled is at the furthest remove from the purpose of the historian."[3]

For instance, merchants have long kept business records in order to keep track of their debtors and creditors. Historians may not be especially interested in who owed what to whom in 1820, but, by reading such account records broadly, they can learn fascinating things about the evolution of modern banking and business techniques, the state of the American economy in the early 1800s, or the ways in which certain segments of the population earned a living.

---

1 Natalie Zemon Davis, *The Return of Martin Guerre* (Cambridge, MA: Harvard University Press, 1983). Professor Davis' book was actually a response to and elaboration upon the award-winning French film, *Le Retour de Martin Guerre*.
2 Robin Winks, ed., *The Historian As Detective* (New York: Harper Colophon, 1970), xvi.
3 Arthur Marwick, *The Nature of History* (New York: Knopf, 1971), 177.

These are things the original documents were never intended to communicate.[4]

When you deal with traditional narrative sources—letters, pamphlets, news stories, diaries, political speeches, memoirs, government press releases and the like—it is still important to be willing to make some reasoned inferences. A political speech, for example, may not necessarily reveal what a candidate really believes. Since politicians often tell people what they want to hear, however, the text of the speech might allow us to make some logical inferences about the fears, aspirations, and preoccupations of the voters the candidate is trying to sway.

Historians cannot function without making inferential "leap[s] of faith."[5] Historical accounts, therefore, will always contain a mixture of the speculative, the probable, and the things we know for sure.

HISTORY BY THE NUMBERS

If inference-making skills are indispensable when dealing with many types of written evidence, they are even more necessary when trying to interpret evidence that comes in numerical form.

Historians have always used quantitative (i.e., numerical) evidence in their work. They tell us how many soldiers died in a given battle, what percent of the population voted for the Republicans in such-and-such election, and how many people lived in Ohio in 1870. They tell us how Congress voted on the Compromise of 1850, how much steel was produced at the turn of the century, and how many immigrants from Ireland came to North America after the Irish potato famine of the 1840s. On the other hand, the most casual glance at the average history book will show that numerical evidence usually takes a distinct back seat to literary or written evidence. Historians, and students of history, are generally more comfortable with words than with numbers.

There are those who argue, however, that in this age of the computer, history should become much more quantitative than it is. Numerical data and statistics are necessary, they say, if history is to become more rigorous, systematic, and scientific. They believe that quantification will help us move beyond the vague and impressionistic style that characterizes so much traditional historical writing.

To this, many traditionalists have reacted with barely controlled outrage. Carl Bridenbaugh, a social and intellectual historian, strongly condemned quantification in 1962. Oscar Handlin lamented that "we have long known the danger of depending on translators; we must now learn the danger of depending on programmers." The eminent intellectual historian, Jacques Barzun, said that when a person examined a chart [of numbers], "he is not *reading history*."[6]

The details of the debate between the quantifiers and traditionalists need not detain us. However, it is important to understand both the advantages and disadvantages of using numbers in history. After all, graphs, tables, and opinion polls have become so common that individuals who desire to understand the world in which they live will have to be able to interpret simple numerical data.

---

4 Another example of creative inference-making can be found in *Salem Possessed* (Cambridge, MA, 1974), by historians Paul Boyer and Stephen Nissenbaum. They used detailed town plans and income records to show how the Salem witch trials, in part, grew out of social, economic, and geographic divisions within the community. Boyer and Nissenbaum saw in these relatively sterile and uninteresting records things that the original record keepers had no intention of revealing.

5 Winks, *Historian as Detective*, xv.

6 Quotations are from Richard E. Beringer, *Historical Analysis: Contemporary Approaches to Clio's Craft* (New York: John Wiley and Sons, 1978), 193–94.

On the positive side, numerical evidence can make history much more precise. As noted earlier, historians talk about quantities all the time, but often in a vague and shapeless manner. We talk about majorities who support such-and-such a proposition; about social classes that are *growing* in strength (the "middle classes were on the rise"); about a *rising* tide of antigovernment opinion, and the like. Our history would be much more convincing if, when possible, some precise numbers could be attached to these statements—a 54 percent majority; a middle class than numbered 37 percent of the population; 63 percent opposed the government on a specific measure.

Statistical data and computer calculations are useful in other areas of historical study. Many issues in modern social history—the study of people as groups, not individuals—can be approached only if we have some meaningful numbers to work with. Quantification is essential if we are to find answers to such questions as: At what age did people get married in New England in the seventeenth century? What was the average life expectancy in Boston, New York, and Charleston in 1850? What percentage of the population lived on family farms in the pre–Civil War South? Were illegitimate births a serious problem in preindustrial America?

In asking these questions we are trying to understand the history of the great mass of people who lived and died without leaving a written legacy. And we cannot answer such questions by studying individuals one by one. We can begin to get answers only when we use parish records, census data, and court records to count heads and compile a collective portrait of a group of people at a given time and place. We can never know these people as individuals, but statistics can provide countless clues to the very real lives they lived.

On the other hand, although quantification is useful for its precision and the social insights it offers, it should not be embraced uncritically for the following reasons. First, most historical evidence is in the form of written records. Quantifi-

Le Retour de Martin Guerre

able evidence may or may not be readily available in most cases, and most historical study will still have to be based on the written record.

Second, many historical questions cannot be answered with numbers or statistics. Arthur Schlesinger, Jr. pointed out in 1962 that "most of the variables in an historical equation are not susceptible to commensurable quantification." Further, said Schlesinger, "almost all important questions are important precisely because they are not susceptible to quantitative answers."[7] We might say that, while quantification can provide many valuable insights, it is necessary to know when such evidence is and is not appropriate to the task at hand.

Finally, numbers can be misleading. Given the scientific bias of our age, many people have a tendency to trust numbers over prose descriptions. Statistics carry weight in debates and discussions, and politicians, journalists, and social reformers are often quick to cite the relevant figures in support of their positions. The problem for the historian is that numbers, like other forms of evidence, do not speak for themselves. Numerical evidence must be interpreted by the historian. Note the difference between saying that "one-quarter of Southern white families owned slaves in 1860," and "*only* one-quarter of those families owned slaves." The first statement is more-or-less neutral, while the second includes a very clear judgment that slaveholding was concentrated in a small minority of families.[8]

It is also useful to pay attention to the source of the numbers you are reading. The way numbers are presented can influence the way they are interpreted, or in the case of modern opinion polls, the wording of the questions can have a significant impact on the answers people give. And, sad to say, sometimes people lie to polltakers for a variety of reasons. The point is, quantitative information that appears in books and in the press should never be accepted at face value or uncritically.

To see how the presentation of data can influence its interpretation, compare the two (fictitious) graphs below. Both show the identical information: that the unemployment rate for the State of Clio went up three percent in a six-year period (1985–91). Graph I uses a percentage scale that begins at 0 percent and ends at 8 percent; Graph II, however, uses an expanded amount scale and grounds the graph at the original 3 percent unemployment rate. Note how much more severe the rise in unemployment appears in Graph II. Yet the numbers are identical. How might unwary readers react differently to the two graphs?

In sum, quantification in history is here to stay. Computers and statistical techniques have enriched and will continue to enrich our understanding of the human past. On the other hand, instead of eliminating the need for historians to draw "legitimate inferences" from the raw, undigested evidence, numerical data demands even more sophisticated inference-making skills.

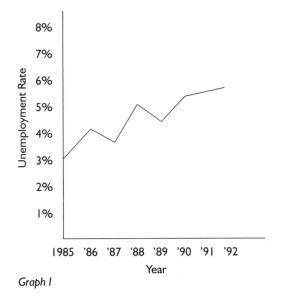

Graph I

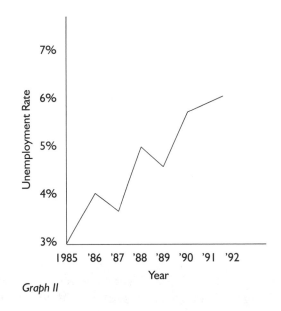

Graph II

7 Quoted in Beringer, *Historical Analysis,* 195.
8 See Peter J. Parish, *Slavery: History and Historians* (New York: Harper and Row, 1989), 28.

I   FROM COMPROMISE TO CONFLICT, 1820–1860

A   *Inference*

Inference, as we noted, is a major tool in the interpretation of evidence. Because the questions that interest historians are often quite different from the objectives of those who created various pieces of primary evidence, historians constantly have to make logical deductions that may not be provable in any absolute sense.

Below are a number of short statements followed by some possible inferences. After reading a statement, indicate for each inference whether it is a VALID inference (V), an INVALID OR "FALSE" inference (F), or an inference for which we have INSUFFICIENT DATA (ID) to determine its validity or invalidity. If you label an inference "F" (False/Invalid), indicate your reasons on the lines provided at the end of each unit.

For the purposes of this exercise assume that the statements reflect the best judgment of the speaker or writer. Also assume that for any statement of fact there exists corroborating evidence. The first unit is already completed as an example.

1. Frances Trollope on American religious institutions in the early 1800s. (Frances Trollope, *Domestic Manners of the Americans,* 1832; reprinted in David Burner, et al., eds., *America Through the Looking Glass,* Vol. I, Prentice-Hall, 1974, 180.)

   We had not been many months in Cincinnati when our curiosity was excited by hearing the "revival" talked of by every one we met throughout the town. "The revival will be very full," "We shall be constantly engaged during the revival," were the phrases we constantly heard repeated, and for a long time without in the least comprehending what was meant; but at length I learnt that the un-national church of America required to be roused, at regular intervals, to greater energy and exertion. At these seasons the most enthusiastic of the clergy travel the country, and enter the cities and towns by scores, or by hundreds, as the accommodation of the place may admit, and for a week or fortnight, or, if the population be large, for a month, they preach and pray all day, and often for a considerable portion of the night, in the various churches and chapels of the place. This is called a Revival.

   Possible Inferences:

   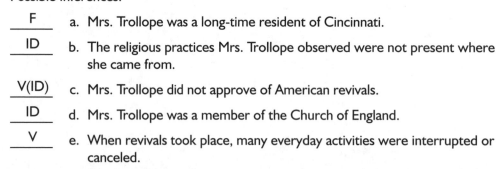

   _____F_____ a. Mrs. Trollope was a long-time resident of Cincinnati.

   _____ID_____ b. The religious practices Mrs. Trollope observed were not present where she came from.

   ____V(ID)____ c. Mrs. Trollope did not approve of American revivals.

   _____ID_____ d. Mrs. Trollope was a member of the Church of England.

   _____V_____ e. When revivals took place, many everyday activities were interrupted or canceled.

Comments: Statement *a* is "False" because of her statement in the first sentence of the passage. We labeled *b* and *d* "ID" because we have no definitive information on these issues, one way or the other. However, we would be tempted to accept an answer of "Valid" for *b*. Statement *c* seems to be a valid inference given the entire tone of the paragraph, although an answer of "ID" would be defensible. Statement *e* is "Valid" in light of her comments on the residents' statements at revival time.

2. Commentary on Irish immigrants digging a canal in Louisiana, circa 1833. (Tyrone Power, *Impressions of America During the Years 1833, 1834, and 1835* [1836]; reprinted in Frederick M. Binder and David M. Reimers, *The Way We Lived*, 2nd ed., Vol I, Heath, 1992, 235.)

I only wish that the wise men at home who coolly charge the present condition of Ireland upon the inherent laziness of her population, could be transported to this spot, to look upon the hundreds of fine fellows labouring here beneath a sun that at this winter season was at times insufferably fierce. . . . At such works all over this continent the Irish are the labourers chiefly employed, and the mortality amongst them is enormous—a mortality I feel certain might be vastly lessened by a little consideration being given to their condition by those who employ them. At present they are, where I have seen them working here, worse lodged than the cattle of the field; in fact, the only thought bestowed upon them appears to be, by what expedient the greatest quantity of labour may be extracted from them at the cheapest rate to the contractor.

Possible Inferences

_____ a. The author is an American.

_____ b. Established Americans considered Irish immigrants inferior.

_____ c. The author probably lives in the United Kingdom (i.e., Ireland or Britain).

_____ d. The Irish were treated as second-class citizens where the author lived.

_____ e. Conditions for Irish immigrants were bad in 1833, but improving.

Reasons for "F" labels:

_____

_____

3. *Declaration of Sentiments* from the women who met at the Seneca Falls Convention in 1848. (Reprinted in David Burner, et al., eds., *America Through the Looking Glass*, Vol. I, Prentice-Hall, 1974, 280–81.)

When, in the course of human events it becomes necessary for one portion of the family of man to assume among the people of the earth a position different from that which they have hitherto occupied, but one to which the laws of nature and of nature's God entitle them, a decent respect to the opinions of mankind requires that they should declare the causes that impel them to such a course.

We hold these truths to be self-evident: that all men and women are created equal; that they are endowed by their Creator with certain inalienable rights; . . .

The history of mankind is a history of repeated injuries and usurpations on the part of man toward woman, having in direct object the establishment of an absolute tyranny over her. To prove this, let facts be submitted to a candid world. [There follows a specific list of grievances.]

• • •

In entering upon the great work before us, we anticipate no small amount of misconception, misrepresentation, and ridicule; but we shall use every instrumentality within our power to effect our object. We shall employ agents, circulate tracts, petition the State and National legislatures, and endeavor to enlist the pulpit and press in our behalf.

Possible Inferences:

_____ a. The authors of this document were probably middle- and upper-class women.

_____ b. The women who wrote this were extreme radicals who were willing to resort to violence to achieve their ends.

_____ c. The authors were familiar with the events of the American Revolution.

_____ d. Political activism among women was unusual at this time.

_____ e. This protest resulted in a number of important reforms.

Reasons for "F" labels:

_____

_____

4. *Recollection of Ben Simpson, a former slave.* (B. A. Botkin, *Lay My Burden Down,* (University of Chicago Press, 1961, 75.)

Boss, I's born in Georgia, in Norcross, and I's ninety years old. My father's name was Roger Stielszen, and my mother's name was Betty. Massa Earl Stielszen captures them in Africa and brung them to Georgia. He got kilt, and my sister and me went to his son. His son was a killer. He got in trouble there in Georgia and got him two good-stepping hosses and the covered wagon. Then he chains all the slaves round the necks and fastens the chains to the hosses and makes them walk all the way to Texas. My mother and my sister had to walk. Emma was my sister. . . .

Massa have a great, long whip platted out of rawhide, and when one the niggers fall behind or give out, he hit him with that whip. It take the hide every time he hit a nigger. Mother, who give out on the way, 'bout the line of Texas. Her feet got raw and bleeding, and her legs swoll plumb out of shape. Then Massa, he just take out he gun and shot her, and whilst she lay dying he kicks her two-three times and say, "Damn a nigger what can't stand nothing." Boss, you know that man, he wouldn't bury mother, just leave her laying where he shot her at. You know, then there wasn't no law 'gainst killing nigger slaves.

Possible Inferences:

_____ a. The events related above occurred before the Civil War.

_____ b. Ben Simpson could read and write.

_____ c. The interviewer was African-American.

_____ d. Ben Simpson's father had died before the family was moved to Texas.

_____ e. Ben Simpson changed his name after the slaves were freed.

Reasons for "F" labels:

_____

_____

B *History by the Numbers*

Although history remains a discipline primarily grounded in a literary and humanistic tradition, a significant number of historians use numerical and statistical evidence in their work. Moreover, since much of the history and journalism read by the general public is accompanied by tables, graphs, and statistical assertions, it is important for students of history to be able to read and interpret evidence that comes in numerical form.

The exercise below will provide a taste of the sort of reasoning and analysis that the use of statistical evidence requires. The tables produced below do not represent primary sources in the purest sense; they were compiled by the author, James Bonner, in his article on the social history of the white farmers in one slave-holding region (Hancock County, Georgia) before the Civil War.[9] The tables represent, in short, the questions Bonner chose to ask and the categories he used to display the data he had gathered.

The tables show the average ages, occupations and economic status of the non-slave population of Hancock County in 1860. "Realty" refers to landed property, or "real estate." "Personalty" refers to other forms of personal property.

TABLE 1: Economic Status of Occupational Groups, 1860

Occupational Group	Number	Total in families	Percent owning realty	Percent owning slaves	Percent owning other personal property
Planters and farmers*					
$10,000 and above	56	267	100.0	100.0	100.0
$9,999 to $1,001	220	1,049	100.0	92.2	100.0
$1,000 and under	85	379	100.0	41.6	91.7
Professional class	48	195	62.4	54.1	77.1
Merchants	29	101	50.0	45.0	75.9
Tradesman	116	414	13.7	7.7	26.9
Overseers	139	367	1.4	6.4	20.8
Farm laborers	198	610	1.2	0.016	8.4
Factory workers	96	157	0.9	0.0	0.0**
All others	110	276	—	—	—

*While the lowest landowning agricultural subdivision (those whose land was valued at $1,000 and under) is placed third from the top in this table, it is evident that its position would be lower than this when measured by other criteria. For example, see the values of land and personalty assigned to the various groups in Table 2.

**The absence of personal property assigned to factory workers is explained by the failure of enumerators to list personal property evaluations of less than $100.

9 James C. Bonner, "Profile of a Late Ante-Bellum Community," *American Historical Review* (July, 1944), 663–80. The tables are recreated from pp. 671–72. Published by permission of the American Historical Association.

TABLE 2: Economic Status of Occupational Groups in 1860

Occupational Group	Average age of each group	Percent owning slaves	Average value of realty	Average value of personalty	Ratio of personalty to realty
Planters and farmers*					
$10,000 and above	49.7	100	$21,786	$45,434	1.99
$9,999 to $1,001	45.8	92.2	4,268	12,904	3.02
$1,000 and under	44.9	41.6	719	2,348	3.26
Professional class	34.85	54.1	2,844	8,025	2.82
Merchants	33.5	45	1,862	5,848	3.14
Tradesman	38.03	7.7	216	874	4.04
Overseers	28.8	6.4	72	1,524	21.16
Farm laborers	30.0	6.01	15	44	2.87
Factory workers	24.09	0	4	0	0

Using the letters A, B, C, indicate whether each statement below:[10]

A. Can be proved using the data in the tables.

B. Can be neither proved nor contradicted using the data in the tables.

C. Can be contradicted using the data in the tables.

Be prepared to defend your answer orally.

Statements:

Unless stated otherwise, assume all statements refer to Hancock County, Georgia.

_____ 1. Planters and farmers constituted the majority of the nonslave population of Hancock County.

_____ 2. The largest single occupational group was that of farm laborers.

_____ 3. Generally, the younger people were the less well-off economically than the older people.

_____ 4. The majority of employed whites owned slaves in 1860.

_____ 5. The economic position of farm laborers in Hancock County was the same as the economic position of farm laborers in all of Georgia.

_____ 6. All planters and farmers owned slaves.

_____ 7. The majority of the nonfarmers supported the institution of slavery.

_____ 8. Industry was as important to the economy of Hancock County as was agriculture.

_____ 9. The same percentage of people in the north as in the south owned real estate in 1860.

_____ 10. Some merchants and members of the "professional class" were better off economically than some farmers.

---

10 The inspiration for this exercise came from Horace T. Morse and George H. McCune, *Selected Items for the Testing of Study Skills and Critical Thinking* (Washington, DC: National Council for the Social Studies, 1964).

Inference from Numbers (Optional)

Using the same numerical tables, write a paragraph in which you try to make some generalizations about class relationships in Hancock County. Your generalizations should be those statements that are either absolutely true or probably true in light of the evidence.

II   WORLD WAR AND COLD WAR, 1941–1963

A   *Inference*

Inference, as we noted, is a major tool in the interpretation of evidence. Because the questions that interest historians are often quite different from the objectives of those who created various pieces of primary evidence, historians constantly have to make logical deductions that may not be provable in any absolute sense.

Below are a number of short pieces of evidence relating to the experience of Americans in World War II. Each statement is followed by some possible inferences. After reading a statement, indicate for each inference whether it is a VALID inference (V), an INVALID OR "FALSE" inference (F), or an inference for which we have INSUFFICIENT DATA (ID) to determine its validity or invalidity. If you label an inference "F" (False/Invalid), indicate your reasons on the lines provided at the end of each unit.

For the purposes of this exercise assume that the statements reflect the best judgment of the speaker or writer. Also assume that for any statement of fact there exists corroborating evidence. The first unit is already completed as an example.

1. General Dwight Eisenhower's reflections on his World War II experiences. (Dwight Eisenhower, *Crusade in Europe,* Doubleday, 1948, 57. Reprinted by permission of Bantam Doubleday Dell Publishing Group, Inc.)

Except during World War I, the U.S. public has habitually looked upon Europe's quarrels as belonging to Europe alone. For this reason every American soldier coming to Britain was almost certain to consider himself a privileged crusader, sent there to help Britain out of a hole. He would expect to be treated as such. On the other hand, the British public looked upon itself as one of the saviors of democracy, particularly because, for an entire year, it had stood alone as the unbreakable opponent of Nazism and the European Axis. Failure to understand this attitude would of course have unfortunate results.

Possible Inferences:

__ID (V)__   a. Eisenhower feared U. S. and British troops would not get along.

__V__   b. Eisenhower feared that arrogance in American troops could create conflicts with the British public.

__F__   c. Eisenhower saw no reason why the Americans and Britons would not get along well.

__V__   d. Eisenhower was familiar with at least some American history.

__ID__   e. There were many conflicts between British troops and American troops during the latter stages of World War II.

Comments: We labeled *b* as a valid inference because of Eisenhower's reference to possible "unfortunate results" if American troops didn't understand British attitudes. Eisenhower's reference to American isolationism in the first sentence makes *d* a valid inference. We labeled *a* and *e* "ID" (insufficient data) because, though perhaps true, Eisenhower makes no direct statement on these matters. One could, however, make a case that statement *a* is "Valid," given the tone of the passage. Statement *c* is "False" (invalid) because Eisenhower does provide a reason for possible misunderstandings.

2. Reflections of Lowell Steward, an African-American aviator in World War II. (Studs Terkel, *"The Good War:" An Oral History of World War II,* Ballantine, 1984, 341–42. Reprinted by permission of Pantheon Books.)

World War Two was not a pleasant experience. It's anti everything I stand for. It was a frustrating and revealing time of my life.

I was born and raised in Los Angeles. I'd never been south. I had not too much experience with discrimination. I went to integrated schools. And the first time I reached manhood, things were frustrating. When I left school to sign up for the air force, I found out I could not go into the service with my friends. . . . [When I was finally called], I was sent to Tuskegee, an all-segregated base, deep in the heart of Alabama. . . .

I had various brushes with Alabama bigotry, such as my wife trying to buy a hat. They'd tell her, "If you put it on, you have bought it." You couldn't try on anything. You had to eat in separate quarters, of course, And live in separate places. . . .

I think the reason the 332nd was trained at Tuskegee was it was down South. As one of the officers in charge put it, if it doesn't work out, it'll be down South and nobody'll see 'em fail anyway. The whole idea was that blacks could not fly an airplane. . . .

It was a tremendous success, beyond their wildest dreams. So they established quotas. They were gettin' so many volunteers for the air force, qualified young men, that they had to limit the size of the classes.

Possible Inferences:

_____   a. During World War II African Americans enrolled in the military in order to advance themselves economically.

_____   b. In the 1940s experiences of African Americans differed greatly from one part of the country to another.

_____   c. African Americans were treated by the military the same as Japanese Americans.

_____   d. Racism was a serious problem in the military during World War II.

_____   e. The success of the Tuskegee airmen disproved the assumption that "blacks could not fly an airplane."

Reasons for "F" labels:

_____

_____

3. Reflections on General Douglas MacArthur by a junior officer in the Pacific War. (William Manchester, *Goodbye Darkness: A Memoir of the Pacific War,* Little, Brown, 1980, 327.)

MacArthur would tolerate no criticism of [Admiral William F. ("Bull")] Halsey in his mess. He slammed his bunched fist on the table and roared, "Leave the Bull alone! He's still a fighting admiral in my book." Halsey had been loyal to him in earlier struggles, and he was reciprocating. Though both men were prima donnas, they remained on the best of terms, perhaps because each recognized himself in the other. Among other things, the admiral admired the general's courage.

Possible Inferences:

_____ a. MacArthur was humble and self-effacing.

_____ b. Members of MacArthur's entourage had criticized Halsey at some time.

_____ c. Manchester admired MacArthur.

_____ d. MacArthur admired Halsey's courage.

_____ e. MacArthur was a good general.

Reasons for "F" labels:

_____

_____

4. Eleanor Roosevelt, wife of President Franklin Roosevelt, writing about a coming trip to visit the Pacific theater of the war. (Joseph P. Lash, *Eleanor and Franklin*, W. W. Norton, 1971, 682.)

This trip will be attacked as a political gesture, & I am so uncertain whether or not I am doing the right thing that I will start with a heavy heart. Well, enough of my doubts. I'll go because other people think I should, & and if I see you that will be a joy, and if I don't I'll try to do a good job on seeing the women's work & where I do see our soldiers I'll try to make them feel that Franklin really wants to know about them.

Possible Inferences:

_____ a. Eleanor Roosevelt is writing to her husband, Franklin.

_____ b. Eleanor Roosevelt was interested in women's issues.

_____ c. She did not want the trip to prove a political liability for her husband.

_____ d. She thought her trip would be politically advantageous for her husband.

_____ e. Mrs. Roosevelt had visited troops on other occasions.

Reasons for "F" labels:

_____

_____

B *History by the Numbers*

For an exercise on the interpretation of numerical evidence, see exercise B in part I.

C *Oral History (Optional)*

(This exercise may also be used as an optional writing exercise in Chapters 8, 9, or 10.)

The excerpt above from Studs Terkel's *"The Good War:" An Oral History of World War II* (exercise A, #2) is an example of an increasingly popular genre of history: oral history. Oral history, as it is currently defined and practiced (See Appendix D), is written from the recorded interviews of people who actually witnessed and experienced the history later generations can only read about. This is the first point in your study of American history at which it is practical to attempt an oral history project, should time and circumstances permit.

To do oral history even moderately well you have to prepare thoroughly and allot sufficient time. Therefore, begin this exercise by reading Appendix D on pages 169–175. A full-fledged oral history project involves the collection, transcribing, editing, dissemination, and storage of the interviews.[11] For the purposes of this exercise we will limit the activity to interviewing subjects and disseminating the findings in a written paper or oral report.

Oral history projects take many forms, but for this exercise we suggest that you attempt an oral history of a significant theme or local or national event—a flood, an election, some aspect of World War II or life in the 1950s, etc.[12] After making the preparations outlined in Appendix D, you should record an interview with at least two individuals who can comment on your chosen event or theme. The interviews will constitute the evidence from which a paper, as assigned by the instructor, will be written.

An abbreviated exercise could take the form of (1) a group interview (in the classroom) of a person who has useful firsthand knowledge to share, or, (2) an oral autobiography assignment in which each student is expected to prepare an account based on an interview with another student in class. In both cases questions and expectations would have to be thoroughly discussed beforehand. Both of these options allow students to practice, and instructors to critique, interviewing skills.

---

11 See Cullom Davis, Kathryn Back, and Kay MacLean, *Oral History: From Tape to Type* (Chicago: American Library Association, 1977).

12 For a list of many oral history project options, see Thad Sitton, George L. Mehaffy, and O. L. Davis, Jr., *Oral History: A Guide for Teachers (and Others)* (Austin, TX: University of Texas Press, 1983), ch. 2. To do your project as family history, see David E. Kyvig and Myron A. Marty, *Your Family History: A Handbook for Research and Writing* (Wheeling, IL: Harlan Davidson, Inc., 1978).

THE STAGES OF WRITING | 8

"If your writing falls apart, it probably has no primary idea to hold it together."

SHERIDAN BAKER

He had already won $500 that afternoon, a fabulous day considering he had started with a desperate two bucks, what he called a "deuce." One horse race left on the program and here was this 3–5 favorite that the smart boys agreed was the best bet of the day. So Martin decided to put his whole bundle right on the nose and that would make his bankroll $800. Great!

The start was good and that odds-on favorite immediately opened up three lengths on the field. After a half-mile he was six in front and coasting. As he turned into the stretch though he began to run out of gas. At the three-six-teenths marker his lead was down to four, at the eighth pole he was laboring to hold on by two lengths, and as he reached the sixteenth pole it was altogether evident that he was through for the day as the rest of the field swept by him.

Up in the grandstand Martin watched grimly as the winning numbers were posted, his dream of big bucks now evaporated. Walking to the exit he ran across an old racetrack friend, and when asked how he had done that afternoon he smiled, and in that resigned attitude peculiar to horseplayers he said "Not so hot. I blew the deuce."

There's an old saying that "All horseplayers die broke." Predicting the outcome of a horse race is a chancy thing, but shrewd horseplayers will tell you that it can be done. It all depends on how well one appreciates the various stages a horse passes through in his running form. The key is never to bet on a race in which several horses are at the same stage—it's too unpredictable. Wait for the race when a single horse in a race is at his stage of peak performance. You won't always win, you may not get entirely rich, but you won't die broke either.

As applied to horse racing the theory of stages can be useful. Moreover it has useful applications in a variety of other areas. About 15 years ago Gail Sheehy wrote *Passages,* a book that details the trials and attitudes of the average person at various age levels: the late teenager, who so often says "I have to get away from my parents," the trying twenties, the discontented characteristic of the 30–35 age group, followed by what she refers to as the "deadline decade" and after that resignation and/or renewal. Author Sheehy provides an interesting and useful framework for understanding of oneself at various stages of life. Yet another application of the idea of stages was developed by historian Crane Brinton. In *The Anatomy of Revolution* (1938) he described revolutions as having six phases: first, discontent with the old regime; then revolution itself; after that the period of moderate rule; then the accession of extremists; following

this, the reign of terror; and, finally, the stage of conservative reaction. Allowing for some variations in individual cases, Brinton's model can be helpful in understanding many revolutions that have occurred.

The act of writing can also be understood as a sequence consisting of various stages. The first is collection and classification of information. The second is formulating a central theme around which the paragraph or essay will be developed. The next stage is creating an outline, or, at least, subordinating the lesser ideas to the major ones. The final stage is writing and revision. With each writer there is considerable variation in how these stages are accomplished. We will now explore each of these stages in more detail.

CLASSIFICATION OF INFORMATION

Collecting information in the library or elsewhere is only half of the process—you also have to classify vital pieces of it. As you deal with an unknown field you must initially use broad categories, because there is so much you don't

know about that field. As you learn more, your classification system can become more sophisticated. In exploring the topic of religion during the colonial period, for example, you might begin with the label Protestantism. It will later become necessary to identify specific major and minor religious groups such as Puritans, Quakers, Episcopalians, Methodists, and many others.

It is also necessary to set up subclasses within your broad categories. Common and relatively simple broad categories of history are: religion (as noted above), politics, economics, society, diplomacy, education, and the military. But, while useful points to begin, such broad categories are never enough. George Washington's role in the Revolutionary War, for example, can be considered under the label "military history," but any serious research would require much more explicit subclasses—his military leadership being broken down into smaller segments such as morale of enlisted men, control of officers, defense against possible British assaults, relations with civilian authorities, etc. This can't happen, of course, without a substantial investment of time and effort.

Historical study and writing begin with division and subdivision of information. Textbook authors, journal article writers, classroom teachers all take this vital step in their professional work. An example of this process in action is that of periodizing the past, which is essentially the act of separating segments of the past from each other so that each segment can itself be broken down into smaller pieces.

THE UNIFYING THEME

The next step in the writing process is to formulate a central theme around which the discourse as a whole will be developed. Many young writers see this as the most frustrating part of the process because they come up empty, "without a clue as to what to write," as they will tell you. Yet it shouldn't be this way. The reason for their frustration is the unrealistic expectation that lightning will strike in the form of sudden inspiration. Tell that to sports writers who have to cover the same major league baseball team 162 times a year, and write a story each day of at least a column length. They will tell you that the daily "angle," is based on developing a distinctive focus for the subject matter they must write about. Much can be learned about the process of writing from these professionals.

The keynote is effort, not inspiration, and there are several ways of going about your task. One of them is to return to your notes, look them over, ask questions, study the details you've accumulated—in general, turn the information over in your mind. Forget about the perfect idea. Take any idea, try it out, measure it, see if it gives you even an inch of progress, which is all you need. You're not looking for a great or powerful idea, but only to explain how or why something happened. A good history essay, whether one paragraph or many, does just that. It explains, always in a limited way, how or why something happened. Nobody ever expects you to give all the causes that made an event happen—one is plenty, if it's reasonably well developed.

What you are looking for is some sort of generalization, one that is quite limited as we've just discussed, and one that can be expressed in a single sentence. That generalization is often called the thesis and it prepares readers for the pieces of information it is intended to explain. The theme you finally select will fit only a relatively small part of the sea of information you've collected. And that should lighten the burden, because you are going to tell your story, from your perspective, using only the information you think is necessary to provide support for your thesis. Beyond this, you can safely junk all the rest of the information you have so laboriously collected.

In addition to developing a thesis, it may also be useful to put a headline on your collected material and write from the lead. Find what you regard as the turning point in a sequence of events, and focus on that as the crucial factor in explaining why things happened as they did. As you collect information, keep an idea card of insights and possibilities, or use other methods you've found to be helpful in this stage of writing.

THE OUTLINE

So far, we've discussed the stage of collection/classification and the stage of finding a central theme to be developed. The final stage before tackling the writing itself is that of putting your thoughts in order so that the central theme can be properly developed. This can be called outlining, a word that somehow or another many students seem to resist. That's fine. Don't outline. Instead, put your ideas in order by identifying and writing down the specific elements of your theme. The hard intellectual work was completed in that second stage when you found a generalization to describe some of the classified information you've collected. You'd never have been able to arrive at that generalization unless your mind had somehow found it an appropriate summary of those specific pieces of information.

An outline is nothing more than a plan or a recipe. If you're going to make a believable short essay, you'd better combine this point, that point, and that other point in a logical order, otherwise your reader won't believe you.

If you do choose to use a formal outline, keep the following in mind:[1]

1. Put the thesis at the top.

2. Use parallel grammatical structure for parallel ideas.

3. Use sentences or fairly complete phrases in the outline. (This helps you keep to the logical structure of the essay.)

4. Use the conventional outline format which allows you to subordinate less-general concepts to more general concepts—e.g.,

  I. National government

    A. State government

      1. County government

        a. Local government,
          Etc.

The traditional outline format is as follows.

  I. First major point/unit
    A.
    B.
      1.
      2.
        a.
        b.
          (1)
          (2)
            (a)
            (b)
  II. Second major point/unit
    A.
    B.
    Etc.

Note, each level of generalization—I, A., 1., a., etc.—must have at least two subordinate points under it.

EXERCISES

1 FROM COMPROMISE TO CONFLICT, 1820–1860

A

American history can be explored in a variety of ways: through films, textbooks, lectures, still pictures, conversations with parents and grandparents, and through newspaper accounts. A few years ago a book entitled *Chronicle of America*[2] offered a novel way of learning about American history. The book presented the events of history as though they happened yesterday, with headlines and the story as they might have appeared in a daily newspaper. The following exercise does much the same thing.

In this exercise we have listed some "news items" of the early- and mid-1800s as they might have appeared in the newspapers of the time, including headlines, and a sentence or two leading into each story. Your job is to classify these items using the several topical categories listed at the end of the exercise, just as you might organize information when writing a paper. To save space and time use only the first two or three words of each headline.

---

1 Diana Hacker, *A Writer's Reference*, 3rd ed. (Boston: St. Martin's Press, 1995), 10.
2 *Chronicle of America* (Mount Kisco, NY: Chronicle Publications, 1989). We are indebted to this volume for the concept of Exercises A and B in both Part I and Part II of this chapter.

ASHLEY EXPEDITION SKIRMISHES WITH INDIANS

St. Louis, Mo., July, 1822

A fur-trading venture led by former General William Ashley was attacked by Ricaree Indians in the area of the great bend of the Missouri above Council Bluffs. A casualty list will be published later.

PASSENGERS HAIL NEW RAILROAD LINE

Baltimore, Md., January, 1830

What is thought to be the first extended rail line in this country, 13 miles long, has received glowing reports from passengers. The Baltimore and Ohio Railroad line will be gradually extended to its western terminus, Cleveland, Ohio.

JACKSON FORMS "KITCHEN CABINET"

Washington, March 1829

In a sharp break with traditional practice President Andrew Jackson consults more often with cronies than with his duly appointed cabinet officers. Some critics refer to this group of friends as Jackson's "Kitchen Cabinet."

CONGRESS PASSES MISSOURI COMPROMISE

Washington, March 17, 1820

After extended debate which often degenerated into bitter name-calling, Congress finally compromised on the Missouri statehood issue by admitting Maine as a free state and Missouri as a slave state. This action maintains the sectional balance in the Senate.

INDIAN TRIBES AGREE TO MOVE WEST

Georgia, 1833

Word has been received here that under federal pressure the Chickasaw and Choctaw Indian nations have agreed to move west to the territory of Oklahoma. The Cherokee and Seminole tribes, however, remain adamantly opposed to the move.

U.S. AND BRITAIN SETTLE BORDER ISSUES

Washington, April 30, 1817

After several days of discussion, Great Britain and the United States have signed the Rush-Bagot agreement, named after the two principal negotiators of the treaty. Its main provision is demilitarization of the U.S.-Canada border.

PRESIDENTIAL ELECTION DECISION GOES TO HOUSE

Washington, December 2, 1824

Although General Andrew Jackson received a plurality in last month's election, the electoral college meeting yesterday failed to give him a majority. The Constitution (Article 2, Section 1, Paragraph 2) requires that the House of Representatives now choose a President from among the highest electoral vote-getters.

NATIONAL ROAD REACHES VANDALIA

Chicago, Ill., December, 1849

What was formerly called the "Cumberland Road" may now be called the "National Road" as it recently reached the Illinois town of Vandalia. The heavily traveled road originates in Maryland and traverses four states.

SOUTH CAROLINA TAKES A FIRM STAND

New York, December 22, 1828

Southern resistance continues to the so-called "Tariff of Abominations" passed earlier this year. Three days ago the South Carolina legislature, influenced it is said by Vice-President John Calhoun, threatened to declare the law unconstitutional within its borders.

MAINE MILITIA ALERTED

Augusta, Maine, February 20, 1839

The border controversy between Maine and the Canadian province of New Brunswick intensified last week as Canadian lumberjacks entered and began working in the disputed

Aroostook River area. Maine Governor Fairfield has called out the militia to assist in breaking up the Canadian lumber operation.

NEW FEDERAL AGENCY ESTABLISHED
Washington, July, 1836

The last few years have seen a variety of problems arise in connection with Indian tribes in the South and West. In order to give central direction to national policy the Congress has authorized creation of the Bureau of Indian Affairs.

MONROE CHALLENGES EUROPEAN ACTIONS IN LATIN AMERICA
Washington, December 3, 1823

In his annual message to Congress yesterday President Monroe declared the Western Hemisphere closed to European interference or colonization. Monroe's policy is thought by many to be directed to Spain because of her interest in reclaiming her lost Latin American empire.

ROAD BILL VETO SUSTAINED BY CONGRESS
Washington, April 12, 1822

Agreeing with President Monroe's view that federal expenditures for internal improvements are unconstitutional, both houses of Congress sustained his veto of a road bill last week. Experts now say the future of the Cumberland Road through west Virginia to the middle west looks dim.

CHEROKEE NATION DECLARES INDEPENDENCE
Atlanta, Ga., June, 1827

In an unprecedented move in U.S.-Indian relations the highly civilized Cherokee nation recently adopted a Constitution declaring itself an independent sovereign nation not bound by any U.S. or state laws. Observers expect a quick, and very negative, response from both authorities.

ERIE CANAL A BONANZA FOR NEW YORK
Albany, N.Y., September 15, 1825

No word except "spectacular" can describe the success of the Erie Canal, opened in April for the 365 miles distance between Albany and Buffalo. Enormous tonnages of midwestern grains now go through here to New York City, and an equal tonnage of manufactured products, as well as immigrants, fill boats going the other way.

JACKSON WINS HUGE VICTORY
New York, November 8, 1828

General Andrew Jackson got his revenge this week in swamping the incumbent President John Quincy Adams by an electoral margin of 178–83. Jackson had been the top vote-getter in 1824 but was denied the presidency in a House election based on a "corrupt bargain," according to Jackson.

U.S. "APPROVES" OF LATIN AMERICAN INDEPENDENCE
Washington, June 15, 1821

Yesterday the House of Representatives passed a resolution endorsing revolutionary efforts of Spanish American provinces to separate themselves from Spain. The House resolution opens the way for early U. S. recognition of any new Latin American republics.

MONROE ELECTION NEARLY UNANIMOUS
Washington, December 6, 1820

After an election most notable for its lack of political battles, President James Monroe was reelected yesterday by a huge margin in the electoral college. Of the 232 ballots cast Monroe received 231 of them, with one going to John Q. Adams. There were three abstentions.

STEAM POWER THE COMING THING

St. Louis, Mo., September, 1826

Steamboat traffic on the Mississippi River has almost doubled over the last year, and that traffic is moving much faster. The average steamboat travels at 25 miles per hour going downstream, and 16 miles per hour upstream.

1. General Categories

Category 1 (Use headlines) Label: Indian Affairs

_____

_____

_____

_____

_____

_____

_____

Category 2 Label: Transportation

_____

_____

_____

_____

_____

_____

_____

Category 3 Label: Politics

_____

_____

_____

_____

_____

_____

_____

Category 4 Label: Western Expansion

_____

_____

_____

_____

_____

_____

_____

2. Now, let's go one step further with classification. Take the largest of your several categories and divide it into two, or even three sub-categories.

Largest Category:

_____

Subcategory A Label: _____

_____

_____

_____

Subcategory B Label: _____

_____

_____

_____

Subcategory C (If used) Label: _____

_____

_____

_____

B

The next exercise is the same as the one just completed except that different aspects of the period are emphasized in these news stories. This time, however, you choose the category headings. Use at least three categories, but no more than four.

NEW LAND POLICY MAKES IMPORTANT CHANGES
Washington, April 29, 1820

The recently passed "Land Act" of 1820 "giveth and taketh away." It does reduce the price of western lands to $1.25 an acre (minimum) and permits purchase of as little as 80 acres. But it eliminates the credit system by which a poorer farmer could pay off the purchase price gradually.

FEDERAL POWER REASSERTED
New York, October 26, 1824

States may regulate as they wish regarding rivers and lakes within their borders, but it's "hands off" of waterways that border another state. In the long anticipated decision in the *Gibbons* vs. *Ogden* case, the court ruled that the national government had exclusive power over interstate commerce.

CONGRESS PASSES OMNIBUS BILL ✓
Washington, September 22, 1850

In yet another effort to solve the red hot slavery issue, Congress yesterday completed eight months of work on the Omnibus Bill. Called by some the "Compromise of 1850," the bill admits California to the Union as a free state, organizes certain Western territories without reference to slavery, and greatly toughens the existing fugitive slave law.

SLAVE PLOT REVEALED IN SOUTH CAROLINA ✓
Richmond, Va., June 1, 1822

In Charleston, South Carolina, the efforts of one Denmark Vesey, a free Negro, to free slaves in the area were nipped in the bud through alert action by local authorities. Thirty-seven participants in the plot were executed.

TREATY OF GUADELOUPE HIDALGO SIGNED
Washington, February 2, 1848

The United States became a much larger nation yesterday, as the Mexican government signed the Treaty of Guadeloupe Hidalgo ending the war with Mexico. Mexico has ceded all of Upper California and the territory of New Mexico to the U.S. Some expansionists wanted to take over all of Mexico, but the negotiators settled for something less.

HOUSE OF REPRESENTATIVES IMPOSES GAG RULE
Washington, May 27, 1836

As tensions over slavery rise in the North and South, House southerners at least made sure the issue will not reach the House floor. The southern faction was able to get passed a resolution that since Congress has no authority over state slavery laws, no petitions on the matter can be debated in the House.

DRED SCOTT DECISION CREATES A STORM
Washington, March 10, 1857

Intense negative reaction has been generated in the North by this week's Supreme Court decision in the *Dred Scott* vs. *Sanford* case. The decision, which essentially meant that Congress has no power over slavery in the territories, is seen by the recently formed Republican Party as a decision that "must be reversed."

HOMESTEAD ACT SIGNED BY PRESIDENT LINCOLN
Washington, May 21, 1862

In recent years federal land policy was primarily shaped by the slavery issue. Now, with the South out of the Union, a Homestead Bill has been signed by the President. The new law virtually gives away western lands if a settler lives on his 160 acre plot for five years, and works improvements on the land.

TRANSCONTINENTAL RAILROAD ISSUE MAY BE RESOLVED
Washington, December 31, 1853

In a move aimed at satisfying the southern bloc in Congress, yesterday the United States purchased from Mexico a rectangular patch of land just south of the Arizona territory. The purchase makes possible a railroad route from New Orleans to California, one of several routes through the West recommended by the Army Corps of Engineers.

NEW ABOLITIONIST SOCIETY FORMED
Boston, Mass., February, 1832

Firebrand editor William Lloyd Garrison, publisher of "The Liberator" newspaper, is the guiding spirit behind the recently established New England Anti-Slavery Society. Garrison, who in his paper promises he "will not retreat a single inch" on this issue, confidently predicts that abolition societies will be formed throughout the country.

SUPREME COURT REPRIMANDS STATE OF WISCONSIN
Washington, November, 1859

In a decision notable for its affirmation of federal supremacy, the Supreme Court denied Wisconsin's judiciary any right to interfere in federal prerogatives. In the case of *Abelman* vs. *Booth,* the Court upheld the full and universal constitutionality of the 1850 fugitive slave law.

SLAVE REBELLION PUT DOWN AFTER MUCH BLOODSHED
Richmond, Va. August 21, 1831

In Southampton County, beginning on August 13, a Negro preacher and former overseer named Nat Turner organized and led an attack on white farmhouses and families. More than 55 whites were killed before the revolt could be put down.

RECENT LEGISLATION AIDS "SQUATTERS"
Washington, June 15, 1829

Once you're on the land, have worked it, and improved it, even though you have no formal title to it, it can no longer be "stolen" from you by an unscrupulous speculator. Such is the intent of the new Pre-Emption Act, which authorizes "first refusal" rights to actual settlers.

SLAVE CODES TIGHTENED IN VIRGINIA
Richmond, Va. October 30, 1833

The Virginia legislature has completed its work on the state slave codes, making them more restrictive than ever. Lawmakers say that toughening the codes was motivated by widespread fears of slave insurrections.

TEXAS BECOMES PART OF THE UNITED STATES
Washington, December 30, 1845

After a nine-year statehood campaign Texas got its wish yesterday as the former independent nation formally entered the Union. The admission of Texas remains controversial, however. Abolitionists don't like the idea of a new slave state, and the Mexican nation still regards Texas as her property.

MCCULLOCH CASE A SUPREME COURT LANDMARK
Washington, March 7, 1819

Yesterday the U.S. Supreme Court decided that the federal government is not to be hog-tied by a restrictive interpretation of the Constitution. In a majority opinion written by Chief Justice John Marshall in *McCulloch* vs. *Maryland,* the court applied the "implied power" doctrine of Alexander Hamilton, thus giving Congress a wide latitude in legislative authority.

NEW ORGANIZATION FOR FREE NEGROES
Boston, June 15, 1817

Announcement has been made of the establishment of the American Colonization Society, which has as its purpose the return of free Negroes and ex-slaves to Africa. A plot of land will be purchased in Western Africa, where, it is hoped, American Negroes will create a new African republic.

NEW LAND ACT REDUCES LAND PRICES IN THE WEST
Washington, August 10, 1854

Against southern protests, Congress has adopted a policy of gradually reducing the price of lands that have been on the market for ten years or more. Southern politicians strongly opposed the measure, suggesting that it would, over a period of time, increase the number of free states in relation to slave states.

UNDERGROUND RAILROAD THRIVES
Philadelphia, Pa. May 20, 1851

Despite the Fugitive Slave Law passed last year, more Negro slaves than ever are being secretly guided to the North by well-organized anti-slavery advocates. Though called a railroad, it is really a series of backwoods and forest paths by which a fleeing slave can make his way north and on to Canada.

EAST FLORIDA NOW A PART OF U.S.
Washington, February 22, 1819

The Adams-Onís Treaty, signed yesterday in this city, finally settled the troubled issue of East Florida. For its part, Spain ceded the East Florida territory to the United States which, in return, renounced all claims to Texas in the West.

SUPREME COURT REJECTS STATE FOREIGN COMMERCE POWER
Washington, June 1849

In a split (5–4) decision, the Supreme Court rejected the claims of New York and Massachusetts that states could regulate foreign commerce. The majority opinion in the so-called "passenger cases" included a ringing defense of the position that regulation of foreign commerce belonged exclusively to the Federal Government.

1. General Categories:

Category 1 (Use headlines) Label: _____

_____

_____

_____

_____

_____

_____

Category 2 Label: _____

_____

_____

_____

_____

_____

_____

Category 3 Label: _____

_____

_____

_____

_____

_____

_____

Category 4 Label: _____

_____

_____

_____

_____

_____

_____

2. Again, take the largest of your categories and divide it into three subcategories in a way that makes the most sense to you.

Largest Category: _____

Subcategory A. Label: _____

Items:

_____

_____

_____

Subcategory B. Label: _____

Items:

_____

_____

_____

Subcategory C (If used) Label: _____

Items:

_____

_____

_____

C

Now it is time to do some writing. For this purpose, let's go back to Exercise B, which gave you a variety of information about the period between 1820 and 1860. You don't have a lot of information, but you do have enough to make a modest statement about how things were in that period of time. Don't try for any wide, expansive, overarching statement that describes the period as a whole. Try instead for a generalization (which will serve as your topic sentence) about a specific aspect of the period—a statement that can be supported or illustrated with the information in one of the categories you have identified.

In the first sentence of your paragraph simply state your generalization, and in the rest of the paragraph put down two or three pieces of information, directly factual or inferential, that make your beginning statement believable. And, if you do this exactly as described, you will have done something that is the essence of history writing, or any other effective writing for that matter: you will have made a generalization backed up by specifics that make it acceptable for a reader, or a listener.

How would things be for women at this time?

_____

_____

_____

_____

_____

_____

_____

_____

_____

_____

American history can be explored in a variety of ways: through films, textbooks, lectures, still pictures, conversations with parents and grandparents, and through newspaper accounts. A few years ago a book entitled *Chronicle of America* offered a novel way of learning about American history. The book presented the events of history as though they happened yesterday, with headlines and the story as they might have appeared in a daily newspaper. The following exercise does much the same thing.

In Exercises A and B we have listed some "news items" of the 1930s and 1940s as they might have appeared in the newspapers of the time, including headlines, and a sentence or two leading into each story.[3] Your job is to classify these items using the several topical categories listed at the end of the exercise, just as you might organize information when writing a paper. To save space and time use only the first two or three words of each headline.

RECONSTRUCTION FINANCE CORPORATION LEADER NAMED
Washington, February 3, 1932
President Hoover yesterday named veteran financier Charles G. Dawes to head the new Reconstruction Finance Corporation. This agency was recently created by Congress to make loans to businesses that have been weakened by prevailing depression conditions.

NIRA BECOMES LAW
Washington, June 16, 1933
One of President Roosevelt's favorite projects, the National Industrial Recovery Act, became law this week in a signing ceremony in the President's office. The act empowers the President, after consultation, to prescribe codes for various industries, these codes having the force of law.

STIMSON REACTS TO JAPANESE MOVEMENT INTO MANCHURIA
Washington, January 8, 1932
Restating a traditional American diplomatic principle, Secretary of State Henry L. Stimson gave Japanese officials a veiled warning about the Japanese occupation of Southern Manchuria. In a note delivered to the Japanese embassy in Washington, Stimson reiterated that the U.S. will insist on the maintenance of Chinese territorial integrity.

DU PONT INTRODUCES NEW FABRIC
Wilmington, Delaware, June, 1938
After ten years of research the Du Pont company will market a super-lightweight fabric tentatively named "nylon." Invented by chemist Wallace H. Carothers, the new product is thought to be potentially useful for making toothbrush bristles and possibly for making women's hosiery, since silk from Japan is in increasingly short supply.

HOLLYWOOD HEARS MIDDLE AMERICA: SETS "PRODUCTION CODE"
Hollywood, Ca. June, 1934
Offended by the gangsterism and open sexuality of recent films, many middle-class Americans have been "turned off" to Hollywood, at least according to box-office numbers. The industry has read the message, and this week set the standards of acceptable film behavior, including restrictions on such matters as language, sexual display, dancing, dress and patriotism.

---

3 We have used the 1930s and '40s in this section (varying slightly from the chronological structure of the book) in order to take advantage of the thematic unity inherent in the prewar and wartime periods.

FDR SAYS "QUARANTINE AGGRESSORS"
Chicago, October 6, 1937
Challenging the isolationist mentality that brought about the Neutrality Acts of the past three years, President Roosevelt spoke out here yesterday against those who make war on their neighbors. It was Roosevelt's first public statement implying that the United States should take a more active role in international affairs.

SCOTTISH PHYSICIST FINDS NEW USE FOR RADIO
London, August, 1934
A system for detecting the distance and motion of remote objects has been demonstrated by Sir Robert Watson-Watt. Because it operates by means of radio waves striking an object and returning the radio impulse to the transmitter, the system has been called "radar," a contraction of "radio detection and ranging."

FDR COURT PLAN BRINGS BIG CONGRESSIONAL BATTLE
Washington, February, 15, 1937
President Roosevelt's proposal to increase the number of Supreme Court justices has run into a wall of opposition on Capitol Hill. Even members of his own party are accusing the President of "subverting the Constitution" in a subterfuge seemingly aimed at destroying the independence of the judicial branch of government.

"SNOW WHITE" GETS RECORD CROWDS
St. Louis, Mo., September, 1938
"Snow White and the Seven Dwarfs," which is cartoon filmmaker Walt Disney's first full-length picture, continues to attract enormous crowds to downtown theaters. "Grumpy," "Doc," and "Sleepy," and the others have become charming new symbols of America.

GOOD NEIGHBOR POLICY IMPLEMENTED
Montevideo, Uruguay, December 27, 1933
Secretary of State Cordell Hull has warmly endorsed a Montevideo Conference declaration: "No state has the right to intervene in the internal or external affairs of another." This declaration, if carried out in practice, signifies the end of American interventionism in Latin America, and is part of President Roosevelt's previously announced "Good Neighbor Policy."

SUPREME COURT BAGS "BLUE EAGLE"
Washington, May, 1935
The "Blue Eagle" is no more. It was the symbol of the NIRA which yesterday was declared null and void by the United States Supreme Court. The Court said the original act of 1933 illegally delegated legislative powers to the Executive Branch.

BRITISH INVENTION BROUGHT TO AMERICA
Boston, November, 1928
American businessman Harold F. Pitcairn has purchased and brought to this country a new type of flying machine called an "autogiro." This machine has a blade mounted above its body enabling it to rise straight up in the air, or so say supposedly reliable witnesses.

"THE BABE" CALLS SHOT: YANKS WIN SERIES
Chicago, October 2 1932
Taunted by Chicago bench jockeys for an earlier strikeout, Yankee star Babe Ruth stepped out of the batter's box, turned to the Cub bench, and pointed to the centerfield bleachers. He then returned to the plate and lashed the ball into the exact spot he had pointed to.

CIVIL WAR EPIC A HUGE HIT
Hollywood, Ca. November, 1939
Margaret Mitchell's novel, *Gone with the Wind,* a best-seller book a few years ago, is close to becoming the top movie of all time. Audiences especially favor Rhett Butler's

(Clark Gable) declaration to the self-centered Scarlett O'Hara (Vivien Leigh) regarding her future: "Frankly, my dear, I don't give a damn."

BIG YEAR IN RAILROAD DEVELOPMENT
Chicago, December 30, 1934
The year's end tomorrow culminates the most successful year ever in railroad innovations. In March passengers enjoyed trips in America's first streamlined high speed trains; November brought the first appearance of diesel-motored trains; and just two weeks ago the streamlined principle was applied to steam locomotives.

NEW ERA FOR MOTION PICTURES: TALKIES ARE HERE
Los Angeles, October, 1927
Box office receipts have been impressive for the recently released "The Jazz Singer" starring Al Jolson. The movie is the first to have a sound track on the film celluloid itself, a major technological advance for the industry.

ACT OF CONGRESS SIGNALS NEW COURSE
Washington, April 10, 1935
The Roosevelt administration is stopping the practice of giving direct relief to depression-stricken families. Instead, under provisions of recent congressional legislation, FDR has established the Works Progress Administration (WPA), which will hire unemployed people to work in the line of their specialty, whether that be construction, music, art, or theater.

ROOSEVELT MAKES APPEAL TO EUROPE
Washington, August 25, 1939
In the face of rapidly deteriorating conditions in eastern Europe, President Roosevelt appealed yesterday to Polish, German, and Italian leaders to accept arbitration of their territorial disputes.

OMAHA WINS BELMONT STAKES, WINS TRIPLE CROWN
New York, June 8, 1935
A horse named after one of America's greatest cities, Omaha, Nebraska, yesterday danced away from his rivals to win the third jewel of the triple crown of horse racing. After the race his owner said, "I'm proud to have named him Omaha, after a city that is the best, just as he is the best."
[Note: One of the authors of this book hails from Omaha, thus explaining the appearance of this particular item.]

JAPANESE-AMERICAN RELATIONS WORSEN
Washington, November 20, 1938
Reacting to Ambassador (to Japan) Joseph C. Grew's mid-October strongly worded protest concerning Japanese policy in China, the Japanese government has declared that the American position is "inappropriate" to the conditions of "today and tomorrow."

1. General Categories:

Category 1 (Use headlines) Label: Government/Politics

_____

_____

_____

_____

_____

_____

Category 2 Label: Technology

_____

_____

_____

_____

_____

_____

Category 3 Label: International Affairs

_____

_____

_____

_____

_____

_____

Category 4 Label: Entertainment

_____

_____

_____

_____

_____

_____

2. Now let's go one step further with classification. Take the largest of your categories and divide it into two subcategories in a way that makes the most sense to you.

Largest Category:

_____

Subcategory A. Label: _____

Items:

_____

_____

_____

Subcategory B. Label: _____

Items:

_____

_____

_____

Classify the following items, all of which deal with World War II, using at least four, but not more than five, categories. Choose your own categories.

IWO JIMA FINALLY IN AMERICAN CONTROL
Honolulu, March 31, 1945
After a month of bitter fighting costing the lives of over 6,500 marines, the island of Iwo Jima in the western Pacific is now firmly in American control. It has become a staging area from which American bombers and fighters are daily pounding the Japanese homeland.

SALLY RAND WILL DO WITHOUT
Chicago, June 2, 1942
Famed balloon dancer Sally Rand, who dances in the nude behind several strategically placed balloons, has announced her own way of helping the war effort. To help the rubber shortage, she announced last week that she would use only one balloon in her dance. "This is my sacrifice," she said. So far her audiences haven't complained.

GERMAN BLITZKRIEG DESTROYS FRENCH OPPOSITION
London, June 18, 1940
In little more than a month, Hitler's war machine has torn apart the Netherlands, Belgium, and now France, the latter considered a mainstay of the western European defense system. In a highly symbolic move Hitler insisted that the German-French armistice be signed at Compiegne, the site of the German surrender that ended World War I.

POTSDAM CONFERENCE CONCLUDES
Berlin, August 2, 1945
President Harry Truman and new British Prime Minister Clement Attlee have gone home after reaching crucial agreements the past few days, most notably a renewed demand for Japan's surrender. Some observers here regard the tone of the demand as so solemn as to be considered an ultimatum, suggesting that the United States may have a military surprise in store for the Japanese.

STRIKES SUSPENDED FOR THE DURATION
New York, April, 1942
Many labor leaders are getting a different sort of message these days from rank and file blue collar union members. Many war production workers take the position that the issues of wages and working conditions are unimportant given the kind of sacrifices made by the millions now in the armed forces.

WAR COMES HOME TO AMERICA
Washington, March, 1942
At the present time the U.S. is losing the battle of the Atlantic, losing it almost within sight of shoreside observers. Twenty-five cargo vessels have been sunk in the past two weeks off the coast of Florida by German "wolf-pack" teams of submarines which fire deadly torpedo patterns.

MOVIE GREATS AID BIG BOND RALLY
Los Angeles, March 18, 1942
At a war bond rally held yesterday near the Federal building in downtown Los Angeles, a dozen or more Hollywood stars, directors, and producers did their bit for the war effort, and the result was a record war bond subscription by the large audience.

ALLIES BEGIN THE LONG ROAD BACK
Casablanca, November 9, 1942
The first step in the war against the Axis was taken yesterday with a combined Allied naval, air, and land operation against Casablanca, Oran, and Algiers in North Africa. Sur-

prisingly, the French defense forces, recent bitter enemies of Hitler, fought on his side this time.

MIDWAY SEEN AS HUGE AMERICAN VICTORY
San Francisco, June 5, 1942

Against a background of Pearl Harbor, Bataan, and Corregidor, all devastating U.S. losses of the past six months, American forces finally won a battle yesterday, and it was a big one. American dive bombers destroyed four major Japanese carriers as their invasion force approached Midway Island, and thus blunted the Japanese drive to dominate the Central Pacific.

UNITED NATIONS DECLARATION SIGNED
Washington, January 1, 1942

Representatives of twenty-six nations, all of them participants in the war against the Axis powers, signed the "United Nations Declaration" yesterday. The agreement, essentially a restatement of the Atlantic Charter, promises full participation in the war and contains a provision that no nation will conclude a separate peace agreement with the enemy.

GAS RATIONING NOW NATIONWIDE
Washington, March 20, 1943

Gasoline has been added to the long list of commodities that are now rationed to the public, including meat, sugar, coffee, butter, even applesauce. Most Americans appeared resigned to the shortages, and when questioned, respond that "it's the least I can do to help out" to win the war.

HUGE BOMB DETONATED OVER HIROSHIMA
Washington, August 7, 1945

At 9:15 A.M. yesterday an incredibly powerful bomb exploded over the manufacturing center of Hiroshima on the main Japanese island of Honshu. Observers in the aircraft "Enola Gay," which dropped the bomb, reported that within an instant four square miles of the downtown area of the city simply vanished.

PATTON ACROSS RHINE, ON WAY TO BERLIN
London, March 22, 1945

General George Patton's Third Army yesterday smashed across the Rhine River, opening a clear path to the heart of Hitler's Germany. The German army in Patton's sector has virtually ceased to exist.

NO NEW HOUSES OR HIGHWAYS FOR THE DURATION
Washington, April 9, 1942

The recently created War Production Board has announced the end of all nonessential residential and highway construction until "further notice." The purpose of this policy is to conserve vital materials for the war effort.

GERMAN U-BOATS PRESENT INCREASING THREAT
New York, July 6, 1942

In the past twelve months more than 1300 British ships, most of them cargo vessels, have been torpedoed and sunk. American naval analysts now say that unless such heavy losses in the Atlantic Ocean can be reduced, Allied plans for an invasion of Europe may have to be scuttled.

PEARL HARBOR DEVASTATED BY JAPANESE ATTACK
Honolulu, December 8, 1941

Yesterday a ferocious Japanese air attack on Pearl Harbor naval installations sank major units of the U.S. Pacific fleet, and killed more than 2,000 sailors. The location of the Japanese carriers that launched the planes is at this time unknown.

U.S. troops fire a volley over officers and men killed at Kaneohe, Dec. 7, 1941

MILITARY DISASTER AVERTED
London, June 3, 1940

Penned in by two German armies which, inexplicably, failed to attack when they were defenseless on the beaches, more than 300,000 British Expeditionary Force soldiers were evacuated from the Dunkirk trap these past seven days. They have survived to fight another day.

DUMBARTON OAKS CONFERENCE CHARTS THE FUTURE
Washington, September 15, 1944

In an ongoing meeting at Dumbarton Oaks, near Washington, representatives of Great Britain, China, the Soviet Union, and the United States have tentatively agreed on the draft of a charter establishing a new international organization to replace the League of Nations after the war.

WOMEN JOIN "SPARS" IN RECORD NUMBERS
New London, Conn., September, 1942

The United States Coast Guard, which in wartime operates under Navy authority, has announced that enlistments of women in the "SPARS" are closed for the time being. Training facilities for the "SPARS" (which means "Semper Paratus Always Ready Service") are overflowing with women enlistees.

ALLIES STORM ASHORE IN NORMANDY
London, June 6, 1944

The massive Allied assault on "Fortress Europa" began today in the morning darkness on Normandy beaches. Dubbed "Operation Overlord," more than 2,800,000 are involved in the undertaking, although only a few thousand went ashore in the first wave.

PAPER BOYS CONTRIBUTE TO WAR EFFORT

New York, October, 1942

More than a million paper boys who deliver the nation's daily newspapers are doing their part for Uncle Sam. When they make weekly collections on their paper routes, they also persuade their customers to buy "war stamps" (cost 10 cents each), which, when accumulated to $18.75 in the stamp book, can be exchanged for a war bond.

HUNTER-KILLER GROUPS PROWL ATLANTIC

New York, December, 1943

A new way of combating the German U-Boat has proven very effective in reducing ship losses. The Navy now uses small aircraft carriers, called "baby flattops" which send out planes to track down submarine wolf packs, and prevent them from attacking convoys, which can now travel the Atlantic sea lanes as though they were highways.

GERMANS LAUNCH MIGHTY ATTACK

Washington, June 23, 1941

German Panzer [armored] units moved quickly through Russian defenses along a 2,000 mile front from the Arctic to the Ukraine. By some reports German forces moved through Russian defenses so fast they lost touch with headquarters units.

OMAHA BEACH OPENS ROAD INTO FRANCE

London, June 10, 1944

Against all odds—weather, fortified positions, superior firepower, and veteran German army units—American forces advanced across Omaha Beach into the interior of France the last few days. They have sustained heavy casualties, however, losing more than 2,000 dead and wounded in just the first day.

General Categories:

Category 1 (Use headlines) Label: _____

_____

_____

_____

_____

_____

_____

_____

Category 2 Label: _____

_____

_____

_____

_____

_____

_____

_____

_____

Category 3 Label: _____

_____

_____

_____

_____

_____

_____

Category 4 Label: _____

_____

_____

_____

_____

_____

_____

Category 5 Label: _____

_____

_____

_____

_____

_____

_____

C

Now it is time to do some writing. Using the information on World War II in Exercise B, write a paragraph on one of the themes you have identified. You don't have a lot of information, but you do have enough to make a modest statement about how things were in that period of time. Don't try for any wide, expansive, overarching statement that describes the period as a whole. Try instead for a generalization (which will serve as your topic sentence) about a specific aspect of the period—a statement that can be supported or illustrated with the information in one of the categories you have identified.

In the first sentence of your paragraph simply state your generalization, and in the rest of the paragraph put down two or three pieces of information, directly factual or inferential, that make your beginning statement believable. And, if you do this exactly as described, you will have done something that is the essence of history writing, or any other effective writing for that matter: you will have made a generalization backed up by specifics that make it acceptable for a reader, or a listener.

_____

_____

_____

_____

_____

_____

_____

_____

_____

_____

_____

_____

_____

MEANINGFUL WRITING: THE PARAGRAPH

Ordinarily we don't think of American presidents as writers. Their public life as leaders and professional politicians somehow obscures their other accomplishments. Yet all of them had to write, due to the nature of the job, and some of them were superb stylists who made a living as authors. Theodore Roosevelt, aside from the 19 books to his credit, published hundreds of articles of commentary about the world in which he lived. Woodrow Wilson, at one time the president of Princeton University, wrote a highly respected study of the American congressional system, in addition to several other scholarly books. Thomas Jefferson wrote "The Declaration of Independence," one of the world's masterpieces of political literature. Abraham Lincoln, a self-educated man from humble beginnings was a writer of enormous sensitivity as shown by the words spoken at Gettysburg: "We are met on this battlefield . . . testing whether this nation or any nation so conceived and so dedicated can long endure."

So here we are on the subject of writing—again. Teachers know how important it is and look for ways to help their students develop this necessary skill. In this chapter we will deal with the two fundamental concepts of effective writing: paragraph organization and the use of transitions within and between paragraphs.

The most vital aspect of quality writing is strong organization. A writer must provide solid organization, along with its accompanying signals to define the path the reader is to follow. In this enterprise the paragraph is the most basic unit of thought. A widely respected authority of the twentieth century, William Strunk, Jr., in his *Elements of Style,* offers this plain and simple counsel: "Make the paragraph the unit of composition," and follows it with some principles of how to structure a paragraph.

The notion of the paragraph as the basic unit of discourse is little more than a century old, having been introduced by Alexander Bain in the 1860s. But Bain was only formalizing with a specific term what effective writers have always done, which is putting related things together in a compartment of their own. In general, there are three basic kinds of paragraph: *narrative,*

which opens with a statement of something happening and follows that with a series of other happenings related to it; *descriptive,* which ordinarily provides an introductory generalization about a person, place, or thing, then follows with a collection of details of concrete imagery; and *expository* (sometimes called discursive), which makes a claim followed by a set of specific statements that make that claim believable to a reader. This type of paragraph is the bedrock of academic writing, and in this chapter and the next we will discuss its elements in detail.

An expository paragraph must have a topic sentence which expresses some sort of generalization, even a limited one, about your subject matter. One authority prefers to use the term "top sentence" because it is like a headline that in a broad way summarizes what is to follow or a signpost that tells the reader what is just ahead. Though not an absolute requirement, placing the topic sentence first in the paragraph does aid the process of communication between writer and reader.

An expository paragraph should also have substance; it must have enough content to make the topic sentence believable. This is a sticky point for many modern students who are used to the staccato, one-sentence paragraph style of many newspapers and newsmagazines. Such publications collect lots of information and then send it out in vaguely organized streams. In expository writing, a paragraph must have specific underlying components, and be long enough to develop the topic sentence. Fewer than four to six sentences, for instance, would not be adequate.

In addition to substance, expository paragraphs also require something called proof structure, or those particular items introduced by a writer that illustrate or support particular aspects of a topic sentence. Most professional writing has a proof structure; in fact most quality student writing has it too, even though you may not be familiar with the term. One of the interesting facets of perceiving writing in this way is that an essay paragraph written by a first year student has the same requirement of having a proof structure as a book hundreds of pages long. In the case of the book, of course, the requirement is fulfilled much more elaborately. But either can be criticized legitimately for its absence.

Proof or support for your points can take many forms. Quoting expert opinion is effective, especially when you can offer two or more sources supporting the same basic conclusion. As impressive as such scholarly opinion might be, however, it is better to provide concrete evidence in support of your case. You should include particular facts or statistical data that lend credence to your position. A series of illustra-

tions can help demonstrate the validity of your thesis. Finally, the strength of your case may depend on how well you explain the logical connections that tie the components of your thesis together. In general you prove something by giving reasons for its validity.

A paragraph is a sequence, a set of things that go together. In order for readers to understand what they read, the elements of the sequence must connect to each other. This is so not only within the paragraph but also between paragraphs. Here is where the third requirement, that of *linkage*, comes into the picture.

One of the things that writers must keep in mind at all times is that their reader is often on unfamiliar ground. Whether the written piece is a student paper, a scientific article, or a newspaper editorial, the reader is often "in trouble" because the sentences and paragraphs aren't fitted together well enough to make clear sense. To most of us distractions come easily, and when a written piece lacks effective connections between sentences a distraction is a welcome relief.

How is effective linkage accomplished? There are a variety of techniques, three of which will be discussed here. The first is the use of *transitional phrases.*

Transitional phrases are best described as the bridges that carry readers into new sentences and paragraphs. They show how each particular idea is related to that which immediately preceded it. One of the most common transitional devices is the expression *for example.* When readers see it they know that the following sentence will provide a specific illustration of the truth of the sentence preceding. Another frequently used transitional device is *as a result,* which tells readers that the sentence to follow will describe an effect of some causal influence that has just been discussed. In using such phrases an author takes his readers with him step by step, thus avoiding those abrupt shifts that can alienate even the most patient of them. In football parlance, by using transitional phrases, a writer "calls signals" to the readers, enabling them to know where the next play is going.

There are several basic types of transitional expressions with which you should become very familiar. One way of classifying them is presented below.

Function	Terms
sequencing	first, next, subsequently, in the end
strengthening	above all, moreover, indeed,
likening	correspondingly, in comparison, similarly
summarizing	all in all, in short, overall, thus
effecting	accordingly, consequently, therefore
illustrating	for example, as an illustration
restating	namely, in other words, to be specific
contrasting	conversely, however, nevertheless
supplanting	rather, alternatively, on the other hand

You should become familiar with all such terms and others like them. They must become a recurrent part of your own writing, for the very good reason that if they are missing, your writing will almost certainly be disjointed, thus lacking in the flow that enables the reader to understand what you have to say.

A second broad linkage technique is the use of *referent terms*, or terms that point backward to something discussed in a recent sentence. One type of referent term is the echo word—repeating an important word or phrase from one sentence or paragraph to another to let the reader know that the discussion is to continue along the same general line. When, for example, shifting to a new aspect of the same subject, it might be presented as follows:

Last sentence of a paragraph:

"All in all, the economic burdens of the *Depression* weighed most heavily on black Americans."

First sentence of the next paragraph:

"However, the *Depression* brought a social climate that was both wholesome and healthy." (The echo word here is "Depression.")

Another type of referent term is the pronoun substituted for an important noun in a preceding sentence. Note the use of pronoun referents in the following:

American bomber crews in England suffered severe casualties early in World War II. *They* had to fly by day, making *them* much easier targets for German gunners. *Their* raid was nearly always conducted without fighter support. *It* was a gamble with death, very often lost.
(*They*, *them*, and *their* refer to the bomber crews; *it* refers to the raid.)

There are other and more subtle forms of showing linkage, such as the use of antonyms ("... the *good* part of his plan was ...: the *bad* part was...."), and the use of repetitions ("he expressed ..., he denied ..., he claimed ..., he insisted ..."), thus enabling the reader to perceive slight shifts.

Perhaps the best way to understand the importance of linkage forms is to see them as devices to move the reader forward in the paragraph. Examine the paragraph below and underline the various linkage elements as you go along.

Women have always sung the blues. In fact, many women became famous singing those blues in the early part of the century. Although there have always been good female instrumentalists, many of them have eluded the pages of history. The singers are remembered. Their voices, as inspired instruments, rise through the gaps of history from the baby's bedside and the church choir to the stage. As the blues gave way to jazz and then to soul and rock 'n' roll, the nation enjoyed the voices of many women. Today women are heard in every aspect of popular music, from country to contemporary. In addition to capturing their voices, modern media have been able to focus on the singers as physical commodities; a new prominence has been bestowed on the sexy lead singer of a band otherwise male.

Through the changing times, women are most often given attention as singers.[1]

(The linkage words and phrases are: *In fact, women, Although, singers, Their, Today, In addition to, Through the changing times*)

To summarize what has been emphasized in this chapter, the effective writers not only supply supportive ideas for their paragraph's topic sentence, but they also connect them, each to the preceding one, in the paragraph.

EXERCISES

I   CIVIL WAR AND RECONSTRUCTION, 1850–1877

A   *The Topic Sentence*

The first exercise involves application of one of the main themes of this chapter, namely the importance of the topic sentence. The following paragraphs lack a topic sentence. Read each paragraph carefully, then compose a topic sentence for it.

1. The first paragraph deals with the role of Southern white women in the Civil War.

   Topic sentence:

   _____

   _____

   Some gained notoriety as spies; others smuggled medicine, guns, clothing, and shoes into the South, often taking advantage of the large hoop skirts then in fashion. Women also spent a good deal of time knitting and sewing clothes for soldiers. "We never went out to pay a visit without taking our knitting along," recalled a South Carolina woman. Perhaps most important, with so many men fighting, women took charge of agricultural production. As one Georgia soldier told his wife, "You must be man and woman both while the war lasts." On plantations, the mistress often supervised the slaves, as well as the wrenching shift from cotton to foodstuffs. "All this attention to farming is uphill work with me," one South Carolina woman confessed to her army husband.

   James Davidson, et al., *Nation of Nations*, Vol. I, 1990. Reproduced with permission of The McGraw-Hill Companies.

2. The next paragraph discusses the attitude of northern and southern leaders toward the American West in the early years of the Civil War.

   Topic sentence:

   _____

   _____

   The government in Washington, determined to hold its western domain, was especially concerned with protecting the supply of gold and silver from western mines, which it vitally needed to help finance war against the Southern states. The govern-

---

1 Therese L. Lueck, "One Voice: The Legacy of Women Singers in Popular Music," *America's Musical Pulse,* ed. Kenneth L. Bindas (Westport: Praeger Publishers, 1991), 221. Reprinted with permission of Greenwood Publishing Group, Inc., Westport, CT

ment in Richmond, driven by its own vision of Manifest Destiny, intended by force of arms to acquire territory in the West for the expansion of its institutions, especially slavery; areas that, to the South's bitter aggravation, were denied to it before the war by the federal government. Additionally, the Confederacy aimed to secure a land corridor to the Pacific stretching westward from the Confederate state of Texas across New Mexico and Arizona to California. Finally, it was determined to seize the Union's western silver and gold mines to shore up its pitiful lack of capital to prosecute the South's war for independence.

3. This paragraph discusses the position of the North and the South as the Civil War began.

Topic sentence:

_____

_____

There were more than 20 million people in the northern states . . . but only 9 million in the South, of whom about 3.5 million were slaves the whites hesitated a to trust with arms. The North's economic capacity to wage war was even more preponderant. It was manufacturing nine times as much as the Confederacy (including 97 percent of the nation's firearms) and had a far larger and more efficient railroad system than the South. Northern control of the merchant marine and the navy made possible a blockade of the Confederacy, a particularly potent threat to a region so dependent on foreign markets.

4. The next excerpt is a commentary on the conditions of the South in the months after the end of the Civil War.

Topic sentence:

_____

_____

The real wealth of the South—buildings, railroads, livestock, factories, and roads—had been destroyed during the war. Financial institutions suffered bankruptcy when the Confederate bonds and currency that they were holding turned out to be worthless and when a high proportion of borrowers were obliged to default on loans. The greatest loss, however, was the 265,000 men who might have rebuilt the ravaged section had they not died for the Confederacy.

5. This paragraph considers the Confederate bombardment of Fort Sumter in April, 1861, the act which touched off Civil War.

Topic sentence:

_____

_____

Secession was not an act of war; millions of intelligent men, in the North as well as in the South, believed that secession was founded on a constitutional right. Even the organization of the Confederate government was not a hostile act, for if states secede they will naturally form a new government. But firing on the United States flag was a warlike proceeding, a direct attack, without any ifs and ands about it. A man in the street could understand that as well as Chief Justice Taney. It was like one man slapping another man's face in an argument. The Confederate administration should have waited, regardless of all considerations to the contrary, for the North to fire the first gun, even if they had to wait a lifetime.

6. The following deals with the economy of the South as the war continued.

Topic sentence:

_____

_____

Loans in specie [coined money] were virtually impossible to gather in a country where wealth was traditionally tied up in land and slaves. The Confederacy's luck with taxes was little better. Like other frustrated governments, it began to print paper money. Three years later, in 1864, a Confederate paper dollar was worth, on average, a cent and a half in specie. Prices soared; speculation and hoarding became rampant. Widespread food shortages, made more difficult to fight by the breakdown of transportation, sapped Confederate morale even more than setbacks in the field.

7. This final excerpt provides a discussion of the political impact of the Dred Scott decision (1857) in which the Supreme Court denied Congress the power to exclude slavery from Western territories.

Topic sentence:

_____

_____

The decision made the position of the Republican party (whose _raison d'être_ was opposition to slavery in the territories) constitutionally impossible; it was forced to denounce the Court, strengthening abolitionist sentiment within party ranks. As for the Democratic party—the only national party and the sole institution for compromise—its fate depended on its Northern and Southern factions accepting popular sovereignty. But, as Lincoln put it to Douglas at Freeport, Illinois, if the Constitution and the Supreme Court prohibited both Congress and the territorial legislatures from excluding slavery, by what authority could the settlers themselves do so? Perhaps they could, Senator Douglas responded, by refusing to pass the police legislation necessary to enforce slavery. This refined logic failed to allay Northern misgivings. And, even if the Northern Democrats had accepted popular sovereignty, how could the Southern Democrats be expected to forgo the certain advantages of _Dred Scott_ for the contingency of a popular decision? When they refused at the national convention at Charlestown in 1860, the Democratic party split and hope for compromise faded. . . .

Sources

1. James W. Davidson, William E. Gienapp, Christine L. Heyrman, Mark H. Lytle, Michael B. Stoff, _Nation of Nations,_ vol. I (New York: McGraw-Hill, 1990), 576.

2. Philip Weeks, _Farewell My Nation_ (Wheeling, IL: Harlan Davidson, Inc., 1990), 76.

3. John A. Garraty, _The American Nation_ (New York: HarperCollins, Publishers, 1991), 416–17. Reprinted by permission of HarperCollins Publishers.

4. Arthur S. Link, et al. _A Concise History of the American People,_ vol. I (Arlington Heights, IL: Harlan Davidson, Inc., 1984), 252.

5. W. E. Woodward, _A New American History_ (New York: The Literary Guild, Inc., 1937), 523.

6. Winthrop D. Jordan and Leon F. Litwack, _The United States,_ Brief Edition, 3/E (Englewood Cliffs: Prentice Hall, © 1990), 199. Reproduced by permission of Prentice-Hall, Inc., Upper Saddle River, NJ

7. R. Kent Newmyer, _The Supreme Court Under Marshall and Taney_ (Wheeling, IL: Harlan Davidson, Inc., 1968), 138–39.

Using appropriate linkage words or phrases, insert three words (no more) in the following passage so that it makes more sense.

After 1830 the allegiance of the vast majority of southerners to the slave plantation system deepened measurably, though their attachment to the peculiar institution varied according to class, region, and occupation. The following considerations help to explain why slavery received such overwhelming support in the decades preceding the Civil War. The extremely heavy concentration of slaves in parts of the South generated deep-seated fears. Southern spokesman declared that antislavery northerners had no inkling of what it was like to live in South Carolina or Mississippi communities where blacks far outnumbered whites. It was widely held in the South that blacks would only be harmed by abolition, a belief strengthened by reports about the deteriorating condition of free blacks in the North. Impoverished southern whites ardently supported slavery as a way of preserving what little status they had. When the time came, they fought for slave property and for a slave-owning class.

Source: (slightly modified) Jordan and Litwack, *The United States,* Brief Edition, 3/E, © 1990, 172–73. Reproduced by permission of Prentice-Hall, Inc., Upper Saddle River, NJ

C

The following excerpts have within them a number of linkage forms. Underline those that show a relationship between one sentence and another, or between one paragraph and another.

1. The following passage describes reactions of whites to slave insurrections that occurred from time to time in the South.

   All this unrest among the slaves, especially that evidenced in Gabriel's attempted insurrection, caused a marked lessening of efforts by the whites to abolish chattel servitude. Such efforts had been actively pursued in the years following the Revolution, albeit without tangible results. But after 1800 the trend was the other way, and the Virginia Abolition Society ceased to function, as did all other such societies in the South. Not only so, but Virginia passed a law in 1806 providing that any slave who was freed had to leave the state within twelve months. This law was later modified to permit local courts to give certain manumitted slaves permission to remain, but passage of the harsh statute showed the tenor of the time.

2. This excerpt discusses Republican policies and public reaction to the party's stance on black suffrage during the Reconstruction years.

   It has been argued, however, that the Republicans' intention in doing this was principled, since they actually lost the votes of angry whites when they enfranchised blacks. In fact, all that this observation proves is that the Republicans miscalculated, since the motive behind an action cannot be deduced from its outcome. Moreover,

---

2 The idea for this exercise, and Exercise B in Part II, came from Irvin Y. Hashimoto, *Thirteen Weeks: A Guide to Teaching College Writing* (Portsmouth: Boynton/Cook Publishers, 1991).

the framers of the suffrage amendment were quite aware of the possible negative effect that enfranchising blacks would have on white voters, so they wrote its provisions in highly qualified terms. Therefore, it did not stipulate that suffrage was to be universal but merely that it could not be denied for other reasons, such as illiteracy or lack of property, a loophole that Southerners later exploited in the 1890s. Yet, even with its cautious phrasing, the amendment provoked considerable opposition in the North, and only the appeal to party necessity got it through the legislatures of the Middle Atlantic and Midwestern states. This deep-seated resistance to equal rights meant that federal Reconstruction policy was burdened by an avowed northern hostility to its central premise of black suffrage.

Sources

1. Virginius Dabney, "Gabriel's Insurrection," in Robert James Maddox, *American History,* vol. 1 (Guilford, CT: The Dushkin Publishing Group, Inc., 1981), 143.

2. Michael Perman, *Emancipation and Reconstruction, 1862–1879* (Wheeling, IL: Harlan Davidson, Inc., 1987), 113.

D

Reflect on 1845–1860 + the prospects for women and minorities (pessimistic or optimistic)

An observer of the American scene in 1860, reflecting on the preceding fifteen years (1845–60), might be quite pessimistic or cautiously optimistic about American prospects. Write a conventionally organized paragraph developing either point of view, making sure you support your topic sentence with at least three pieces of evidence. Use your course text(s) for your information.

President John F. Kennedy watches Caroline and John dance in the Oval Office.

MODERN AMERICA, 1960–PRESENT

A *The Topic Sentence*

The first exercise involves application of one of the main themes of this chapter, namely the importance of the topic sentence. The following paragraphs lack a topic sentence. Read each paragraph carefully, then compose a topic sentence for it.

1. The first paragraph deals with traditional America's reaction to the emergence of rock and roll in the 1950s.

   Topic sentence:

   _____

   _____

   In the South, white church groups attacked it as part of an NAACP plot to corrupt the morals of southern youths and foster integration. In Hartford, Connecticut, Dr. Francis J. Braceland described rock and roll as "a communicable disease, with music appealing to adolescent insecurity and driving teenagers to do outlandish things. . . . It's cannibalistic and tribalistic." Particularly between 1954 and 1958, there were numerous crusades to ban rock and roll from the airways.

2. This excerpt comments on John F. Kennedy's relationship to television.

   Topic sentence:

   _____

   _____

   His tall, thin body gave him the strong vertical line that cameras love, and his weatherbeaten good looks appealed to women without intimidating men. He had a full head of hair, and even in winter he maintained a tan. Complementing his appearance was his attitude. He was always "cool" in public. This too was tailor-made for the "cool medium," television. Wit, irony, and understatement, all delivered with a studied nonchalance, translate well on television. Table thumping, impassioned speech, and even earnest sincerity just do not work on television.

3. The next paragraph discusses the 1960s.

   Topic sentence:

   _____

   _____

   In 1967 nearly 27 percent of American marriages were ending in divorce; this reflected a growing instability in family life. Crime and juvenile delinquency were rising steadily; in many cities the streets were unsafe at night. Alcoholism grew at an alarming rate; by 1967 more than 5 million Americans were classed as alcoholics. Mental illness, some of it associated with alcoholism, rose with the growing tensions of modern life. Hospitals and outpatient clinics were clogged with disturbed and worried people. In the 1960s personal experimentation with hallucinatory drugs shocked and dismayed citizens who saw danger in such behavior. Added to these and other matters were the controversies and conflicts over race relations and civil rights.

   Norman Graebner, et al., *A History of the United States*, Vol. II, 1970. Reproduced with permission of The McGraw-Hill Companies.

4. This passage describes President Eisenhower's basic way of conducting his day-to-day management of the presidency. Eisenhower, though often criticized by historians, had learned much in a versatile career.

Topic sentence:

_____

_____

He [Eisenhower] delegated authority, never forgetting Marshall's rule that nothing was more important than the "choice of those to be near you." Drawing on his experience as supreme commander, he reversed the practice of most politicians by creating mechanisms to generate good advice, giving credit to subordinates for accomplishments, and, when possible, personally taking the blame for failures. At cabinet meetings he required that reports be prepared in advance and played devil's advocate to ensure full discussion during their presentation. There were "awful fights in front of him," recalled his son, John, a staff member during the second term, but his method brought results.

5. The following describes the relationship of Vice-President Richard M. Nixon to the Republican party in early 1960.

Topic sentence:

_____

_____

His office had provided him with experience, as well as news coverage, as he attended high-level conferences and embarked on official tours of the Far East, Latin America, and Europe. Perhaps no American had conversed with so many of the world's political and diplomatic leaders. His willingness to carry the campaign burdens in 1954, 1956, and 1958 had won the approval of party managers everywhere. Throughout his years in Eisenhower's shadow, Nixon had performed as an able and active public figure, learning and giving evidence of maturity and judgment. By early 1960 Republican spokesmen agreed that Nixon not only merited the party's nomination but also offered the greatest promise of success at the polls in November. At Chicago in July, Nixon gained the nomination on the first ballot with scarcely an opposing vote.

Norman Graebner, et al., *A History of the United States*, Vol. II, 1970. Reproduced with permission of The McGraw-Hill Companies.

6. In the mid-1950s it had become apparent that the federal highway system was inadequate to the needs of modern society. In 1956 Congress considered and passed an Eisenhower initiative to create an interstate highway system, discussed in the excerpt below.

Topic sentence:

_____

_____

Few individuals at the time would have believed that within twenty years the average American family could drive anywhere in the country on expressways complete with rest stops and information booths, zipping through the largest cities at 65 miles per hour in tunnels or on skyways. Likewise, few businesspeople realized that before too long their products and goods could be shipped anywhere in the nation by semitrailer. The undertaking of the immense project enabled Eisenhower to obtain "greatest direction over economic movements" by holding some highway funds for distribution to states during downturns in the economy.

7. During the mid-1950s, a group of radicals calling themselves the "Beat Generation" emerged to challenge traditional American values, as developed in this excerpt.

Topic sentence:

_____

_____

Beats scorned materialism and traditional family life, religion, sexuality, and politics. They renounced the American Dream. Instead, they valued spontaneity and intuition, searching for truth through Eastern mysticism and drugs. Although whites formed the rank and file of the Beat Generation, they glorified the supposedly "natural" life of black Americans, a life representing (at least for whites) pure instinctual drives. They adopted black music and jive words of the black lexicon. *Cat, sold, chick, Big Apple, square,* were all absorbed into the Beat vocabulary.

Sources

1. James K. Martin, Randy Roberts, et al., *American and Its People* (Glenview: Scott, Foresman and Co., 1988), 907. Reprinted by permission of HarperCollins Publishers.

2. Martin, Roberts, et al., *American and Its People,* 1988, 915. Reprinted by permission of HarperCollins Publishers.

3. Norman A. Graebner, Gilbert C. Fite, Philip L. White, *A History of the United States,* vol. 2 (New York: McGraw-Hill Book Company, 1970), 954.

4. William B. Pickett, *Dwight David Eisenhower and American Power,* (Wheeling, IL Harlan Davidson, Inc., 1995), 195.

5. Graebner, *A History of the United States,* vol. 2, 961.

6. Pickett, *Dwight David Eisenhower and American Power,* 157.

7. Martin, Roberts, et al., *America and Its People,* 1988, 909. Reprinted by permission of HarperCollins Publishers.

B | Linkages

Using appropriate linkage words or phrases insert three words (no more) in the following passage so that its makes more sense.

The election of 1984 was significant in several respects. The Democratic party broke precedent by nominating a woman, Geraldine Ferraro of New York, for vice-president. In the Democratic primaries, moreover, the Reverend Jesse Jackson, a former co-worker of Martin Luther King and a black civil-rights activist, became the first black candidate to win substantial support for the presidential nomination of a major party. Ronald Reagan scored a landslide victory, winning forty-nine states and further fragmenting the old New Deal coalition. Walter Mondale, the Democratic candidate and former senator and vice-president, managed to win only his home state of Minnesota and the District of Columbia. The census of 1980 confirmed the substantial movement of Americans from the Northeast to the Sunbelt states of the South and West, where suspicion of federal power and conservative political principles had long been entrenched; those regions gave Reagan his most substantial majorities.

Source: (slightly modified) Jordan and Litwack, *The United States,* Brief Edition, 3/E, © 1990, 497. Reproduced by permission of Prentice-Hall, Inc., Upper Saddle River, NJ

C

The following excerpts have within them a number of transitional devices. Underline those that show a relationship between one sentence and another, or between one paragraph and another.

1. The first excerpt deals with President Lyndon Johnson's attitudes toward the Vietnam War.

Yet to say Johnson had little experience in foreign affairs is not to suggest that he did not have strong opinions on the subject. Like most politicians of the period, Johnson was an unquestioning Cold Warrior. In addition, along with accepting the domino theory and a monolithic view of communism, Johnson cherished a traditionally southern notion of honor and masculinity. It was his duty, he maintained, to honor commitments made by earlier presidents. . . .

Furthermore, Johnson believed that any retreat from Vietnam would destroy him politically. Soon after becoming president, he told America's ambassador to Vietnam, "I am not going to be the President who saw Southeast Asia go the way China went." No, he would not "lose" Vietnam and allow Republican critics to attack him as they had Truman. . . .

Before winning in Vietnam, however, he had to win in the United States. The presidential election in 1964 was his top priority. . . .

2. This passage discusses President John F. Kennedy's domestic program in the early 1960s.

Kennedy thus sought, with skill and success, to ensure his expansionist [economic] policies against inflationary aftereffects. At the same time, he recognized that general fiscal stimulus, while it would increase aggregate output and employment, would not reach into pockets of localized and "structural" poverty. Income tax reduction, for example, was of limited help for people too poor to pay income taxes. The plight of the demoralized and inarticulate poor greatly concerned him. He had seen them in the black valleys of West Virginia when he campaigned for the Democratic nomination in 1960. He began to attack the "culture of poverty" with the Area Redevelopment Act of 1961 and the Appalachia program. . . .

In economic management, Kennedy was a most effective President. But his ambition for larger social programs—Medicare, federal aid to education and to the cities, civil rights—was frustrated by his parliamentary situation. For he had been elected President in 1960 with a slim margin of 120,000 in the popular vote. . . . Like every Democratic President since Roosevelt after 1938, he faced a House controlled by a conservative coalition made up of Republicans and Southern Democrats. . . .

Sources

1. Martin, Roberts, et al., *America and Its People,* 1988, 924. Reprinted by permission of HarperCollins Publishers.
2. Arthur M. Schlesinger, Jr., "What the Thousand Days Wrought," *American History,* vol. 2, ed. Robert J. Maddox (Guilford: The Dushkin Publishing Group, Inc., 1985), 193.

D

An observer of the American scene in early 1970, reflecting on the preceding ten years (1960–70), might be quite pessimistic or cautiously optimistic about American prospects. Write a conventionally organized paragraph developing either point of view, making sure you support your topic sentence with at least three pieces of evidence. Use your course text(s) for your information.

STRUCTURED WRITING: PARAGRAPH STRATEGIES 10

"A page of history is worth a volume of logic."
OLIVER WENDALL HOLMES

"Writing history is a perpetual exercise in judgment."
CUSHING STROUT

Some historians say that history is essentially the lengthened shadow of great individuals. If so, to understand the twentieth century one has to read a lot of biographies. Joseph Stalin's Russia was his version of a society on its way to a communist Utopia; Adolf Hitler's Germany made a battlefield of an entire continent in the early 1940s; and the England that Winston Churchill inspired survived the darkest days of World War II. In America there have been any number of major figures in this century: Theodore Roosevelt, who initiated new forms of federal activism; his cousin, Franklin D. Roosevelt, who fathered the New Deal; John F. Kennedy, a symbol of a new generation of Americans; and Lyndon B. Johnson, the man at the center of major social, political, and international changes of the 1960s.

Johnson, or LBJ, came to the Oval Office with a very clear model in mind. He sought to be a new age Franklin D. Roosevelt, the political hero of his youth. He was a conciliator, as FDR had been. Rarely letting ideology interfere with getting something done, he was a pragmatist and practiced one-on-one politics in the Roosevelt manner. He used a "brain trust" collected from eastern universities, as had Roosevelt. His program, dubbed the "Great Society," was reminiscent of Roosevelt's New Deal of the 1930s.

LBJ did what all of us quite naturally do—use models as a basic resource to guide our actions. Everyone has role models, heroes who are wor-

thy of imitation. Every cook follows a recipe to balance food ingredients in the right way. Every construction foreman uses a blueprint, a small scale model of the building-to-be. There are other high-powered words for this, such as paradigm or prototype, but they all mean the same thing: a model used to select the right way of proceeding. It should be no surprise that writing good paragraphs can be made easier by using model forms. More about this shortly.

In their book *Beat Not the Poor Desk*[1], writing instructors Marie Ponsot and Rosemary Deen recommend an efficient way of getting started on a writing project once you have collected your information: use paragraph models to release, or stimulate, thought. Such models are widely used by professional writers and can be very helpful to less experienced writers. They provide a frame within which information can be comfortably organized.

In an earlier chapter we described critical thinking as the willingness to evaluate propositions in the light of evidence and from that evaluation, form a clear, well-based opinion. This is what your instructors expect of you. In examinations and papers teachers aren't looking for a simple summary of events or a parroting of textbooks views. They want you to *evaluate, analyze, compare,* and *contrast.* They want you to articulate your position in a well-reasoned fashion, backed up with solid evidence. To do

---

1 Marie Ponsot and Rosemary Deen, *Beat Not the Poor Desk* (Portsmouth: Boynton-Cook Publishers, Inc., 1982).

this, you have to write organized expository paragraphs that advance a claim and support it with clear and convincing evidence—i.e., a proof structure (see Chapter 9). And here is where some simple models might be helpful. They provide strategies for organizing your ideas.

Of the variety of models that may be used the *comparison paragraph* is one of the best. It provides an excellent short essay format. Typical of this model is the relationship (and development) implied by the construction: "Although . . . , nevertheless. . . ." For instance, note the example below:

> *Although* the South had certain advantages as the Civil War began, *nevertheless* it was decidedly the underdog in warmaking potential. The South did have superior military commanders, many of them having had experience in the Mexican War. It had the moral advantage of fighting on its own soil against an invader, as well as the further edge of fighting a defensive war, which usually requires much less manpower. Nevertheless, it faced an enemy with enormous assets. The North had industries to supply massive firepower, as well as the financial resources to afford it. The North had a navy capable of throwing a blockade around all major southern ports. It had a railway transportation system of considerable efficiency. Northern population outnumbered the South by more than two to one. Its own advantages notwithstanding, the South faced a formidable enemy as the war began.

Note several things about this sample paragraph. It provides a format in which to present what you know. It is not a substitute for knowledge, but a way to categorize the information you possess. Further, the comparison model covers both sides of an issue. It shows that the writer is aware of the complexity of the issue (in this case, warmaking potential) and managed to simplify those complexities into opposing lists and to develop a critical evaluation. For this reason, the comparison model is an excellent framework to use in answering essay questions. It tells the reader (i. e. the professor) that you have achieved a certain sophistication in your thinking.

Another model that can be used to structure thought is the *generalization/list paragraph*. The generalization is presented as the paragraph topic sentence followed by a sequence listing the factors or elements composing the whole. Each item of the sequence is preceded by an adverb such as "first," "second," "third," "finally," or

any terminology that indicates the elements of a sequence. (Sometimes this numeration is implicit.) The following textbook paragraph discussing mid-nineteenth century industrial development is illustrative:

> Yet industry in the 1850s had certain characteristics indicating the United States was still in the early stages of the Industrial Revolution. *First*, most of the manufacturing involved the processing of the products of American farms and forests. In 1860 the leading industry was the milling of flour and meal, whose value was about one-eighth of the total value of manufac-

> tures. Other important industries included lumber-milling, distilling, brewing, leather-tanning, and meat-packing. A *second indication* of industrial immaturity was the smallness of the typical manufacturing enterprises; on the average they employed fewer than ten workers and had a capital value of less than $7,500. *Finally*, as we have seen, the United States was still a large consumer of foreign manufactured goods and primarily an exporter of agricultural products.[2] (Italics added by authors.)

Note how well the reader is "tipped off" to each new aspect as it appears. Also, each element could be separated to form a paragraph of its own. In general, this format is most often

---

2 John M. Blum, Bruce Catton, Edmund S. Morgan, Arthur M. Schlesinger, Jr., Kenneth M. Stampp, C. Vann Woodward, *The National Experience*, 2nd. ed. (New York: Harcourt, Brace and World, 1968), 314.

used when discussing a situation having several influences or elements.

The third model, the *coordinate paragraph,* is a particularly effective framework for expressing an opinion. A coordinate paragraph is simply one in which, after a clearly phrased topic sentence, the writer supplies two or more supporting elements that confirm the truth of that topic sentence. Each of the supporting elements is called a coordinate; a paragraph with a single supporting element would be an ordinate paragraph.

As an example consider the following paragraph from Garry Wills' award-winning account of the genesis of Abraham Lincoln's Gettysburg Address:[3]

> Some think, to this day, that Lincoln did not really have *arguments* for union, just a kind of mystical attachment to it. That was the charge of Southerners, who felt they had a better constitutional case for secession than he had for compelling states to remain. Alexander Stephens, who had served as vice-president of the Confederacy, was an influential formulator of the view that Lincoln's attitude was not reachable by mundane arguments: "The Union with him, in sentiment, rose to the sublimity of a religious mysticism." But even Northerners like Whitman felt that "the only thing like passion or infatuation in the man [Lincoln] was the passion for the Union of these states." Edmund Wilson was following a long tradition when he called his Lincoln essay (later included in his book on the Civil War) "The Union as Religious Mysticism."

Notice how Wills begins with the generalization that, over the years, many have thought Lincoln's attachment to the union was based more on emotion than reason. Wills then proceeds to provide three pieces of evidence in support of that claim: the opinions of contemporaries Alexander Stephens and Walt Whitman, and the judgment of twentieth-century scholar Edmund Wilson. For all his examples Wills underscores his point by quoting the actual words of the representative figures, backed up with appropriate source citations. (To be fair we should mention that Wills goes on to challenge this traditional view by arguing that Lincoln did indeed have reasoned arguments, in addition to sentiments, in favor of union.) This is the sort of writing—opinions, backed up by solid evidence—that we most want to encourage. Remember, "evidence" is anything you need to include in your paragraph that makes your point "evident" to your intended reader.

EXERCISES

I   CIVIL WAR AND RECONSTRUCTION, 1850–1877

A

History involves argument. Historians must make reasoned arguments—the presentation of a thesis along with the reasons that support it. Effective writing is essentially a matter of writing a thesis as the topic sentence of a paragraph, and providing supporting evidence for that conclusion in the remainder of the paragraph.

The following excerpts each present a topic sentence generalization along with specific supporting reasons or subpoints. In some cases a subpoint is followed by further detail before the next subpoint is addressed. Your task is to analyze the paragraph and, in the parenthesis preceding each sentence, assign a number (1, 2, 3, etc.) to each subpoint; use a "d" for those sentences that provide detail for a subpoint; and use an "s" for a sentence that appears to summarize the paragraph contents. In all cases the first sentence is the topic sentence. We have completed the first excerpt as an illustration.

1. This passage deals with southern advantages as the Civil War began.

---

3 Garry Wills, *Lincoln at Gettysburg: The Words that Remade America* (New York: Touchstone, 1992), 125.

Other considerations favored the Confederacy. (1) One was the South's superior officers. (d) For twenty years before Lincoln's inauguration, southern officers dominated the United States army. (2) Another source of southern confidence was cotton. (d) Secession leaders expected to exchange that staple for the foreign manufactured goods they needed, without having to sacrifice fighting men to factory work. (3)Probably the South's most important advantage was that it had to defend only relatively short interior lines against invaders who had to deal with long lines of communication and attack on a broad front. (d) The Confederacy had no need to divert fighting men to tasks such as garrisoning captured cities and holding conquered territory.

2. This passage provides a summary of executive branch actions implementing "reconstruction" of the South in the late 1860s and early 1870s.

Presidential action took several forms. ( )The first was political. ( )Grant intervened in Virginia and Mississippi in 1869 to have Confederate disfranchisement removed from the new constitutions. ( )That same year, he helped rescue the Republican government in Georgia by commencing Reconstruction anew, only to withdraw when Governor Bullock wanted to prolong the state's reliance on Washington. ( )Then, in the 1872 elections, he sided unequivocally with the regular party in the South in its campaign against the dissident Liberal Republicans, a stance which of course aided his own reelection prospects. ( )Another kind of involvement was military. ( )Sometimes he sent troops to put down disorder, as in North Carolina's armed struggle with the Klan in 1870. ( )At other times, federal forces were dispatched to restore calm when violence threatened to erupt over a contest for control of a legislative body, such as occurred in Alabama after its disputed election of 1872. ( )A third type of intervention was undertaken to supervise federal elections and thereby enforce the Fifteenth Amendment, which provided for universal suffrage.

3. This paragraph provides a commentary on Lincoln's Emancipation Proclamation, issued in September, 1862, to become effective on January 1, 1863, freeing slaves in Confederate territory.

Thus in many ways the Proclamation affected the course of the war as well as Lincoln's way of thinking about the problem of blacks in the United States. ( )Abroad, it rallied large numbers of people to the North's side and became a valuable instrument of American foreign policy. ( )At home it sharpened the issues of the war and provided a moral and humanitarian ingredient that had been lacking. ( )It fired the leaders with a new purpose and gave to the President a new weapon. ( )Small wonder that he no longer promoted the idea of colonization. ( )Small wonder that he began to advocate education and the franchise for blacks. ( )They were a new source of strength that deserved to be treated as the loyal citizens that they were.

4. This passage also discusses the Emancipation Proclamation.

Nevertheless, both by what it said and what it did not say, the Proclamation greatly contributed to the significant shift in 1863 in the way the war was regarded. ( )It recognized the right of emancipated slaves to defend their freedom. ( )The precise language was that they should "abstain from all violence, unless in necessary self-defense." ( )It also provided that former slaves could now be received into the armed services. ( )While it was clear that they were to fight to save the Union, the fact remained that since their own fate was tied to that of the Union, they would also be fighting for their own freedom. ( )The black who, in December 1862, could salute his own colonel instead of blacking the boots of a Confederate colonel, as he had been doing a year earlier, had a stake in the war that was not difficult to define. ( )However loyal to the Union the black troops were—and they numbered some 190,000 by April 1865—one is inclined to believe that they were fighting primarily for freedom for themselves and their brothers in the months that followed the issuance of the Emancipation Proclamation.

5. This paragraph deals with the new legal and constitutional situation brought about by the "Reconstruction Amendments," particularly the Fourteenth Amendment.

   All of this momentously affected the way the Constitution operated. (   )For one thing, here were significant new stretch-points in the Constitution's wording—depending on what the courts wished to make of them. (   )For another, here was a whole new grant of authority to the federal government. (   )For, it was the federal government which had to enforce the new protections on behalf of citizens. (   )As originally designed, the Constitution did not contemplate a direct relationship between citizens and the federal government. (   )It was the states that governed the lives of individuals; the federal government did general things like coin money and provide defense. (   )Now the individual could turn to the federal government if the state violated his rights.

6. This paragraph gives some idea of the political impact of the Civil War on the American system.

   Fought to preserve the Constitution, the war in fact laid siege to it. (   )The magnitude and unprecedented nature of that crisis called forth a flood of decisions that went beyond the regular channels of constitutional law and swept over the classic constitutional barriers against governmental abuse of power. (   )An effective two-party system faded into Republican dominance, though it remained theoretically alive. (   )Separation of powers gave way, in fact if not theory, as wartime decision-making shifted to the President. (   )The delicate balance between state and federal powers which the Court had labored to establish was permanently disrupted as the federal government consolidated the duties—military, financial, and administrative—which the states could not perform. (   )The necessities of war took priority over individual freedom and private property. (   )Order and the rule of law grappled feebly with chaos and expediency.

7. This excerpt examines a variety of interpretations of the causes of the Civil War.

   Ever since 1861, writers have disputed what caused the Civil War and whether it was an "irrepressible conflict" in the sense of being inevitable. (   )Southerners have argued that the war was fought not over slavery but over the question of states' rights; . . . . (   )Economic determinists have contended that the Northern public never would support the abolitionists on any direct question (which is certainly true), . . . and that the conflict was really between an industrial interest which wanted one kind of future for America and an agrarian interest which wanted another. (   )Other historians, going a step beyond this, have pictured the North and the South as two "diverse civilizations," so dissimilar in their culture and their values that union between them was artificial and unnatural. (   )In recent years another group of writers, known as revisionists, have emphasized the idea that Northerners and Southerners had formed distorted and false concepts of each other and that they went to war against those images rather than against the people they were really fighting. (   )The war, they would argue, grew out of emotions, not out of realities.

Sources:

1. Winthrop D. Jordan and Leon F. Litwack, *The United States,* Brief Edition, 3/E (Englewood Cliffs: Prentice Hall, © 1990), 190. Reproduced by permission of Prentice-Hall, Inc., Upper Saddle River, NJ

2. Michael Perman, *Emancipation and Reconstruction, 1862–1879* (Wheeling, IL: Harlan Davidson, Inc.,1987), 108–09.

3. John Hope Franklin, *The Emancipation Proclamation* (Wheeling, IL: Harlan Davidson, Inc., 1995), 126–27.

4. Franklin, *Emancipation Proclamation,* 113–14.

5. Excerpted from *America: A Study in Heritage* by Frank W. Fox and Clayne L. Pope. Copyright 1993 by Kendall / Hunt Publishing Company. Used with permission.

6. R. Kent Newmyer, *The Supreme Court Under Marshall and Taney* (Wheeling, IL: Harlan Davidson, Inc., 1968), 143–44.

7. Louis B. Wright, et al., *The Democratic Experience* (Chicago: Scott, Foresman and Co., 1963), 197. Reprinted by permission of HarperCollins Publishers.

This exercise again focuses on paragraph organization but in a somewhat different way. What follows are two scrambled paragraphs. Your task is to unscramble them, using a "1" for the topic sentence, and numbering the rest from "2" on in the order that makes the most sense.

1. The first passage deals with the Russian view of the Emancipation Proclamation of 1863.

_____ The Russian ruler was at a loss, he said, "to understand how you Americans could have been so blind as to leave the Negro slave without tools to work out his salvation."

_____ Perhaps their general reaction was reflected in the editorial comment by the St. Petersburg *Vedomosti,* which found the Proclamation important "regardless of the motivations or necessity, therefore, a great benevolent deed."

_____ Several years later he told his American friend, Wharton Barker, that he did more for the Russian "in giving him the land as well as personal liberty, than America did for the Negro slave set free by the Proclamation of President Lincoln."

_____ This statement, made in 1879, reflected the benefit of both wisdom in general and knowledge of the years of reconstruction in particular.

_____ The Russians, having so recently emancipated their own serfs, were particularly interested in the emancipation policy in the United States.

_____ The Czar was a bit more reserved in his praise.

2. This excerpt examines the attitudes of the South and the North towards the expansion of slavery into the western territories, all of them in the process of waiting to become states.

_____ And, since the North also possessed a numerical, political, and economical preponderance, it was not inclined to temper its demand.

_____ The South considered the right to extend slavery basic to its future existence.

_____ Here, then was the explosive political issue which the Supreme Court boldly undertook to solve in 1857.

_____ But the North was not in an obliging mood.

_____ The fugitive slave problem aroused bitter sectional feeling, but it was the question of slavery in the territories that fully—and fatally as it turned out—joined the issue between the North and the South.

_____ The admission of new slave states would also bolster the declining political strength of the South, especially in the Senate.

_____ Convinced that slavery and free labor were incompatible and that it had a moral duty to make the nation over in its own image, the North insisted the new territories should be free.

_____ And Southern honor demanded the right as a reward for its services to the Union and as an indication of the good intentions of the North.

_____ The constant acquisition of new land was an economic imperative for the slave economy, the *sine qua non* of southern agrarian capitalism.

Sources:

1. Franklin, *Emancipation Proclamation,* 111.
2. Newmyer, *Supreme Court,* 127.

The following passage describes with sharp detail the famous (or infamous) march of General William T. Sherman's army through Georgia in 1864. Using the *comparison* "although-nevertheless" model, write a fully developed paragraph expressing your opinion in the matter of Union military necessity vs. humane conduct in regard to the advancing Northern army. In other words your topic sentence might be something along the lines of either (1) Although Sherman's march was dictated by the necessities of war, nevertheless it was carried out in an unnecessarily harsh and cruel manner, or (2) Although Southern civilians along the line of Sherman's march suffered greatly, nevertheless the march was a prudent and necessary military operation.

The army as it proceeded, having little or no fighting to do, devoted itself to organized plunder. A Georgia news-writer pictured the scene as follows:

Dead horses, cows, sheep, hogs, chickens, corn, wheat, cotton, books, paper, broken vehicles, coffee-mills, and fragments of nearly every species of property that adorned the beautiful farms of this county, strew the wayside, monuments of the meanness, rapacity, and hypocrisy of the people who boast that they are not robbers and do not interfere with private property. . . .

The Yankees entered the house of my next door neighbor, an old man of over three score years, and tore up his wife's clothes and bedding, trampling her bonnet on the floor, and robbing the house and pantry of nearly everything of value.

The business of destroying material susceptible of warlike use was done with the thoroughness of an expert. In destroying a railroad, for instance, the rails were loosened from the ties; the ties were placed in piles with the rails on top; the piles were set on fire; and the heated rails were bent and twisted with specially constructed hooks till they were beyond hope of restoration except by re-rolling. Bridges were destroyed, cars burned, driving wheels and trucks broken and cast into deep water, connecting rods bent and hidden away. . . .

Public buildings were often destroyed; foodstores were taken; horses, mules, and livestock were removed. Importance was attached to the removal of horses; for such supplies as were left were useless for military purposes if they could not be hauled. Special details were sent out to "forage," the men selected for the purpose being significantly called "bummers." Along with the systematic business of foraging there was a shocking amount of downright plunder and vandalism. Dwellings were needlessly burned; family plate was seized; wine cellars were raided; property that could not be carted away was wantonly ruined. It was a sorry chapter of the war, made worse than Sherman's intentions; for the army was in harum-scarum spirit and, being recruited in part by conscription, it included Northern riff-raff, drifters, vagabonds, and even criminals. . . .

Sherman's name became a by-word in the South. Though told that Yankees were brutes and barbarians, many Southerners had discounted such stories as Confederate propaganda. But when Sherman came though, the deeds of his "bummers" made it seem that the Yankees were trying to justify their unsavory reputation. The elaborate story as to irregular methods of warfare (on both sides) during the Civil war cannot be sketched here; nor is this the place for rationalization concerning the use of such methods as distinguished from battles and sieges. If the war was ever to end otherwise than by a draw, if it was to be terminated by a military decision, its final aspects would unavoidably present to the invaded area an intolerable cup of bitterness. The dragon's teeth had been sown in years past; the war had been raging for three and a half years; and by the autumn of 1864 it was believed by both governments that it could not be ended by the attainment of any partial objective or the acceptance of any compromise. Indeed, once the appeal to arms had been made, the motive of winning, and winning completely, became the dominant purpose on both sides; and such was the grim nature of American resolution North and South that the wretched struggle had to go on from slaughter to slaughter until one side or the other was down and out. To fight to the end and die in the last ditch might make even defeat honorable; but to quit while there still remained a shaky line of ragged troops would seem a dishonor. . . . The factors being as they were in 1864, such a peace seemed impossible for the North and South. Under these circumstances, on the eve of his "march to the sea" Sherman wrote:

. . . I propose to act in such manner against the material resources of the south as utterly to negative Davis's boasted threat and promises of protection. If we can march a well-appointed army right through his territory, it is a demonstration to the world—foreign and domestic—that we have a power which Davis cannot resist. This may not be war . . . ; nevertheless, it is overwhelming to my mind that there are thousands of people abroad and in the south who will reason thus: If the north can march an army right through the south, it is proof positive that the north can prevail in this contest, leaving only open the question of its willingness to use that power. . . .

It cannot be denied that Sherman's march was marred by unjustifiable excess; yet his campaign, being directed against property and Southern resources, was conceived as a substitute for further human slaughter. That it did in fact contribute materially toward ending the war is the general opinion of authorities. Sherman was in the South with the sorry job of helping to conquer the South. To gallant Southerners, animated by pride of country and praying for success to Confederate arms, that was, after all, the most detestable thing about him. Furthermore, the fact that he was operating, not against substantial armies but against Southern morale and upon the people, made his presence particularly offensive. Beyond the attainment of a military decision, however, Sherman had no desire to persecute the South, nor to promote a hateful policy of reconstruction.

Reprinted with permission from *The Civil War and Reconstruction,* 2/e by J. G. Randall and David H. Donald, copyright © 1969 by D. C. Heath and Company.

D

Using the excerpt above as a basis, write a *coordinate* paragraph expressing your opinion as to whether or not Sherman's march to the sea, as conducted, was necessary. In writing your paragraph be sure to begin with a clearly phrased topic sentence, followed by at least two subpoints justifying your opinion. Your paragraph should be in the neighborhood of six to seven sentences.

II MODERN AMERICA, 1960–PRESENT

A

History involves argument. Historians must make reasoned arguments—the presentation of a thesis along with the reasons that support it. Effective writing is essentially a matter of writing a thesis as the topic sentence of a paragraph, and providing supporting evidence for that conclusion in the remainder of the paragraph.

The following excerpts each present a topic sentence generalization along with specific supporting reasons or subpoints. In some cases a subpoint is followed by further detail before the next subpoint is addressed. Your task is to analyze the paragraph and, in the parenthesis preceding each sentence, assign a number (1, 2, 3, etc.) to each subpoint; use a "d" for those sentences that provide detail for a subpoint; and use an "s" for a sentence that appears to summarize the paragraph contents. In all cases the first sentence is the topic sentence. We have completed the first excerpt as an illustration.

1. The first paragraph discusses the Vietnam war opposition that emerged within the Lyndon Johnson administration during the 1960s.

   Yet opposition to the war continued to grow and even appeared within the administration itself. (1)Undersecretary of State George Ball, who had questioned American policies in Vietnam, quietly left the administration. (2)Johnson's press secretary, whom the President regarded almost as a son, also resigned over Vietnam. (3)National Security Advisor McGeorge Bundy, one of the major planners of the war, came to have doubts and quit the administration to take a job with the Ford Foundation. (4)The most significant policy maker to have second thoughts was Secretary of Defense Robert McNamara. (d)Returning from a trip to Vietnam in October 1966, McNamara began to question optimistic predictions of U.S. military officials. (d)He assigned a special assistant in the Defense Department, Daniel Ellsberg, to compile a thorough historical study of American involvement in Vietnam. (d)Ellsberg, who already had some reservations about the war, uncovered classified documents, recording a long history of deception and deceit . . . .

2. This excerpt describes the political background to John F. Kennedy's presidential victory in 1960.

   New sources of Democratic strength also contributed to Republican setbacks. (   )The Democrats became more competitive at the state and local levels through a kind of delayed realignment, which political scientist James L. Sundquist has called "aftershocks of the New Deal earthquake." (   )A new and more attractive Democratic leadership began to emerge in such states as North Dakota, Minnesota, Wisconsin, Iowa, Michigan, Pennsylvania, Vermont, Maine, California, and Oregon, a leadership that was active and liberal and had a program. (   )Another reason for Democratic vitality was the revival of liberalism in the second half of the 1950s. (   )Follow-

Marines in the streets of Hue, Vietnam, 1968

ing the election of 1956, Paul Butler, the Democratic national chairman, helped form an advisory council in order to give the party a more liberal and progressive program than that provided by congressional leaders between presidential campaigns. ( )This body reflected the new Democratic liberalism, which gave special attention to civil liberties, civil rights, and the need for greater economic growth. ( )A liberal program began to take shape, as it had in 1948 and 1949, and it embodied national solutions to such problems as education, health care, and economic development.

3. The following paragraph provides a comparison of the foreign policies of John F. Kennedy in the 1960s with those of Ronald Reagan twenty years later.

Historical analogies always are imperfect, but it seems fair to say that Reagan's rhetoric and policy toward the USSR and its allies during his first term (Jan. 1981–Jan. 1985) bore considerable resemblance to the approach of one of Reagan's favorite presidents, John F. Kennedy. ( )Like Kennedy, Reagan and his advisers saw Russia as an obvious and immediate threat to world peace and stability, and they viewed Soviet expansion in the Third World with particular alarm. ( )Reagan, too, harbored a deep-seated hatred of Castro's Cuba and of revolutionaries in Latin America with ties to Castro. ( )Both presidents sponsored a major buildup of U.S. military power that eased public and Congressional concerns about American "weakness." ( )And both, after acting and talking tough during their first years in office, moved toward a more conciliatory relationship with Russia that—perhaps partly because of the presidents' earlier toughness—gained widespread public support.

4. This paragraph goes back to the World War II years, a time when women were entering the blue collar work force in large numbers.

For all of the excitement, there was frequent frustration as well. ( )Women constantly faced [a] . . . cold welcome . . . —particularly in jobs formerly held only by men—and simply had to wait for attitudes to change. ( )Women also chafed under restrictions imposed by managers who were concerned about the mixing of the sexes in their plants. ( )General Motors fired any male supervisor and female employee found "fraternizing." ( )The company argued that questionable conduct by either party could hurt labor-management relations and compromise the policy of hiring women. ( )Unions too imposed restrictions on women. Flint Local 599 of the United Automobile Workers voted that committeemen should ignore the grievances of any women "indecent in her wearing apparel or actions."

5. This passage provides a commentary on the evangelical movement of the late 1970s; "evangelical" refers to Christians who emphasize the importance of being "born anew" to the requirements of the Christian gospel.

George Gallup, Jr. termed 1976 "the year of the evangelical," and the late 1970s and early 1980s saw a burgeoning of the movement. ( )Books by evangelical authors became best sellers. ( )Billy Graham's *How To Be Born Again* (1977) had an initial printing of eight hundred thousand copies, ... ( )Widely sold in supermarkets and drugstores, evangelical books became so successful that, as one critic noted, "customers could find books on Christian weight loss and Christian money management." ( )In many large cities, there were "Christian Yellow Pages," directories that would only sell space to an advertiser who "accepts Jesus Christ as . . . personal Lord and Savior and acknowledges Jesus as the Son of God." ( )One million school children were soon attending five thousand elementary and high schools where subjects were taught from an evangelical perspective. ( )In Christian night clubs patrons could order grape juice cocktails and listen to gospel songs. ( )By 1978 there were 1300 radio stations . . . that were Christian owned and operated, and one new such station was being added every week.

6. The long Vietnam War finally ended in January, 1973, with the United States getting none the best of the cease-fire agreement.

President Nixon hailed the face-saving cease-fire agreements as "peace with honor," but the boast rang hollow. ( )The United States was to withdraw its remaining 27,000 or so troops and could reclaim some 560 American prisoners of war. ( )The government of South Vietnam would be permitted to continue receiving limited American support but no more American fighting forces. ( )An election was eventually to be held to determine the future of the country. ( )The North Vietnamese were allowed to keep some 145,000 troops in South Vietnam where they could be used to spearhead a powerful new offensive when the time seemed ripe. ( )Ominously, the North Vietnamese still occupied about 30 percent of South Vietnam. ( )To many observers, the shaky "peace" seemed little more than a thinly disguised American retreat.

7. The final passage deals with Russian motivations for the beginnings of U.S.-Russian détente in 1963. The first sentence refers to Nikita Khrushchev, Russian leader at the time.

Khrushchev, for his part, was eager to improve relations with the West at a time of intense Sino[Chinese]-Soviet hostility. ( )The Russians needed a positive achievement to balance the humiliation in Cuba [the Cuban missile crisis] the previous fall, and they also needed concrete agreements with the West to demonstrate to other communist parties that their policy of peaceful coexistence was more beneficial than Beijing's outspoken insistence on hostility toward the capitalist nations. ( )Far behind the West in nuclear missiles and bombers, the Russians needed time to move toward equality in strategic weapons before risking another confrontation with the United States. ( )As Soviet Deputy Foreign Minister Vassily Kuznetsov bitterly warned U.S. diplomat John McCloy shortly after the missile crisis, "You Americans will never be able to do this to us again." ( )Most important, the Russians needed agreements with the West in order to ensure that they would be able to meet the challenge from their populous enemy in the East. ( )Indeed, negotiations in Moscow between Russia and China broke off—without any progress toward resolving outstanding issues—on July 21, just four days before Soviet, British, and U.S. negotiators completed the test ban treaty.

Sources:

1. Douglas T. Miller, *Visions of America* (St. Paul: West Publishing Company, 1988), 210. Reprinted by permission of West Publishing Co.

2. Dewey W. Grantham, *Recent America* (Wheeling, IL: Harlan Davidson, Inc., 1987), 98.

3. Ralph B. Levering, *The Cold War: A Post–Cold War History* (Wheeling, IL: Harlan Davidson, Inc., 1994), 166.

4. Allan M. Winkler, *Home Front U.S.A.* (Wheeling, IL: Harlan Davidson, Inc., 1986), 54.

5. Walter LaFeber, Richard Polenberg, Nancy Woloch, *The American Century* (New York: Alfred A. Knopf / Random House, 1986), 529.

6. Reprinted with permission from *The American Pageant,* 10/e by Thomas A. Bailey and David M. Kennedy. Copyright © 1994 by D.C. Heath and Company.

7. Levering, *The Cold War,* 103.

B

This exercise again focuses on paragraph organization but in a somewhat different way. What follows are two scrambled paragraphs. Your task is to unscramble them, using a "1" for the topic sentence, and numbering the rest from "2" on in the order that makes the most sense.

1. This excerpt discusses the China policy of President Richard Nixon and Secretary of State Henry Kissinger in 1971.

_____ But most Americans were as pleased as they were surprised by Nixon's announcement.

_____ Others complained that Chiang Kai-Shek [in Taiwan] was being abandoned—indeed, the General Assembly of the United Nations voted three months later to seat Mao Tse-Tung's regime [the People's Republic].

_____ Nixon began it in July by announcing that he would visit the People's Republic of China early in 1972.

_____ Kissinger's efforts for détente with the great powers were apparently paying off.

_____ Critics grumbled that the proposed trip was a public relations stunt.

_____ Still others pointed out that Red China, which felt threatened by the Soviet Union, was simply using the United States, and that the visit would poison American relations with Japan, the most highly industrialized nation in Asia.

_____ In mid-1971 the administration began a turnabout that dramatically improved its fortunes.

_____ The Cold War was thawing at last.

2. This passage deals with the emergence of political rivals to President Lyndon B. Johnson early in the election year of 1968.

_____ On March 12, 1968, their efforts gave McCarthy an incredible 42 percent of the Democratic votes and twenty of the twenty-four convention delegates.

_____ The charismatic Kennedy, heir to his fallen brother's mantle of leadership, stirred a passionate response among workers, blacks, Hispanics, and young people.

_____ Going "clean for Gene," with shaven faces and shortened locks, these idealistic recruits of the "Children's Crusade" invaded the key presidential primary state of New Hampshire to ring doorbells.

_____ Four days later Senator Robert F. Kennedy of New York, the murdered president's younger brother and by now himself a "dove" on Vietnam, threw his hat into the ring.

_____ The president meanwhile was being sharply challenged from within his own party.

_____ President Johnson was on the same ballot, but only as a write-in candidate.

_____ The soft-spoken McCarthy, a sometime poet and devout Catholic, gathered a small army of antiwar college students as campaign workers.

_____ Eugene McCarthy, a little-known Democratic senator from Minnesota, had emerged as a contender for the 1968 Democratic presidential nomination.

Sources:

1. James T. Patterson, _America in the Twentieth Century_ (New York: Harcourt Brace Jovanovich, Inc., 1976), 500.
2. Bailey and Kennedy, _The American Pageant_, 936.

C

The passage below explores the many-faceted role the automobile has played in America over the past seventy-five years. Using the _comparison_ "although-nevertheless" model, write a fully developed paragraph (five to seven sentences) expressing your opinion as to whether, on balance, the automobile has made life in America better or worse.

Nothing made the Good Life better—or worse—than the automobile did. To the Consumer Society it provided everything that Aladdin got out of his magic carpet and a lot of what he got out of his magic lamp—including trouble.

In the beginning, motorcars were regarded as curiosities —playthings for the wealthy. But when Henry Ford made them both cheap and dependable, they quickly transformed society. The car changed the house by adding a garage. It changed the city by multiplying its streets and causing them to be paved. It changed rural living by bringing urban stores and amusements to within driving distance. It changed the concept of travel with inexpensive motels and drive-in restaurants. It fashioned new entertainment in the Sunday-afternoon drive and the Saturday-night cruise. It revolutionized social mores by introducing short skirts for female drivers, drive-in movies, and the pastime of "parking." It consolidated education by means of school buses, streamlined the postal service with rural free delivery, and souped up law enforcement with the high-speed chase. Labor leaders complained that it emptied the union halls, and ministers, that it emptied the churches. . . .

Cars made the suburbs possible. Dad could scoot off to the office on the boulevard while Mom piled kids and groceries into the station wagon and headed for Little League. In time, of course, the kids had to have cars too; no sense being stuck at home. The single-car garage became the double and then the triple. Houses began to look odd—the garage with attached dwelling.

It was not the only thing. The cars themselves looked odd, with massive grills, wraparound windshields, and spaceshiplike tailfins. The boulevards looked odd. They were filled with gas stations, used car lots and drive-in fast-food places, and they were littered with dented hubcaps and broken tape cassettes. The traffic looked odd. There was so much of it and it moved slower and slower every year. Even the air looked odd. You couldn't see things at a distance any more, and it made eyes itch and burn.

The problems compounded. Cars were falling apart before their time. People were mortgaging away their lives just to remain mobile. There was no place to park. The highway death toll mounted into the tens of thousands, then the hundreds of thousands. Freeways were blighting the landscape with multitiered concrete monstrosities, and even they couldn't handle the traffic. Commutes of twenty and thirty minutes lengthened into commutes of two and three hours. Los Angeles, symbol of twentieth-century America, was becoming the city that everyone loved to hate.

And then, one day, a small group of Arabs figured out that the automobile had become America's Achilles' Heel. It was no longer anyone's plaything but everyone's vital necessity, and they, the Arabs, could choke it off at the carburetor if they wanted to. And given the world situation, especially in the Middle East, they decided they did want to—just to see what would happen. It was the beginning of the end for American automobility—and perhaps for the American good life.

Excerpted from *America: A Study in Heritage*, by Frank Fox and Clayne Pope. Copyright 1993 by Kendall / Hunt Publishing Company. Used with permission.

D

Using your textbook's discussion of the presidency of Jimmy Carter (1977–80), write a *coordinate* paragraph expressing your opinion as to whether or not Jimmy Carter was an effective president. In writing your paragraph be sure to begin with a clearly phrased topic sentence, followed by at least three subpoints justifying your opinion—that is, cite the specific pieces of evidence upon which your judgment is based. Your paragraph should be in the neighborhood of six to seven sentences.

TELEVISION, FILM,
11 AND HISTORY

"The camera never lies."

CONVENTIONAL WISDOM

"Of course the camera lies."

THE AUTHORS

"History is the enemy of art."

EDWARD ANHALT[1]

"Art is the enemy of history."

THE AUTHORS

History is quintessentially a discipline of the written word, however, we live in an age in which the written word is fighting a losing battle with television and the motion picture industry. Whatever history people think they know is as likely to have been learned from films and television as from books. This is not altogether a bad thing, given the growing body of respectable historical video and film produced in recent years (e.g., Ken Burns' series on the Civil War). It is not an altogether good thing either. But, whether the trend is welcome or not is immaterial. Moving-image history is here to stay, and historians have recognized this by incorporating a variety of films and videos into their history classes.

Historians and students of history should become as adept at reading and analyzing film and television as they are at evaluating the more traditional written documents and books. In this chapter we will provide a brief introduction to the critical analysis of film historical artifacts and historical reconstructions.[2] More detailed guidance can be found in the source references to this chapter.[3]

FILM AS RECORD, REPRESENTATION, AND CULTURAL ARTIFACT

"A rose is a rose is a rose," said Gertrude Stein. The same cannot be said of film. Films vary widely in character and historians use films in quite distinctive ways. Before viewing and analyzing a film it is important to understand the type of film you are viewing and the perspective your instructor wants you to take. To begin it might be useful to distinguish between film as record, as representation, and cultural artifact.

FILM AS RECORD

On the most basic level, film can provide a visual record of an event. Taped footage on the nightly news, amateur videos/films of significant events (e.g., Abraham Zapruder's film of the Kennedy assassination), and the raw footage taken by documentary filmmakers can provide the historian with an invaluable visual record of the personalities and events that have shaped our century. At this level, film is the equivalent of a primary source—the raw material out of which historians reconstruct their accounts of the past.

---

1 Quoted in John E. O'Connor, ed., *Image as Artifact: The Historical Analysis of Film and Television* (Malabar, FL: Robert E. Krieger Publishing Co., 1990), 35.

2 Although there are technical and perceptual differences between videotape and film, we will use the term "film" to refer to both moving-image technologies, including films that have been transferred to video format. When it is important to make the distinction between film and video, we will do so.

3 The amount of scholarship devoted to film and television is growing exponentially, and students and instructors can benefit from reading some of the essays published in O'Connor, *Image as Artifact*, and in Steven Mintz and Randy Roberts, eds., *Hollywood's America: United States History Through Its Films* (St. James, NY: Brandywine Press, 1993). For instructors a place to begin would be John O'Connor and Martin A. Jackson, *Teaching History with Film* (Washington, DC: AHA, 1974). An excellent recent addition is Mark C. Carnes, *Past Imperfect: History According to the Movies,* (NY: Henry Holt & Co., 1995.)

However, even when dealing with "actuality footage," historians should use discretion because cameras can indeed lie. Every piece of film is shot from a specific angle, showing some things but not others. What wasn't in the viewfinder, the historian wants to know. Further, it is a rare piece of film that hasn't been edited to fit time constraints, eliminate unwanted material, or conform to a censor's mandate.[4] Taped television interviews are often edited down from hours of footage to the few minutes that are actually put on the air. In the 1930s and 1940s there was a tacit agreement among news professionals not to show that Franklin Roosevelt was confined to a wheelchair due to an earlier bout with poliomyelitis. The footage was edited out

before the newsreels were released to the public.[5] Finally, visual evidence can be falsified. The advent of digital computer technology has made this easier to do today than ever before.

FILM AS REPRESENTATION

More complex are those films, crafted by filmmakers, intended to represent a segment of the past. Representational films are carefully scripted and produced historical reconstructions, and are the visual equivalent of secondary sources (see pp. 75–76). They attempt to narrate and explain events in a manner analogous to books and essays. Most classroom films are of this type. Within this category are nonfiction documentaries (which often contain excerpts of the actuality footage discussed above), and docudramas[6] which use actors and modern movie-making magic and are said to be based on a true story. *Roots, Reds, JFK, Malcolm X,* and *Nixon* are some examples.

Many docudramas tend to play fast and loose with the facts, and need to be evaluated carefully and critically. However, documentaries, which use original footage and interviews with participants, eyewitnesses, and academic experts, are generally accepted at face value. But even documentaries should be considered with the same skepticism as Hollywood potboilers. Documentaries are still constructions that present a filmmaker's point of view, and are as much in need of critical analysis and commentary as any written version of history.

FILM AS CULTURAL ARTIFACT

Finally, films of all types—whatever their historical content—can be used by historians to gain insights into the era in which they were created. Just as raw documentary footage can be considered a primary source, all films, whether made to educate or entertain, are primary sources when used to study the values, behaviors, psychology, and myths that were predominant during a given time period. For example, D.W. Griffith's *Birth of a Nation* (1915), which portrays the post–Civil War south and the rise of the Ku Klux Klan, would be a *secondary* source if we were interested in how it represented the Reconstruction period of American history. It would be a *primary* source, however, if we were viewing it as an early twentieth-century cultural

---

4 Even in countries that value freedom of the press, there are societal and institutional constraints that limit and color what is presented to the public in the mainstream media. For an analysis of political and economic elites managing the media in this way, see Daniel Hellinger and Dennis Judd, *The Democratic Facade,* 2nd ed. (Belmont, CA: Wadsworth Publishing Co., 1994), chapter 3, "Political Elites and the Media."

5 Robert E. Herzstein, "News film and Documentary as Sources for Factual Information," in O'Connor, *Image as Artifact,* 180.

6 The representational category can also include those films that use fictional characters but try to present an accurate portrait of a piece of the past. Examples would be *Platoon* and *Full Metal Jacket* (about the Vietnam War), *The Winds of War* (World War II), *All Quiet on the Western Front* (World War I).

artifact which could be used to measure America's attitudes about race relations in 1915.

THINKING ABOUT HISTORICAL FILMS[7]

Films have a language all their own, which is in some ways similar to the written language of books, but unique enough to require very different interpretation and analysis.[8]

Film has certain advantages over the written word. It can communicate the look of people, places and events that even the best written descriptions can't equal. Also, film creates an emotional intensity and immediacy that captivates audiences in ways that writers can only envy. "Film can open our minds to another, more vivid and human, less literary understanding of the past."[9] In a word, it can make the past come alive.

On the other hand, the emotional power of film is, from the historian's perspective, not always a good thing. Film is inherently manipulative, using clever editing, calculated lighting and camera angles, emotion-laden sound tracks, and special effects of various kinds, to create illusions that appeal less to our intellects than our emotions.[10] In fact, film's often nonlinear narrative style (rapid-fire, nonsequential or unrelated images, used for example on MTV, television commercials, quick cuts in film chase scenes), may be antithetical to the very enterprise of history. Good historical writing is based on linear thinking. Historians must lead their readers in a logical sequence from one event to another, or make a systematic argument using linear logic— if A, then B, therefore C. Film often does not communicate in this way.

In comparing words and images, two other points should be made. First, written or spoken language is a medium of *intercommunication* in which an ongoing dialogue is possible. This is not true of film. According to James Monaco, "Cinema is not strictly a medium of intercommunication. . . . Whereas spoken and written languages are used for intercommunication, film, like the nonrepresentational arts in general . . . , is a one-way communication."[11] Additionally, it is much more difficult to check on a film's use of source materials than it is to evaluate the documentary basis of a piece of written history. The source citations in history books can be checked for accuracy and contextual le-

---

7 Most of the comments that follow refer primarily to the representational films (documentaries and docudramas), which are most commonly used in history classrooms.

8 See especially James Monaco, *How to Read a Film*, Rev. ed. (New York: Oxford University Press, 1981); also Art Silverblatt, *Media Literacy: Keys to Interpreting Media Messages* (Westport, CT: Praeger Publishers, 1995).

9 Pierre Sorlin, "Historical Films as Tools for Historians," in O'Connor, *Image as Artifact*, 50.1

10 As a further example of the manipulative powers of film, the pictures in moving pictures (film, not video, in this context) do not technically move at all. Every second, a movie projector individually stops and illuminates 24 still images, creating a psychologically compelling illusion of movement. The illusory capabilities of modern film and video technology should be kept in mind by all of us who enjoy the creations of Hollywood directors.

11 Monaco, *How to Read a Film*, 132.

gitimacy, but the relationship between content and sources in a film is often difficult to discover. How, for instance, can we find out whether the film footage and interviews in a documentary do justice to the original uncut footage and interviews? How do we discover where docudrama writers get their facts and interpretations? In most cases, the answer is, we can't. The credibility of a historical film must be tested by using already existing written histories.

ASKING QUESTIONS

When trying to "read" a film, the old cliché still applies: the more you know, the more you will get out of it. And the questions you should ask are the same as when you analyze a written document or piece of historical scholarship: What does the content tell us? How was the film produced? How was it received?[12]

Content
Analysis of content is still the heart of the historical enterprise and applies to both the written word and to film. Every documentary or docudrama has a distinctive point of view and often, especially in the case of documentaries, contains an identifiable thesis. Once you identify point of view and thesis, consider the following: Is the reconstruction accurate? What does the filmmaker want the audience to think about the events being presented? What does the filmmaker want the audience to feel? Are the film's conclusions defensible in the light of what is already known about the event in question? You should also ask yourself how particular techniques—lighting, use of camera position, sound, color, editing—have contributed to the overall message of the film.[13] (See the insert on film language.)

Docudramas pose challenges all their own. Like history books they are historical reconstructions. However, the historian's primary responsibility is to the evidence while the filmmaker's priorities are artistic and financial. Films require artistic integrity and entertainment value in or-

der to be successful in the Nielsen Ratings or at the box office. As James Davidson and Mark Lytle comment:

> For filmmakers, far different principles of construction are paramount. They involve questions of drama, not fidelity to the evidence. Does the screenplay move along quickly enough? Do the characters "develop" sufficiently? Does the plot provide enough suspense? These matters dominate the making of a film even when that oft-repeated claim flashes across the screen: *Based on a True Story.*[14]

Since filmmakers alter the historical record for the sake of creating more entertaining films, there are no simple, clear-cut, criteria for determining whether a film is historically accurate or true. Films can communicate two kinds of truth—literal truth and a larger, human truth that we still recognize as good history. For this reason, individuals will differ on the truth-value of a given film, based on their perspective. The movie *Platoon* (a gritty, close-up look at the Vietnam war experience through the lives of the members of a single platoon), did not aim for literal truth—the characters were fictional. Yet many would argue that *Platoon* is good history because it captured the larger truth of the war better than most of the other commercially produced films about Vietnam.

Although it is important to determine the historical accuracy of a piece of film history, even inaccuracies have their uses as cultural myth. As one commentator wrote, "historians who tried to list the historical inaccuracies in *The Birth of a Nation* would be ignoring the fact that their job should not involve bestowing marks for accuracy but describing how men living at a certain time understood their own history."[15] While it is important to address the accuracy issue, even misrepresentations of history can provide invaluable insights into the minds of those who originally made and viewed a film.

Production and Reception
In addition to content, students of filmed history should also ask questions about the production and reception of a film. "It is necessary to ask of

---

12 The trinity of Content, Production and Reception is based on a number of the essays in O'Connor's, *Image as Artifact.*
13 Leni Riefenstahl's famous Nazi propaganda film *Triumph of the Will* is an interesting example of how the visual language of film can be used to arouse or intimidate audiences.
14 James Davidson and Mark Lytle, *After the Fact,* 3rd. ed. (New York: McGraw-Hill, Inc., 1992), 360. This updated edition adds a chapter on "History and Myth in the Films of Vietnam," which provides an excellent essay-length introduction to the analysis of historical films.
15 Daniel Leab, "The Moving Image as Interpreter of History," in O'Connor, *Image as Artifact,* 89.

any visual source as one would of any other source how did it come into being, who created it and why, what was or is its impact."[16]

Effective book analysis requires that we know something about the times in which the book was written as well as something about the author's values, background, and intent. The same is true of film analysis. *Platoon*, for example, was made in 1986 when Americans were finally willing to confront the agonies and traumas of the Vietnam experience. This helps us understand why *Platoon* could portray American soldiers less as mythic heroes (a common approach in dramatic films about World War II), than as frightened, confused, sometimes callous young men who didn't want to be in a war they didn't understand. It is also helpful to know that the film was made by Oliver Stone, a twice-wounded Vietnam veteran, many of whose films *(Born on the Fourth of July, JFK)* display a gut-level bitterness about the war as well as a distrust of the U.S. government and military.[17] Stone's world view explains not only the convincing realism of Platoon, but its antiwar message as well.

The popularity of a film or television show also tells us a good deal about the era in which it was made. This is especially useful if we are studying the film as a cultural artifact—i.e., as evidence for social and cultural history. One could hardly argue that a given television show was an accurate reflection of American popular culture if no one watched it, or if it was taken off the air after a few episodes. Similarly, a popular historical film, even if more myth than fact, can tell us how people at the time viewed (or wanted to view) their own history.

CONCLUSION

Moving-image history is here to stay. The danger of moving-image history is not the enjoyment we get from it but whether we accept it passively and uncritically. When the lights go down it is too easy to turn off the brain and wait to be entertained. What we see on the screen must be analyzed, discussed and challenged if we are to avoid becoming passive receptacles for whatever messages are broadcast in our direction. The critical skills discussed in this book must be used to examine all serious ideas, whatever the medium of their transmission.

---

16 Leab, "Moving Image," *Image as Artifact*, 88.
17 The discussion of *Platoon* is based largely on Davidson and Lytle, *After the Fact*, 379–82.

Students interested in historical film should know something about film language. Below are a few important terms and concepts used in much formal film analysis.[18]

SHOT, SCENE, SEQUENCE

The basic unit of a film is the single shot. A series of shots make a scene and connected scenes form a sequence. Some commentators (e.g., John O'Connor) like the analogy that shot, scene, and sequence can be equated to sentence, paragraph and chapter in written language. Critiques of historical films should begin with an analysis of the individual shots *(mise-en-scène)* and how the shots are edited into scenes and sequences *(montage)*.

MISE-EN-SCÈNE

Mise-en-scène (French for "putting together") is a commonly used term in film criticism for the contents and photographic look of a single unbroken shot, no matter how long its duration. In evaluating a historical film you might consider the accuracy of the set and costumes, and take notice of how the scene is photographed. Important photographic elements in a single shot are:

- *Duration*, or the length of time a shot is on the screen. A shot can be short and simple or quite long and complex. In *tracking shots* the camera moves while filming, often going from a distance shot to a close-up, or even following an actor or sequence of events without any editorial cutting. Directors occasionally try to enhance a sense of naturalistic realism by filming tracking shots

with hand-held cameras.
- *Lighting and Color* The intensity and direction of the lighting, and the colors used, can be powerful emotion-shapers. Dark shadowy images, for example, convey a sense of danger and apprehension. Colors have psychological correlates (red=anger; blue=sadness) as well as culturally significant symbolic meanings.
- *Camera Position* includes the elements of composition, camera angle, and camera movement. Composition refers to the arrangement of objects and people on the screen, camera angle to how high or low the camera is placed, and camera movement speaks for itself. All of these elements can play a role in influencing the emotions of the audience. The single variable of camera angle, for instance, can influence greatly the audience's reading of a film. Leni Riefenstahl, the film genius responsible for the Nazi propaganda film *Triumph of the Will*, often photographed Hitler, his entourage, and German soldiers from below to make them appear heroic and larger than life.

MONTAGE

Montage refers to film editing—that is, the sequencing of the individual shots. If mise-en-scène refers to the modification and manipulation of space, montage refers to the filmmaker's manipulation of time. Since history is the systematic study of events as they happened in time, historians should pay close attention to how filmmakers manipulate emotions through the editing process. *Hearts and Minds*, a 1974 documentary critical of U.S. involve-

---

18 For a more in-depth discussion see Monaco, *How to Read a Film*, Ch. III, "The Language of Film: Signs and Syntax," or O'Connor, *Image as Artifact*, Ch. V, "An Introduction to Visual Language for Historians and History Teachers."

ment in Vietnam, includes an interview with U.S. General William Westmoreland in which he states that Asians don't respect life the same way Westerners do. During this section of the interview the filmmaker, Peter Davis, undercut Westmoreland's credibility by inserting a scene of a Vietnamese woman weeping over the grave of a loved one. Skillful editing can also telescope or compress time in a way that can compromise the historical truth of a given sequence or film. Editing can also create the impression that you are seeing something entirely different from what you are actually looking at. In the television series, *Victory*

at Sea (1952), a chronicle of the U.S. Navy in World War II, the entire episode on the Battle of Leyte Gulf in the Philippines was created out of whole cloth by editing together stock pieces of war footage and adding appropriate narration. There had been no cameras at the actual battle![19]

SOUND

The use of sound helps give a film a certain mood. Compare the emotional impact of the same film viewed with and without the soundtrack. When analyzing a historical film, pay conscious attention to the soundtrack and the feelings it creates.

Lincoln's assassination, as depicted in D. W. Griffith's The Birth of a Nation

19 For the anecdotes about *Hearts and Minds* and *Victory at Sea* we are indebted to O'Connor, *Image as Artifact*, 318, 314.

Films can be a component of any segment of an American history course. Therefore we have no set of specific exercises designed to accompany a given unit. What we do suggest is that you think of classroom films as something more than mere entertainment, or as a "day off." The following form might be a useful tool for the critical analysis of films.

Film Analysis

Name of Film: _____ Release Date: _____

Type of Film (documentary or drama): _____

Analysis of Content

      Thesis (documentary) or Central Historical Message (drama):

      Major Points:

Context

      Information about director/producers:

      What does the film reveal about the period in which it was made?

      How was it received then or later?

Visual Analysis

(Here you should note those elements of film language that contributed significantly to the overall "message" or impact of the film—editing, sound, camera placement, set, costumes, etc. Refer to the insert on film language on pages 157–158.)

      The "Look" of the Film (mise-en-scène):

      Editing (montage):

      Sound:

Overall Conclusion

How does the film hold up as a piece of history?

A Note on Film Research

A legitimate question is: "Where do I go to find out background information on a specific historical film?" A good place to start would be with newspaper and magazine reviews of the film when it came out. Also, consult Mark C. Carnes, *Past Imperfect,* John O'Connor's *Image as Artifact,* Steven Mintz's and Randy Roberts' *Hollywood's America* and the bibliographies in each book. Especially noteworthy is the section in O'Connor's bibliography entitled, "Sources on the Connections between History and the Moving Image." The journal *Film & History* is a valuable source, and a number of historical journals have begun to review pertinent films and publish articles on the use of film in the classroom.

READING HISTORY

"Books are not made to be believed, but to be subjected to inquiry."

WILLIAM OF BASKERVILLE IN UMBERTO ECO'S
THE NAME OF THE ROSE

"Facts may be detailed with the most minute exactness, and yet the narrative, taken as a whole, may be unmeaning or untrue."

FRANCIS PARKMAN

In this book we have defined history as the account created by a historian. It stands to reason, therefore, that to learn history, you have to read books—lots of them! That is why many history instructors assign supplementary readings on more specialized topics—usually collections of excerpts or paperback histories that cover a period, event, or theme in some depth. In this appendix we want to suggest some techniques that will help you get the most out of these supplementary readings and any work of nonfiction you decide to read.

History books (along with articles and essays) are reservoirs of information, but they also attempt to explain and interpret the past. And those interpretations and explanations often differ markedly from book to book. As we have seen, there is no single, unanimously accepted version of American history, instead there are many versions that often conflict with one another. In the words of Dutch historian Pieter Geyl, history is "an argument without end."

Certainly, no student of history can ignore important pieces of information, for facts are the bricks out of which historical interpretations are built. But facts do not speak for themselves, and often the known facts will bear the weight of more than one interpretation. This is the primary reason historians keep rewriting the history of a single event or period.

Reading history, therefore, cannot be a passive activity in which you simply attempt to absorb various pieces of information; it is a pursuit that requires active thought and reflection. Not all interpretations are equally credible. It is simply not true that "one opinion is as good as another." The validity of a historical interpretation rests on how well it is supported by the known evidence. Some interpretations fit the facts better than others, and those based on shoddy scholarship or faulty reasoning should be exposed and rejected.

FINDING THE THESIS

When reading a book or article you should first try to discover the author's central thesis or major explanatory conclusions or interpretations.[1] You should also pay attention to the important information the book contains, but that information will be more easily assimilated if you understand the author's broader purpose in writing the book. It is an author's interpretation (thesis) that makes a book or article distinctive, and this thesis is the glue that ties together the disparate facts that can otherwise overwhelm the reader.

Usually the thesis of a book can be discovered quickly. If it's not immediately obvious, either the book is poorly constructed (not uncommon) or you are missing something. Many times the author states the thesis explicitly ("My argument is . . ."); on other occasions you must do the work yourself. Most authors summarize their central arguments in a preface, introduction, or first chapter, and recapitulate the main points

---

1 This discussion of thesis-finding and skimming techniques is indebted to Norman E. Cantor and Richard I. Schneider, *How to Study History* (Wheeling, IL: Harlan Davidson, Inc., 1967), especially Chapter Five.

again at the end of a book or article. These are the sections you should read first. In the case of an article, read the first few paragraphs and the last few in order to isolate the thesis. Don't be afraid to read the last chapter (section) before those in the middle; a historical narrative is not a murder mystery where the reader needs to be kept in suspense until the end.

It is important to identify the thesis early so that as you read the rest of the book you need not read every detail with equal diligence. The facts in the book should support and illustrate

---

TOPIC VS. THESIS

Don't confuse the *topic* of a book with the *thesis.* The topic refers to the specific subject matter the book covers. The thesis refers to the distinctive argument the author makes about the topic—i.e., the interpretation. For instance, many, many authors have written on the origins of the American Civil War (that is, they have written on the same topic), but they have presented very different theses about the cause or mix of causes that led to the Civil War. To some the war was fought over slavery; to others it was a war that grew out of the economic differences between the South and the North; and still others have said the war was caused by a conflict over the issue of states' rights.

Remember:

Topic refers to the subject matter. When you say "This book is about _____," you are describing the topic.

Thesis refers to the author's central argument about the topic under discussion. No sentence can be a thesis statement unless it can be prefaced with the words: "The author argues/states that . . . ."

---

the thesis, and if you have identified the thesis from the beginning, you will find it much easier to read the rest of the book. As you become more and more familiar with a given topic, you will find it easier to master additional books on that topic. Most importantly, you will be thinking creatively, not just absorbing masses of information.

Finally, although the thesis is the most important single element in a book, you should by no means ignore the rest. As you read you should take note of the important generalizations made in each chapter or subsection of the book, for often chapters and subsections will have subtheses of their own. You should also make a mental or written note of what factual material is covered to have a clear idea of what the book does and does not contain. That way, if you need a specific piece of information in the future you will know where to find it.

SKIMMING

Reading a book is like mining for precious gems—the valuable stones must be separated from the surrounding rocks. A valuable technique for mining historical literature is skimming. After you have read carefully to establish the thesis, the rest of the book can be more-easily digested. A well-constructed book will contain regular patterns that can be used as shortcuts by the reader. For instance, just as an author's major points are usually summarized at the beginning or end (or both) of a book, the same is often true of chapters. Likewise, topic sentences summarize the key generalizations of individual paragraphs. Once you have established where a particular author tends to locate the ideas he or she considers most important, it is easier to concentrate on those ideas and skim over much of the supportive and illustrative factual material.

This technique is only valuable for books on topics for which you already have a basic textbook knowledge. We don't recommend that you skim when reading a book on a brand new subject. Further, we are not talking here about "speed-reading" (a questionable and highly overrated technique), but about *selective* reading. The advice given above is intended to help you discriminate between the sections of a book that should be read with relative care, and those that can be read less intensively.

WRITING A BOOK REVIEW

"We would rather read a good book review than a bad book."

THE AUTHORS

The book review is one of the most common and useful literary forms. Newspapers and magazines are full of reviews that inform readers about the content and quality of recently published titles. Such reviews serve as a brief guide to the newest offerings in every subject area, and help readers choose which of the hundreds of new titles would be worth reading. And, at some point in their college career, students will be asked to write a book review.

The subject of any book review is the book and its author, not the subject matter of the book you are reviewing. That is, if you are reading a book on the Indian Wars in the late 1800s, your review should not become an abbreviated paper on the Indian Wars. Instead, your review should discuss how this particular author, in this particular book, treats the subject of the Indian Wars. (Remember, a history book presents but one of many versions of the past. See Appendix A, Reading History.)

To help you to focus your review on the author, and not the author's subject, remember that authors make countless choices about topic, information to be included or excluded, the organizational scheme, and much more. Such choices make every book unique, and it is your job as a reviewer to describe and evaluate the choices the author has made.

A good book review provides both a summary and an evaluation of the book in question. A common mistake is to concentrate almost exclusively on the summary and make no attempt to provide the necessary critical commentary. After a brief summary of the book's content, the bulk of your review should be devoted to providing a thoughtful reaction to the author's ideas, evidence, and methods. Following is a list of questions you should attempt to answer in the book reviews you write.

BEGINNING

First, provide a complete bibliographic citation—author, title, place of publication, date—for the book you are reviewing. The date alone can provide many clues to the quality and orientation of a book. For instance, a history of World War II written in 1946 might be less objective and less substantive than one written in 1980, because the 1980 author would have had the opportunity to incorporate evidence that would not have been available in 1946.

THE SUMMARY

In your summary you might try to answer (not in any particular order) the following basic questions:

1. *What specific topic(s) does the book cover? That is, what subject matter did the author choose to discuss?*

In addition to noting the general subject area (World War II, the Cold War, Labor conflicts in the 1920s), you might also identify for your reader the type of history the book represents. Most authors choose to emphasize some aspects of the past at the expense of others: economic relationships (economic history), political issues (political-institutional history), the single individual (biography), the role of social groups (social history), the evolution of ideas (intellectual history), war (military history), diplomacy (diplomatic history), everyday life (social history again), or any number of other facets of past life. In any event, the emphasis an author chooses in writing a work of history reflects a conscious decision, a decision you should be aware of as you write your review.

2. *What is the geographic and chronological setting—i.e., time and place?*

Many students overlook this very obvious question because they forget that what is now totally familiar to them after reading a book may not be familiar to a reader. So it's important to let the reader know the where and the when of the subject matter of the book: Spain in the time of Columbus? Atlanta during the Civil War? California in 1848?

3. *How is the book organized?*

In addition to choosing subject matter, time-frame, and emphasis, the author decides whether to organize a book chronologically or topically. Books organized chronologically present material the same way many college survey courses do—year by year or period by period. Those organized topically or analytically have chapters or sections based on thematically similar materials. Each chapter in Clinton Rossiter's *The First American Revolution* (1956), an example of topical organization, covers the same chronological period (the colonial era before 1776), but explores different "compartments" (thematic units) of colonial life—the economy, religion, politics, social structure, etc. Often the two forms of organization are combined by alternating the chronological narration of events with periodic analyses of specific issues or topics. Taken as a whole, though, most books will conform predominantly to one organizational scheme or the other.

4. *Does the book have illustrations, maps, or other aids for the reader?*

THE COMMENTARY

The most important part of the review is the critical commentary. Essentially a book review should answer the question: "Is this a good book?" "Why or why not?" To help you answer that, you should think about the following:

1. *What is the author's major point or thesis?*

This, along with the question below, is the most important. (See Appendix A for a discussion of thesis-finding.)

2. *How does the author support his or her thesis? What types of evidence, arguments and examples are used? Does the author make a convincing case?*

Here it is appropriate to comment on the author's sources and how well they are used. Are there extensive source references? Few? None? Is the bibliography large? Small? Missing altogether? This sort of information can give you a clue as to the seriousness and perhaps the credibility of the book, although it would be a mistake automatically to equate extensive sources with quality. Also, a lack of such research apparatus does not necessarily mean that the book is worthless. It could have been the author's intention to write an introductory study (like this one) intended for a general audience.

You should also note what type of sources the author used. Are the sources appropriate to the subject matter? For instance, a history of American slavery using only material written by southern plantation owners would be highly suspect, as would a history of the labor movement based only on the observations of the factory owners.

Note whether the author used extensive primary sources, or if the book written on the basis of secondary works. The answer to this question can help you discover whether the author was attempting to break new ground by examining original sources or attempting to synthesize the research findings of a number of other historians.

3. *Does the book reflect an identifiable bias or point of view, and how might the author's bias have influenced the book's subject matter or conclusions?*

Often books reflect the political, national, religious or ideological values of their authors. For instance, books on religious history sometimes reflect the religious convictions of the authors. Similarly, British accounts of the American Revolution often differ quite markedly from American accounts. Critical readers should look for clues to an author's biases in order to weigh more intelligently the arguments made in the books. Remember that the intrusion of bias does not automatically discredit an author's thesis. The test of a historical interpretation is how well it conforms to and explains all of the evidence.

It often helps to know something about the author. Is the author a scholar? Journalist? Politician? What is the author's political persuasion? Religion? Nationality? Gender? Many times such information can be found on a jacket cover or in a brief biographical sketch in the book itself. If you know of some other books the author has written it might be helpful to read some reviews of those works.

4. *How does the book compare with others you have read on similar topics?*

5. *Was the book well-written? Clear?*

6. *What did you get out of the book? Would you recommend it to others?*

Again, these questions need not be answered in any specific order, but all of them should be addressed, however briefly, somewhere in the review. Finally, a book review, like any piece of writing, should observe the basic requirements of literary discourse. There should be an introduction (in this case an overview of your thesis concerning the book you are reviewing—"This was a good book because. . ."), a middle section in which you support your assertion, and a brief conclusion. As always, clarity and grammatical precision are important if you want your reader to understand what you are saying.

THE TERM PAPER: AN OVERVIEW

By Harry James Cargas
Professor of Literature and Language
Webster University
Published by permission of the author

Papers are, among other things, expressions of individual personalities. Papers written by a class group are not meant to be uniform in content or style. Nevertheless, they do have a common purpose and each of them should contain all of the elements necessary for a successful effort. Each paper is meant to be a thoughtful, disciplined, honest piece of work on which you, the writer, are willing to rest your reputation as a thinker, based on observable, replicable facts—not opinions, gut responses or contemporary fads. When I take a student's paper home with me, I take a part of that student with me. That student's mind is accompanying me and will speak to me via the written/typed word. And, of course, there is this limitation: we cannot dialogue. Everything that the student has to say on the subject under consideration must be said, and said convincingly, in the paper.

WRITE TO THE POINT

Generally, a paper is written to make a point. The writer's task is to make that point so persuasively that the skeptical reader will, when finished, be in total agreement with the student. This means the work must be well written, logical and supported with evidence.

A double caution must be made regarding the point being discussed in a paper. If the instructor allows you to choose the topic of your paper, you must be sure to limit the scope of your investigation and you must make it worthwhile. In other words, you should concentrate on making one point and it should be significant. For example, if you decide that the focus of your paper will be the American Civil War, you have decided almost nothing. You must narrow your aim to a particular theme such as the importance of a certain battle to the outcome of the war or how the journals of several southern women throw new light on the conduct of the war, etc. Otherwise the problem you set out to resolve may prove too large, too overwhelming, too difficult on which to get a handle. And remember, you must prove it convincingly—and this is especially true if you are free to select the topic of your paper. If you find that you cannot totally prove your point, drop it and search for a new one. Begin again.

Remember, too, that the point must be a significant one. To work on a paper to prove that Shakespeare was a good writer is to waste a lot of time. A much more acceptable topic would be how a particular passage contributes to the overall meaning of a Shakespeare play.

THE TITLE

Incidentally, the title of your paper should tell the focus of your topic. If your paper is titled "The Depression Years," it is unacceptably vague. Better is "Why Herbert Hoover Could Not Have Prevented the Depression." Thus, the reader knows quite fully what the effort is on. But then it is important that this one point not be diluted, Everything you select for inclusion in your paper must be to this one point and everything else is irrelevant and should be omitted. A good paper is tightly written, with nothing of importance to the point being made left out and with absolutely no padding.

CONSTRUCTION

One way in which tightness (and logic) may be built into a paper is to see it as a composition based on the traditional construction of a beginning, a middle and an end. This sounds simple, but too often a student will approach an essay as if it were a work of fiction and develop it not logically but very tentatively—circuitously. Too often, students perform like beginning basketball players who want to start out like Harlem Globetrotters, doing all of the fancy things the Globetrotters do: pass the ball behind their backs, dribble between their legs, perform trick shots and other acts of wizardry. What these potential basketball stars forget is that the Globetrotters all learned the basic skills of their game extremely well and then individualized their approaches. What follows, then is a suggested basic approach to a paper; individual styles can be developed after such a method is mastered.

The beginning of the paper, often no more than a paragraph or two, tells the reader what the problem is that the writer is presenting and the approach to be used in solving that problem. Often, the conclusion to be achieved will also be indicated. (The paper is not meant to be a mystery presentation. Stating the purpose of the paper as early as possible will help the reader; the major purpose of your paper is to be totally clear and convincing in your presentation.) All of this means that your paper is firmly outlined, at least in your mind, preferably in writing. Sometimes a paper is begun with the idea that a certain conclusion will be reached but instead, after close scrutiny of the facts, another conclusion occurs. That is fine. The writer shows an ability to learn and an open mind. However, this no doubt means that much of the paper will have to be rewritten. The aim of the paper is not to show how you changed your mind; that is usually irrelevant to your purposes. Rather it is to present a single, logical, well-developed and significant conclusion.

The second section of the kind of paper being described is the middle. Here, after you have told what you are going to do in the beginning part, you do it. This is the bulk of the paper. Here is where you present powerful arguments to support your thesis. Here is where you prove you are right. As in all parts of your paper, write clearly and simply and be sure that you follow this guide: overprove rather than underprove your point. So often students will try to buttress an argument with a quotation or two on the topic in question when in fact, ten or fifteen references or examples would be better. Remember, your paper is your whole presentation. You will not be there to amplify or to clarify when your reader is looking it over. Cite as many sources as necessary to leave no doubt in the reader's mind that what you say is absolutely true.

One important reminder here: documentation is a very important part of paper writing. Every time you use a quotation, or a point unique to a given document or author, you must indicate the source. The reader must be able to locate that source from the information you give. There are proper forms for such documentation which must be followed. Be sure to learn how to use these forms—particularly footnotes or endnotes—or learn where to go for assistance on this important matter. And remember this little verse:

Every quote
requires a note!

(Certain unique pieces of information and paraphrases of an author's ideas should also be documented, but the verse above is too brief to accommodate these addenda.)

The final part of the paper is the conclusion. In this wrap-up you tell the reader what it was that you had set out to do and then, briefly, the method by which you did it. If the conclusion follows logically from the middle, and if it states essentially what was given in the beginning, then you have—in basic form at least—a well organized paper.

STYLE AND MECHANICS

A few more points should be made. One is: have pride in your effort. Do not hand in sloppy work, torn papers, sheets which fell on the floor and were stepped on. All teachers prefer typed (or word processed) papers (double-spaced with adequate margins on all four sides) to handwritten ones. If yours is typed, be certain that the ribbon on your typewriter or printer is in decent condition; when you strike a wrong key, don't back up and strike over the letter with another one leaving the product either unreadable or of unknown quantity. (Which letter is meant? The reader has no way of knowing which letter got there first!) Proofread your work. You are absolutely responsible for this; there is no blaming the typist, no saying "I was rushed and had to get it in on time." From a teacher's point of view, many excuses about shoddy or late papers are marvelous, imaginative, even sometimes true. I personally give many grades of "A" for the excuses. The papers themselves, however, earn much different grades—and only these latter grades count.

There is a point to be made about late papers. Nearly always students have sufficient notice about deadlines for papers. Since life has a way of interfering with schedules, including those for writing papers, it is a good idea to plan to finish papers well before they are due. This way, emergency situations can be absorbed and papers will not seem to be rush jobs.

You might wish to refer to a basic grammar text on the uses of semicolons, colons, commas, ellipses and other forms of punctuation. A basic rule here is to be certain that you know how to use properly all of the punctuation which you do use. This applies to spelling as well. You are free to use any words you choose for your paper. Select only those of which you are certain either because you know their spelling and meaning or because you can verify them. Needless to say (but, alas, not needless in all cases), when you cite a quotation there should be no misspelling. It is simply a matter of copying correctly. If there is a misspelling within the quotation, indicate that the error is not yours.

As far as the technical aspects of papers go, there are several helpful works which you may wish to consult. From them you can learn how to go about writing a paper, how to do research, how to cite sources, and other important mechanics. Two of the best works are:

A Manual for Writers of Term Papers, Theses, and Dissertations, 4th edition (Chicago: University of Chicago Press, 1973).

MLA Handbook, Second Edition (New York: Modern Language Association, 1984).

ORAL HISTORY

"We have agencies aplenty to seek out the papers of men long dead. But we have only the most scattered and haphazard agencies for obtaining a little of the immense mass of information about the more recent American past—the past of the last half century—which might come fresh and direct from men once prominent in politics, in business, in the professions, and in other fields; information that every obituary column shows to be perishing."

ALLEN NEVINS, *THE GATEWAY TO HISTORY* (1938)[1]

"The memories of the living, one soon discovers, are no more reliable or free of wishful recollection and the adjustments of hindsight than the memoirs of the dead."

BARBARA TUCHMAN (1972)[2]

Oral history is older than the practice of writing about the past, and, at the same time, a true child of the last half of the twentieth century. Historians have always interviewed living witnesses, as can testify any reader of Herodotus or Thucydides. Yet, as an organized enterprise, oral history dates its existence from the government-sponsored interview projects of the New Deal and from Allan Nevins's 1938 plea for the collection of the living memories of important individuals.

Oral history weds the ancient practice of interviewing witnesses to the modern technology of the tape and video recorder. Defined by Charles Morrissey as "recorded interviews which preserve historically significant memories for future use,"[3] oral history provides the contemporary historian with a wealth of source materials that did not exist 50 or 60 years ago.

Oral history refers to the source materials and not the final product created by the historian. Recorded interviews, even if transcribed, are oral documents roughly equivalent to the printed and manuscript sources that have for generations been the lifeblood of historical scholarship. Historians must sift, analyze, and interpret oral sources in precisely the same manner as they would scrutinize diaries, letters, or government documents. Thus, when students do an oral history project, they are both (1) collecting sources in the interviewing process and (2) actually doing history when they use those sources to write a narrative or commentary.

As Allan Nevins's 1938 plea implies, oral history projects first targeted the prominent individuals who had always been the objects of historical scholarship: politicians, intellectuals, business leaders, generals, etc. But it was not long before historians realized that the magic of the tape recorder opened up dramatic new possibilities. It was now possible to tape the remembered experiences of the not-so-famous people who had previously slipped through history's net: the poor, the illiterate or uneducated, marginalized members of minority groups, women, workers who rarely wrote journals or diaries, and the anonymous soldiers and sailors who usually bear the brunt of war.

Critics have argued that the quest to interview anyone who would sit still in front of a microphone has created a mountain of trivia of questionable accuracy and merit that few historians will ever use. While there is some truth to the

---

1 Quoted in Louis Starr, "Oral History," *Oral History: An Interdisciplinary Anthology*, ed. by David K. Dunaway and Willa K. Baum (Nashville, TN: American Association for State and Local History, 1984), 8.
2 Barbara Tuchman, "Distinguishing the Significant from the Insignificant," in Dunaway and Baum, *Oral History*, 76.
3 Dunaway and Baum, *Oral History*, xix.

charge, the influence of the telephone and rapid air travel make oral sources increasingly important to historians of the twentieth century. Whereas political leaders in the past wrote lengthy letters and kept extensive diaries, today they pick up the phone or fly a few hours to have a person-to-person conference. Oral history, then, necessarily replaces the manuscript sources that have disappeared in our high-technology age. Further, oral history is something even novice historians can get involved in. It is personally satisfying and can render a valuable community service.

DOING ORAL HISTORY: INTERVIEWING

Oral history involves much more than turning on a tape recorder in front of an interviewee. In this appendix we will attempt to single out the most important considerations fledgling oral historians should keep in mind. For a more detailed discussion of the process of oral history, however, and for project suggestions, we recommend that you turn to one of the many guides written to help teachers and students get started.[4]

The scouting motto, "be prepared," is also relevant for oral history. After making sure that your tape recorder works, you have to (1) choose with care the people you intend to interview, (2) do background research on your subject and prepare for the interview, and (3) familiarize yourself with the legal and ethical constraints that responsible interviewers observe.

1. Choosing Narrators

Almost anyone, young or old, can be a good source for the oral historian, depending on the subject under investigation. Still, you will want to select interview subjects with care. Choose individuals who have good memories and who have the potential of making a valuable contri-

bution to your particular study. Build a list of prospects by soliciting suggestions from parents, friends, and teachers. If you are studying events a few decades in the past, inquire at retirement centers, local churches, and nursing homes. Excellent possible sources are members of your own family, whose testimony might be incorporated into a family history project.[5]

2. The Interview

Never do an interview unless you have done some preliminary research on the topic in question. It is difficult to ask meaningful questions about the Depression, Vietnam War, or the Flood of '48 unless you already know something about them. Prior reading allows you to test the generalizations you find in textbooks against the individual experiences of the people you interview.

You should also prepare yourself to be an effective interviewer. One expert notes, "The interviewer's paramount objective is to help the narrator reconstruct his/her personal history with as much accuracy and vivid detail as possible."[6] To accomplish this it is wise to prepare some questions in advance. Then, at the interview itself:[7]

- Ask the questions who? what? where? when? how? why? Keep questions broad and general so that interviewees have to do more than answer "yes" or "no."
- Ask about specific events or experiences. "Why did you vote as you did in the 1968 election?" "Where were you when you watched the telecast of the first moon landing?" "What was it like to work on the Ford assembly line in the 1940s?"
- Ask the person to recall actual feelings about the events and experiences you are discussing.
- Ask your narrator to reconstruct specific conversations and physical locations. Concrete details often help people recall a wealth of interesting particulars.

---

4 For example, Cullom Davis, Kathryn Back, and Kay MacLean, *Oral History: From Tape to Type* (Chicago: American Library Association, 1977); Thad Sitton, George L. Mehaffy, and O. L. Davis, Jr., *Oral History: A Guide for Teachers (and Others)* (Austin: University of Texas Press, 1983); James Hoopes, *Oral History: An Introduction for Students* (Chapel Hill: University of North Carolina Press, 1979). Section V ("Oral History and Schools") of Dunaway and Baum, *Oral History* (1984) is also valuable. The bibliography of this work lists a large number of additional oral history manuals.
5 See David E. Kyvig and Myron A. Marty, *Your Family History: A Handbook for Research and Writing* (Wheeling, IL: Harlan Davidson, Inc., 1978).
6 Davis, et al., *Oral History*, 20.
7 These questions were drawn from lists suggested in Davis, et al., *Oral History*, 20–21, and William Bruce Wheeler and Susan D. Becker, *Discovering the American Past: A Look at the Evidence*, Vol. II (Boston: Houghton Mifflin, 1986), 228.

- Don't argue with the person you are interviewing. You are there to solicit their experiences and opinions, not convert them to your way of thinking.
- Save controversial issues until the end of the interview. By that time the narrator may feel more comfortable talking about sensitive matters.
- Make sure you have written down all pertinent personal information: name, age, educational and family background, occupation at time of events being investigated, etc.
- Make sure the interviewee signs the release form.

3. *Ethical and Legal Considerations*

At some point in the interviewing process, preferably at the beginning, it is necessary to obtain the interviewee's signature on a legal release. The legal release (see sample release below) "acknowledges the legal (and legitimate) rights of interviewees to shield themselves from public ridicule or the betrayal of confidences. Generally, legal releases either give complete access to an interview or stipulate the conditions under which all or portions of the interview will be released."[8] Without such a signed release you do not have the legal right to allow others to have access to the collected materials.

There are other rules which, though not mandated by law, are dictated by common sense and good manners. The Oral History Association, founded in 1967, encourages practitioners to "recognize certain principles, rights and obligations for the creation of source material that is authentic, useful and reliable."[9] There follows a set of guidelines for interviewees, interviewers, and institutional sponsors which we have reprinted in full below.

DOING ORAL HISTORY: THE NARRATIVE

Perhaps a reminder is in order: oral testaments are primary sources—not history as we have defined it in this book. The most important phase of an oral history project is to use your newly created sources to write some history. The length and nature of what you write depends on individual classroom circumstances, but something should be written, however brief or tentative. It is at this point that you actually do the work of the historian, and, it is the most meaningful phase of the project.[10] That said, have fun.

---

8 Sitton, et al., *Oral History*, 78.
9 Reprinted in Dunaway and Baum, *Oral History*, 415–416.
10 Another important aim of oral research projects is to catalog and store the oral histories (often in written transcriptions) for the use of future historians. Given the nature of this book, these elements have not been discussed. See the sources in footnote 4 for further information.

Sample Release Form

Tri-County Historical Society

For and in consideration of the participation by *Tri-County Historical Society* in any programs involving the dissemination of tape-recorded memoirs and oral history material for publication, copyright, and other uses, I hereby release all right, title, or interest in and to all of my tape-recorded memoirs to *Tri-County Historical Society* and declare that they may be used without any restriction whatsoever and may be copyrighted and published by the said *Society*, which may also assign said copyright and publication rights to serious research scholars.

In addition to the rights and authority given to you under the preceding paragraph, I hereby authorize you to edit, publish, sell and/or license the use of my oral history memoir in any other manner which the *Society* considers to be desirable and I waive any claim to any payments which may be received as a consequence thereof by the *Society*.

PLACE *Indianapolis, Indiana*

DATE *July 14, 1975*

Harold S. Johnson

(Interviewee)

Jane Rogers

for *Tri-County Historical Society*

Source

From Collum Davis, Kathryn Back, and Kay MacLean, *Oral History: From Tape to Type* (Chicago: American Library Assn., © 1977, p. 14.) Reprinted by permission of the American Library Association.

PRINCIPLES AND STANDARDS OF THE ORAL HISTORY ASSOCIATION

(Published by permission of the Oral History Association)

The Oral History Association promotes oral history as a method of gathering and preserving historical information through recorded interviews with participants in past events and ways of life. It encourages those who produce and use oral history to recognize certain principles, rights, and obligations for the creation of source material that is authentic, useful, and reliable. These include obligations to the interviewee, to the profession, and to the public, as well as mutual obligations between sponsoring organizations and interviewers.

Oral history interviews are conducted by people with a range of affiliations and sponsorship for a variety of purposes: to create archival records, for individual research, for community and institutional projects, and for publications and other media productions. While these principles and standards provide a general framework for guiding professional conduct, their application may vary according to the nature of specific oral history projects. Regardless of the purpose of the interviews, oral history should be conducted in the spirit of critical inquiry and social responsibility, and with a recognition of the interactive and subjective nature of the enterprise.

RESPONSIBILITY, TO INTERVIEWEES:

1. Interviewees should be informed of the purposes and procedures of oral history in general and of the aims and anticipated uses of the particular projects to which they are making their contribution.

2. Interviewees should be informed of the mutual rights in the oral history process, such as editing, access restrictions, copyrights, prior use, royalties, and the expected disposition and dissemination of all forms of the record.

3. Interviewees should be informed that they will be asked to sign a legal release. Interviews should remain confidential until interviewees have given permission for their use.

4. Interviewers should guard against making promises to interviewees that they may not be able to fulfill, such as guarantees of publication and control over future uses of interviews after they have been made public.

5. Interviews should be conducted in accord with any prior agreements made with the interviewee, and such preferences and agreements should be documented for the record.

6. Interviewers should work to achieve a balance between the objectives of the project and the perspectives of the interviewees. They should be sensitive to the diversity of social and cultural experiences, and to the implications of race, gender, class, ethnicity, age, religion, and sexual orientation. They should encourage interviewees to respond in their own style and language, and to address issues that reflect their concerns. Interviewers should fully explore all appropriate areas of inquiry with the interviewee and not be satisfied with superficial responses.

7. Interviewers should guard against possible exploitation of interviewees and be sensitive to the ways in which their interviews might be used. Interviewers must respect the right of the interviewee to refuse to discuss certain subjects. to restrict access to the interview, or under extreme circumstances even to choose anonymity. Interviewers should

clearly explain these options to all interviewees.

RESPONSIBILITY TO THE PUBLIC AND TO THE PROFESSION:

1. Oral historians have a responsibility to maintain the highest professional standards in the conduct of their work and to uphold the standards of the various disciplines and professions with which they are affiliated.

2. In recognition of the importance of oral history to an understanding of the past and of the cost and effort involved, interviewers and interviewees should mutually strive to record candid information of lasting value and to make that information accessible.

3. Interviewees should be selected on the basis of the relevance of their experiences to the subject at hand.

4. Interviewers should possess interviewing skills as well as professional competence or experience with the subject at hand.

5. Regardless of the specific interests of the project, interviewers should attempt to extend the inquiry beyond the specific focus of the project to create as complete a record as possible for the benefit of others.

6. Interviewers should strive to prompt informative dialogue through challenging and perceptive inquiry. They should be grounded in the background of the persons being interviewed and, when possible, should carefully research appropriate documents and secondary sources related to subjects about which the interviewees can speak.

7. Interviewers should make every effort to record their interviews. They should provide complete documentation of their preparation and methods, including the circumstances of the interviews. Interviewers, and when possible interviewees, should review and evaluate their interviews and any transcriptions made from them.

8. With the permission of the interviewees, interviewers should arrange to deposit their interviews in an archival repository that is capable of both preserving the interviews and eventually making them available for general use. Interviewers should provide basic information about the interviews, including project goals, sponsorship, and funding. Preferably, interviewers should work with repositories prior to the project to determine necessary legal arrangements. If interviewers arrange to retain first use of the interviews, it should be only for a reasonable time prior to public use.

9. Interviewers should be sensitive to the communities from which they have collected their oral histories, taking care not to reinforce thoughtless stereotypes or to bring undue notoriety to the communities. They should take every effort to make the interviews accessible to the communities.

10. Oral history interviews should be used and cited with the same care and standards applied to other historical sources. Users have a responsibility to retain the integrity of the interviewee's voice, neither misrepresenting the interviewee's words nor taking them out of context.

11. Sources of funding or sponsorship of oral history projects should be made public in all exhibits, media presentations, or publications that result from the projects.

12. Interviewers and oral history programs should conscientiously consider how they might share with interviewees and their communities the rewards and recogni-

tion that might result from their work.

RESPONSIBILITY FOR SPONSORING AND ARCHIVAL INSTITUTIONS:

1. Institutions sponsoring and maintaining oral history archives have a responsibility to interviewees, interviewers, the profession, and the public to maintain the highest professional and ethical standards in the creation and archival preservation of oral history interviews.

2. Subject to conditions that interviewees set, sponsoring institutions (or individual collectors) have an obligation to prepare and preserve easily usable records; to keep accurate records of the creation and processing of each interview; to identify, index, and catalog interviews; and to make known the existence of the interviews when they are open for research.

3. Within the parameters of their missions and resources, archival institutions should collect interviews generated by independent researchers and assist interviewers with the necessary legal agreements.

4. Sponsoring institutions should train interviewers, explaining the objectives of the program to them, informing them of all ethical and legal considerations governing an interview, and making clear to interviewers what their obligations are to the program and to the interviewees.

5. Interviewers and interviewees should receive appropriate acknowledgement for their work in all forms of citation or usage.

SUGGESTIONS FOR FURTHER READING

THE NATURE OF HISTORY—THE PHILOSOPHY OF HISTORY

Becker, Carl. *Everyman His Own Historian.* New York: Appleton-Century-Crofts, 1935.

Beringer, Richard E. *Historical Analysis: Contemporary Approaches to Clio's Craft.* New York: John Wiley and Sons, 1978.

Bloch, Marc. *The Historian's Craft.* New York: McGraw, 1964.

Braudel, Fernand. *On History.* Chicago: University of Chicago Press, 1980.

Butterfield, Herbert. *Man on His Past.* Cambridge: Cambridge University Press, 1955.

———. *The Whig Interpretation of History.* London: G. Bell, 1931.

Carr, E. H. *What is History?* New York: Random House, 1967.

Collingwood, R. G. *The Idea of History.* Oxford: Clarendon Press, 1946.

Commager, Henry Steele. *The Nature and Study of History.* New York: Garland, 1984.

Conkin, Paul K., and Roland N. Stromberg. *Heritage and Challenge,* Wheeling, IL: Harlan Davidson, Inc., 1989.

Dray, William H. *Philosophy of History.* Englewood Cliffs, NJ: Prentice-Hall, 1964.

Fischer, David Hackett. *Historian's Fallacies: Toward a Logic of Historical Thought.* New York: Harper and Row, 1970.

Gardiner, Patrick L. *The Nature of Historical Explanation.* New York: Oxford University Press, 1952.

Gottschalk, Louis. *Understanding History.* New York: Knopf, 1969.

Gustavson, Carl G. *The Mansion of History.* New York: McGraw-Hill, 1976.

———. *A Preface to History.* New York: McGraw-Hill, 1955.

Hexter, J. H. *The History Primer.* New York: Basic Books, 1971.

Hughes, H. Stuart. *History as Art and as Science.* New York: Garland, 1985.

Kitson Clark, George. *The Critical Historian.* London: Heinemann, 1967.

Marwick, Arthur. *The Nature of History.* London: Macmillan, 1970.

Meyerhoff, Hans, ed. *The Philosophy of History in Our Time.* New York: Doubleday, 1959.

Nash, Ronald H., ed. *Ideas of History.* 2 vols. New York: E.P. Dutton, 1969.

Nevins, Allan. *The Gateway to History.* Chicago: Quadrangle Books, 1963.

Norling, Bernard. *Timeless Problems in History.* Notre Dame, IN: University of Notre Dame Press, 1970.

Smith, Page. *The Historian and History.* New York: Knopf, 1964.

Tholfsen, Trygve R. *Historical Thinking.* New York: Harper and Row, 1967.

Trevelyan, G. M. *Clio, a Muse and Other Essays.* New ed. London: Longmans, Green, 1930.

Vaughn, Stephen, ed. *The Vital Past: Writings on the Uses of History.* Athens, GA: University of Georgia Press, 1985.

Walsh, W. H. *An Introduction to Philosophy of History.* 3rd ed. rev. London: Hutchinson University Library, 1967.

HISTORICAL METHODOLOGY

Altick, Richard D. *The Scholar Adventurers.* Columbus: Ohio State University Press, 1987.

Aydelotte, William O. *Quantification in History.* Reading, MA: Addison-Wesley, 1971.

Barzun, Jacques. *Clio and the Doctors: Psycho-history, Quanto-history and History.* Chicago: University of Chicago Press, 1974.

———, and Henry F. Graff. *The Modern Researcher.* Rev. ed. New York: Harcourt, Brace, 1985.

Benjamin, Jules R. *A Student's Guide to History.* New York: St.Martin's Press, 1987.

Brundage, Anthony. *Going to the Sources.* Wheeling, IL: Harlan Davidson, Inc., 1989.

Cantor, Norman F., and Richard I. Schneider. *How to Study History*. Wheeling, IL: Harlan Davidson, 1967.

Daniels, Robert V. *Studying History: How and Why*. 3rd ed. Englewood Cliffs, NJ: Prentice-Hall, 1981.

Davis, Cullom, Kathryn Back, and Kay MacLean. *Oral History: From Tape to Type*. Chicago: American Library Association, 1977.

Davidson, James W., and Mark Lytle. *After the Fact: The Art of Historical Detection*. 2nd ed. New York: McGraw-Hill, 1985. 3rd ed., 1992.

Dunaway, David K. and Willa K. Baum, eds. *Oral History: An Interdisciplinary Anthology*. Nashville: American Association for State and Local History, 1984.

Elton, G. R. *The Practice of History*. London: Sydney University Press, 1967.

Furay, Conal and Michael J. Salevouris. *The Methods and Skills of History*. Wheeling, IL: Harlan Davidson, Inc., 1988.

Gray, Wood, et al. *Historian's Handbook: A Key to the Study and Writing of History*. 2nd ed. Boston: Houghton Mifflin, 1964.

Handlin, Oscar. *Truth in History*. Cambridge, MA: Harvard University Press, 1979.

The History Teacher. Long Beach, Calif.: The Society for History Education. Published Quarterly.

Kyvig, David E. and Myron A. Marty. *Your Family History*. Wheeling, IL: Harlan Davidson, Inc., 1978.

Lichtman, Allan J. and Valerie French. *Historians and the Living Past*. Wheeling, IL: Harlan Davidson, Inc., 1978.

Lowenthal, David. *The Past is a Foreign Country*. Cambridge: Cambridge University Press, 1985.

Marwick, Arthur. *What History Is and Why It Is Important; Primary Sources; Basic Problems of Writing History; Common Pitfalls in Historical Writing*. Bletchley, England: The Open University Press, 1970.

Renier, G. J. *History: Its Purpose and Method*. Macon, GA: Mercer University Press, 1982.

Shafer, Robert Jones, ed. *A Guide to Historical Method*. 3rd ed. Belmont, CA: Wadsworth Publishing, 1980.

Shorter, Edward. *The Historian and the Computer*. Englewood Cliffs, NJ: Prentice-Hall, 1971.

Sitton, Thad, George L. Mehaffy, and G. L. Davis, Jr. *Oral History: A Guide for Teachers (and Others)*. Austin: University of Texas Press, 1983.

Stephens, Lester D. *Probing the Past: A Guide to the Study and Teaching of History*. Boston: Allyn and Bacon, 1974.

Teaching History, a Journal of Methods. Emporia, KS. Division of Social Sciences and the College of Liberal Arts and Sciences, Emporia State University. Published semiannually.

Tuchman, Barbara W. *Practicing History*. New York: Knopf, 1981.

Winks, Robin W., ed. *The Historian as Detective*. New York: Harper Colophon, 1970.

HISTORIOGRAPHY

Appleby, Joyce, Lynn Hunt, and Margaret Jacob. *Telling the Truth About History*. New York: W. W. Norton, 1994.

Barnes, Harry E. *A History of Historical Writing*. 2nd rev. ed. New York: Dover, 1963.

Benson, Susan P., Stephen Brier, and Roy Rosenzweig. *Presenting the Past: Essays on History and the Public*. Philadelphia: Temple University Press, 1986.

Breisach, Ernst. *Historiography: Ancient, Medieval, and Modern*. Chicago: The University of Chicago Press, 1983.

Gay, Peter, and Gerald J. Cavanaugh, eds. *Historians at Work*. 4 Vols. New York: Irvington, 1975.

Geyl, Pieter. *Debates with Historians*. New York: Meridian Books, 1958.

Gilbert, Felix, and Stephen R. Graubard, eds. *Historical Studies Today*. New York: Norton, 1972.

Gilderhus, Mark T. *History and Historians*. Englewood Cliffs, NJ: Prentice-Hall, Inc., 1987.

Gooch, George Peabody. *History and Historians in the Nineteenth Century*. Rev. ed. London: Longmans, Green, 1952.

Halperin, S. William, ed. *Some Twentieth-Century Historians*. Chicago: University of Chicago Press, 1961.

Higham, John, Leonard Krieger and Felix Gilbert. *History: The Development of Historical Studies in the United States*. Englewood Cliffs, NJ: Prentice-Hall, 1964.

Himmelfarb, Gertrude. *The New History and the Old*. Cambridge: The Belknap Press of Harvard University Press, 1987.

Kren, George M., and Leon H. Rappoport, eds. *Varieties of Psychohistory*. New York: Springer, 1976.

Noble, David W. *The End of American History*. Minneapolis: University of Minnesota Press, 1985.

Novick, Peter. *That Noble Dream*. Cambridge: Cambridge University Press, 1988.

Stannard, David E. *Shrinking History*. New York: Oxford University Press, 1980.

Stephens, Lester D. *Historiography: A Bibliography*. Metuchen, NJ: Scarecrow Press, 1975.

Stern, Fritz, ed. *The Varieties of History from Voltaire to the Present*. New York: Random, 1956.

Sternsher, Bernard. *Consensus, Conflict, and American Historians*. Bloomington, IN: University Press, l975.

Thompson, James Westfall. *A History of Historical Writing*. 2 Vols. New York: Irvington, 1942.

Wise, Gene. *American Historical Explanations*. Minneapolis: University of Minnesota Press, 1980.

Wolman, Benjamin B., ed. *The Psychoanalytic Interpretation of History*. New York: Harper and Row, 1971.

WRITING SKILLS

Anderson, Richard. *Writing That Works*. New York: McGraw-Hill Publishing Company, 1989.

Barnes, Gregory A. *Write for Success*. Philadelphia: ISI Press, 1986.

Bennett, James D. and Lowell H. Harrison. *Writing History Papers*. Wheeling, IL: Harlan Davidson, Inc., 1979.

Cuba, Lee. *A Short Guide to Writing About Social Science*. 2nd ed. New York: HarperCollins College Publishers, 1993.

Hacker, Diane. *Writer's Reference*. 3rd ed. Boston: St. Martin's Press, 1995.

Hashimoto, Irvin Y. *Thirteen Weeks: A Guide to Teaching College Writing*. Portsmouth: Boynton/Cook Publishers, 1991.

Meyer, Herbert E., and Jill M. Meyer. *How to Write*. Washington: Storm King Press, 1987.

Ponsot, Marie, and Rosemary Deen. *Beat Not the Poor Desk*. Portsmouth: Boynton/Cook Publishers, 1982.

Rathbone, Robert R. *Communicating Technical Information*. Reading: Addison-Wesley Publishing Company, Inc., 1966.

Strunk, William, Jr., and E. B. White. *The Elements of Style*. New York: The Macmillan Company, 1979.

FILM AND HISTORY

Carnes, Mark C. *Past Imperfect: History According to the Movies*. New York: Henry Holt and Co., 1995.

Ferro, Mark. *Cinema and History*. Detroit: Wayne State University Press, 1988.

Mintz, Steven and Randy Roberts. *Hollywood's America: United States History Through Its Films*. St. James, NY: Brandywine Press, 1993.

Monaco, James. *How to Read a Film*. Rev. ed. New York: Oxford University Press, 1981.

O'Connor, John, ed. *Image as Artifact: The Historical Analysis of Film and Television*. Malabar, FL: Robert E. Krieger Publishing Co., 1990.

———, and Martin A. Jackson. *Teaching History with Film*. Washington, DC: American Historical Association, 1974.

Rollins, Peter, ed. *Hollywood as Historian: American Film in a Cultural Context*. Lexington: University Press of Kentucky, 1983.

Short, K.R.M., ed. *Feature Films as History*. Knoxville: University of Tennessee Press, 1981.

Smith, Paul, ed. *The Historian and Film*. Cambridge: Cambridge University Press, 1976.

Saturday May 8, 2004

"Polarization of Politics" Panel

Live 7AM (CA time) Fairfax, VA Capitol Books Festival

A Celebration of National

Panel   moderated by

Eleanor Clift
Alan Colmes

Ken Starr
Laura Ingraham

---

② Gen Peter Schoomaker (Army Chief of Staff): Discipline is doing what's right when nobody's watching. This was a breakdown of discipline, & a void of effective leadership."

① Gen. Richard Myers (Joint Chiefs): "We didn't need a leader standing over these individuals on these nights, Oct thru Dec, to remind them that what they were doing was not only illegal, but its immoral; its unethical. And yes we have things to fix, and yes leadership can help, but... this is a failure of individuals."

Learning American History:
  Critical Skills for the Survey Course

Development editors: Maureen Hewitt
  and Andrew J. Davidson
Copy editor: Katy Heider
Book design and production: Lucy Herz
Photo editor and proofreader: Claudia Siler
Typesetter: Bruce Leckie
Printer: Thomson-Shore, Inc.

Cover design: DePinto Graphic Design